Explorers, Fortunes & Love Letters

A WINDOW ON
NEW NETHERLAND

GWC NEW NETHERLAND INSTITUTE

MOUNT IDA PRESS

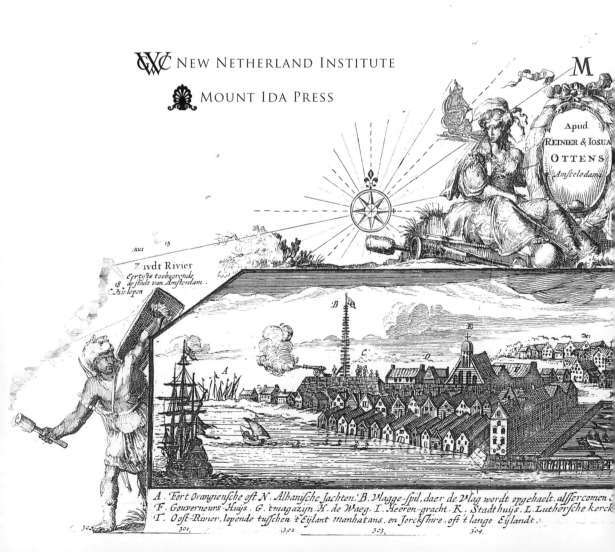

M

Apud
REINIER & IOSUA
OTTENS
Amstelodam

Zuidt Rivier
Eertijts toebehorende
18 de stadt van Amsterdam.
Fuir lopen

A. Fort Orangiensche oft N. Albanische Jachten. B. Vlagge-spil, daer de Vlag wordt opgehaelt. alsser comen
F. Gouverneurs-Huijs. G. 't magazijn. H. de Waeg. I. Heeren-gracht. K. Stadthuijs. L. Luthersche kerck
T. Oost-Rivier, lopende tusschen 't Eijlant Manhatans, en Jorckshire, oft 't lange Eijlandt.

Explorers, Fortunes & Love Letters

A WINDOW ON
NEW NETHERLAND

EDITED BY
MARTHA DICKINSON SHATTUCK

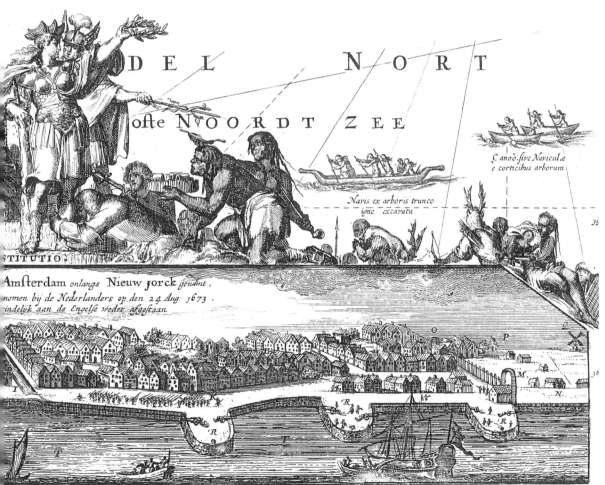

DEL NORT

ofte NOORDT ZEE

Canoö, five Naviculæ
e corticibus arborum

Navis ex arboris trunco
igne excavata

ſTITUTIO.

Amſterdam onlangs Nieuw jorck genaemt.
nomen bij de Nederlanders op den 24 Aug. 1673.
indelijk aan de Engelſe weder afgeſtaan

Haven. C. Fort Amſterdam, genaemt Jeams-fort bij de Engelſche. D. gevangen-huijs. E. Gereformeede kerck.
rt. N. Smidts-valleij. O landtpoort. P. Weg na tverſche Water. Q. Wint-molen. R. Ronduijten. S. Stuijveſants-huijs.

NEW NETHERLAND INSTITUTE
Box 2536
Empire State Plaza
Albany, New York 12220
518-486-4815   www.nnp.org

MOUNT IDA PRESS
111 Washington Avenue
Albany, New York 12210
518-426-5935   www.mountidapress.com

Distributed by State University of New York Press
www.sunypress.edu

Published 2009. Printed in the United States of America.
Design: The Market Street Group www.marketstreetgroup.com
Printing: Thomson-Shore www.tshore.com

ISBN: 978-0-9625368-5-4

Library of Congress Cataloging-in-Publication Data
Explorers, fortunes, and love letters : a window on New Netherland /
edited by Martha Dickinson Shattuck.
      p. cm.
Includes bibliographical references and index.
 1. New Netherland—History. 2. New York (State)—History—
Colonial period, ca. 1600-1775. 3. Dutch—New York (State)—
History—17th century. I. Shattuck, Martha Dickinson.
F122.1.E96 2009
974.7'102--dc22
                                        2009001132

Endpapers and title page: Details from *Totius Neobelgii Nova Et
Accuratissima Tabula* (The Restitutio View), 1673, published by
Carolus Allard. Museum of the City of New York, The J. Clarence
Davies Collection, 29.100.2199.

This book is dedicated to Charles T. Gehring, translator and director of the New Netherland Project, in appreciation and admiration for his years of devotion to continuing the important work of making the Dutch records of New Netherland available in English translation. Added to this is the gratitude of untold numbers of students and scholars of New Netherland's history who have benefitted from his unstinting generosity in providing advice and support.

ACKNOWLEDGEMENTS

The initial impetus for publishing a book in celebration of the Hudson-Fulton-Champlain Quadricentennial came from the Board of Directors of the New Netherland Institute as part of their plans for the 2009 festivities. Thanks go to them and to the Institute's Board president, Charles W. Wendell, and the vice president, Marilyn E. Douglas, for their support. Jippe Hiemstra, as chairman of the Institute's 2009 Committee, worked tirelessly to obtain financial backing for both the book and the traveling exhibit, Light on New Netherland. The many donors have our grateful appreciation. Special thanks go to Leonard Tantillo for permission to reproduce his fine paintings of seventeenth-century New Netherland and to James F. Sefcik, the 2009 project coordinator, who was an integral part of the publication. The final and important stages of publication were ably handled by Diana S. Waite, president of Mount Ida Press, assisted by project manager Melissa M. Bramble and editorial assistant Maya E. Rook.

CONTENTS

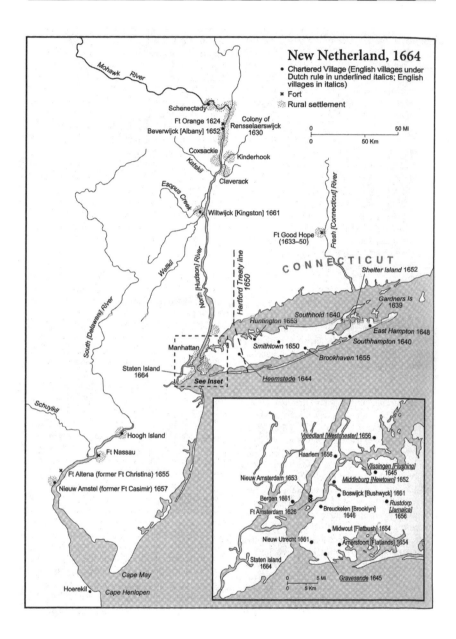

New Netherland, 1664

- Chartered Village (English villages under Dutch rule in underlined italics; English villages in italics)
- × Fort
- ░ Rural settlement

0   50 Mi
0   50 Km

Mohawk River

Schenectady
Ft Orange 1624
Colony of Rensselaerswijck 1630
Beverwijck [Albany] 1652
Coxsackie
Kinderhook
Katskil
Claverack
Espous Creek
Wiltwijck [Kingston] 1661
Wallkil
Ft Good Hope (1633–50)
Fresh [Connecticut] River

C O N N E C T I C U T

Shelter Island 1652
Gardners Is 1639

North [Hudson] River
Hartford Treaty line 1650

Southhold 1640
Huntington 1653
East Hampton 1648
Smithtown 1650
Southhampton 1640
Brookhaven 1655

Manhattan
Staten Island 1664
See Inset
Heemstede 1644

South [Delaware] River

Schuylkil

Hoogh Island
Ft Nassau

Ft Altena (former Ft Christina) 1655
Nieuw Amstel (former Ft Casimir) 1657

Cape May
Hoerekil
Cape Henlopen

Inset:

Vreedlant [Westchester] 1656
Haarlem 1656
Vlissingen [Flushing] 1645
Nieuw Amsterdam 1653
Middleburg [Newtown] 1652
Boswijck [Bushwyck] 1661
Bergen 1661
Rustdorp [Jamaica] 1656
Ft Amsterdam 1626
Breuckelen [Brooklyn] 1646
Midwout [Flatbush] 1654
Nieuw Utrecht 1661
Amersfoort [Flatlands] 1654
Staten Island 1664
Gravesende 1645

0   5 Mi
0   5 Km

Map of New Netherland in 1664. From Peter Eisenstadt, ed., Encyclopedia of New York State *(Syracuse University Press, 2005), 1048. Reprinted with permission of the publisher. Map drawn by Joe Stoll.*

MARTHA DICKINSON SHATTUCK

*I*n this, the four-hundredth anniversary of Henry Hudson's discovery in 1609 of the river that now bears his name, it is possible to suggest that without his voyage, and without his report to the Dutch East India Company noting the abundance of furs that he found, New Netherland might never have existed.

While the river was not the conduit to the northern passage that Hudson had hoped to find, his report opened up a new and profitable vista for the merchants in the Dutch Republic. Between approximately 1611 and 1621 they would sail upriver to the area that is now Albany, New York, to trade with the Indians. Competition among trading companies, along with the Dutch government's attempt to consolidate that competition, ceased with the founding in 1621 of the Dutch West India Company.

Not until 1624, however, did the story of New Netherland as a settlement finally start with the arrival on Noten Island (now Governor's Island) of the first settlers, the first set of laws, and the first appointed officials. The colony grew slowly at first and was almost destroyed by the ill-advised Indian wars in the early 1640s; however, by the 1650s, during the administration of Petrus Stuyvesant and his council, emigration from Holland had considerably improved. In 1664, when the English commandeered the colony, even though they were not at war with the Dutch Republic, the population of New Netherland is estimated to have been around nine thousand.

During its forty-year existence the colony, which stretched north-south from Beverwijck (now Albany) to the Delaware Bay, was comprised of sixteen villages, the city of New Amsterdam (Lower Manhattan), and the patroonships of Nieuw Amstel (New Castle, Delaware) and Rensselaerswijck (Albany and Rensselaer counties and part of Columbia County). It was America's original melting-pot society, containing not only the Dutch but also Scots, English, French, Germans, Scandinavians, Jews, Africans, and the indigenous population of Indians. It was run under Dutch law until the advent of the English control. Yet Dutch customs and people dominated society, as they would for generations. This book's twelve essays are not concerned with a single thematic argument; instead, they illuminate separate but equally important aspects of life in New

Netherland. Little would be known about New Netherland's place in American colonial history, however, without the English translation of the colony's governmental archives by the New Netherland Project, which since 1974 has been the work of Charles T. Gehring. Well before that date lies the history of the archives' remarkable survival from the time of the English takeover in 1664 to the Revolution. Woven into Russell Shorto's essay are his conversations with Charles Gehring about the archives, the work of the New Netherland Project, and the history of the nineteenth- and early-twentieth-century translators who preceded its founding.

Some time ago two historians rendered inaccurate views on New Netherland society: one called it a place where "the roots of a distinctively Dutch society were never firmly established," and another stated that it "never developed into anything more than a congeries of trading posts."[1] The eleven essays that follow Shorto's "Three Conversations" clearly refute those allegations, describing instead a viable and active society. The essays relate historians' fresh interpretations on Hudson and the growth of navigational science that he undoubtedly used in his voyages; Indian and Dutch relations in the Mohawk Valley; problems faced by Jews in New Amsterdam; a case study of how one citizen rose from little to much wealth; the practice and practitioners of medicine; the various stages of childhood; the prominent place of bread in daily life; the Dutch celebration of St. Nicholas that yielded the American Santa Claus; what Kiliaen van Rensselaer's love letters tell about him and early-seventeenth-century courtship; the effect of intricate marriage and family relationships on colonial politics; and finally, the reasons why the Dutch and New Netherland have an important place in the story of America's beginnings. These analyses provide a window on what life must have been like for settlers in New Netherland.

A last comment. The end notes following each essay contain an abundance of bibliographical references and can suggest further reading on the subjects at hand. A general bibliography is also available in the New Netherland Project's Web site, www.nnp.org.

---

1. The first quote comes from Thomas J. Condon's *New York Beginnings: The Commercial Origins of New Netherland* (New York: New York University, 1968), 119. The second quote appears in Sung Bok Kim's *Landlord and Tenant in Colonial New York* (Chapel Hill: University of North Carolina Press, 1978), 5.

Three Conversations

RUSSELL SHORTO

One day in September of 2000 I picked up the telephone and dialed a number in Albany, New York. A man answered: a deep, caramelly voice undulating over the syllables of what was clearly a well-worn greeting, "New Netherland Project." I'm a fairly thorough note-taker, and in this case, looking back through the file I kept, I see that I even recorded how I planned to introduce myself: "I'm a journalist. I write for the *New York Times* and other publications. I've been interested in the Dutch roots of New York City lately. I wonder if I might talk to someone about your organization."

At the time, I was living with my wife and our two young daughters in the East Village of Manhattan, and the nearest open space to take our older daughter to play was the churchyard of St. Mark's in the Bowery. One day, while Anna skipped among the tombs of some of the first families of old New York, I stood in front of the plaque marking the burial place of the graveyard's most famous inhabitant, Peter Stuyvesant. As I read the arcane details of his life recorded on the plaque (several of which I would later realize are incorrect), I felt my own ignorance of New York's Dutch beginnings. I didn't even know that I was living in what had once been Stuyvesant's *boerderij*, or farm (from which "the Bowery" would derive), though I had heard of Stuyvesant and his wooden leg. I asked a few knowledgeable people where I could go for information; few had anything to tell me—even the couple of historians I spoke to professed ignorance of the topic. I surmised the reason the Dutch period was so little known was that there were few records. Still, the historical hook had set in me, and I had a mind to do some exploring. Eventually someone suggested I contact a man in Albany who was leading a project to unearth New York's Dutch roots.

It was Charles Gehring who answered the phone. He told me that the New Netherland Project was a tiny nonprofit organization founded in 1974 to translate and publish the archives of the Dutch colony that was centered on Manhattan Island. He said that most of this archive had never seen the light of day. He told me that this colony had given birth to New York City and much else. These archives, he said, consisted of 12,000 pages of wills, letters and court cases; that they comprised intricate, and sometimes intimate, details in the life of a nearly forgotten society.

I was bewildered by numbers; I asked him to repeat. "I have been working for twenty-six years now," he said. "I'm about halfway through the archives."

I wanted to know more, and as it happened I had called at an opportune moment. Gehring told me he hosted an annual seminar on the topic of New Netherland, and that it was to be held the following week in Albany. He suggested I drive up for it. The following weekend I sat in on every talk on offer, and in between I interviewed the attendees. There were maybe 120 people: historians, archaeologists, genealogists, teachers. New Netherland had ended its life three and a half centuries earlier, but here it was still alive. People were researching "Dutch foodways" in the Hudson Valley in the seventeenth century, the place of women in the Dutch colony, the application of Dutch law in New Netherland. The focus was intense, yet it was all a bit confusing. People made casual references—"Van Tienhoven," "the South River"—that assumed familiarity. I felt I'd walked into the middle of a conversation that had been going on for years.

The next week, I phoned Charly Gehring again (we were now on a first name basis). I needed some context. Looking over my notes of that conversation, however, I see that I began on the opposite tack, asking about the particularities of his work, and especially about the archives that he was in the process of translating and publishing. Exactly where and what were these materials? "The records were kept in the office of the provincial secretary, above the main gate of the fort," he told me. This would have been the fort at the southern tip of Manhattan, on the site of what is now the Old Customs House. "They were kept in bound ledger books, labeled *a* through *z*, then *aa* through *pp*. Each letter code indicates either a certain type of record or a series—that was the way the Dutch organized them. The records tell you on almost a day-by-day basis how the Dutch administered the province. They show aspects of how they administered government, the relations with the natives, with the English neighbors. New Netherland was later dismissed as an aberration, but the records show that something was developing there. People were transmitting their culture from the Old World to the New. There was a blending of cultures."

This was what I wanted to hear more about: this mostly forgotten colony, it seemed, had *mattered* in some way. What the conference speakers were talking around—taking for granted, perhaps, as people who spend their lives in a subject are likely to do—was something whose outlines seemed so vast that I was a bit nervous stating it. "Tell me," I said, "about the treatment of New Netherland in American history." This colony developed alongside the Pilgrim settlement to the north and Jamestown to the south. Why was it overlooked?

"There's a simple reason for that," Gehring said. "The English won. To the victors go the textbooks. What you find in reference books is that the contributions of the Dutch are minimized. Meanwhile, over the years the Pilgrim story developed into a nice myth that everyone could feel good about."

And what exactly was the overlooked significance of the Dutch colony? Gehring talked a bit about it then, and later I was to explore it for myself. The

Dutch Republic of the seventeenth century was the melting pot of Europe: people who were fleeing oppression or war or seeking freedom to publish made their way to its relatively liberal cities. As a result, the populations of Amsterdam, Rotterdam, Utrecht, and The Hague had unusually high concentrations of minorities. Diversity was almost universally frowned on as a weakness at the time; it was generally held that in order for a society to be strong it had to be unified, which meant, above all else, being comprised of a single religious bloc. The Dutch being an eminently practical people, they made a virtue of their diversity. They gave birth to the notion of "tolerance." This Dutch tolerance was not anything like what today would be called "celebrating diversity." It was a far more limited notion—something more like "putting up with" people of different religions and ethnicities. In the scheme of things, however, it was a step forward—a major step in the development of modern society, which includes as hallmarks individual freedom and tolerance of differences.

When the Dutch Republic founded a colony in the New World, then, it took on many of the features of the multiethnic society of the home country. The colony of New Netherland had a mixed population from the start: Dutch, English, German, Swedish, and Norwegian settlers figured in its narrative, as well as Africans, Jews, and American Indians. It was America's first melting pot. You might say its capital, New Amsterdam, was New York City right from the beginning. But New Netherland gave birth to more than New York City. Eventually, of course, the English took control of the colony, but its character by and large remained, and over time its influence extended. As Europeans emigrated to America in great numbers in the eighteenth and nineteenth centuries, many came first to New York, and the mixed society they found there—turbulent, vital, fecund—they took to be a hallmark of "America." As they migrated further west—Pennsylvania, Ohio, Indiana, Illinois, and beyond—they brought this notion with them. So it was that the legacy of the Dutch colony became magnified; its impact would grow.

All of this, Charly Gehring told me in our second phone conversation, was to be found there in the records. "New Netherland was an inconvenient problem for historians, but the records show that something was taking root here before the English arrived," he said. "And this persisted for generations, and became part of what we call American culture."

I wanted to know more about the documents themselves. Why were they forgotten? How had they survived? In 1664 the English took over the colony, and they were very matter-of-fact about maintaining its archives. "What happens is the English provincial secretary takes over the quarters of the Dutch provincial secretary, over the gate, and the English secretary just begins to add to them, with one administration blending into another," Gehring said. "So you get a very continuous series of books. The first major disruption occurs in 1688. James, the Duke of Albany, becomes king of England, and he decides to reorganize the colonies under the 'dominion of New England.' This makes Boston the capital, and in order to supply records for the new administration, they take all the records to Boston. A lot of records were lost during that transfer—maybe they fell off a wagon. Then the dominion fails during the Glorious Revolution, when William and Mary come to the throne, and all the records are brought back to New York again. More are lost: entire books."

The papers were housed once again in the fort at the tip of Manhattan. In 1741, during one of the most infamous episodes in early American history—the so-called slave revolt on Manhattan (it's unclear exactly what ignited the chaos, but it was blamed on rebellious slaves)—someone set fire to the main gate of the fort. People rushed to the secretary's office and began tossing documents out the window, down onto the street. "There was a heavy wind that day," Gehring told me. "Papers were seen flying off up the street. So you had more records lost."

The records even played a part in the American Revolution. With fire and mayhem in the streets of Manhattan, New York's British governor, William Tryon, had the archives of the colony—including those documenting its Dutch beginnings—brought with him onto a ship in the harbor, where he spent much of the war. "They were there for a number of years," Gehring said. "It was damp in the hold—a very unaccommodating environment for paper. So there is more damage, this time from mold and rot."

Eventually the papers were brought to New York's capital, Albany. "By this time their value is considered negligible, because they are in a poor state, not to mention the fact that they are in Dutch, so nobody can read them." A Dutchman named Francis Adrian van der Kemp was asked to translate them. Despite failing eyesight, he did a rapid-fire longhand translation, glossing over what he thought unimportant or scurrilous, focusing on political material and ignoring social and personal matters, summarizing without annotation. His work was never published, but it was catalogued under the title "Albany Records," and historians relied on it in creating some of the first histories of New York.

Another attempt at translating and making available records from the New Netherland period began in the 1840s. The state of New York sent an agent named John Romeyn Brodhead on a mission to European archives in search of materials related to the founding of the state. Brodhead returned with thousands of pages of material, and in 1849 Edmund B. O'Callaghan, who had taught himself Dutch, set to work on it. O'Callaghan eventually produced a four-volume work entitled *Documentary History of the State of New York*. O'Callaghan and another translator, Berthold Fernow, then produced a fourteen-volume work of material on the state's early period, entitled *Documents Relative to the Colonial History of the State of New York*.

In 1881, meanwhile, the Dutch colonial records themselves were moved to the New York State Library in Albany. In the early twentieth century another translator set to work on them. This time, the man—A. J. F. van Laer—was thorough, painstaking, and highly skilled. He translated four volumes of material, but then in 1911 a fire broke out in the library—one of the major losses to American historical records, in which two million volumes would be destroyed. Most of the Dutch records, however, survived. "Ironically, they survived because of their lowly status," Gehring told me. "They were kept on the lower shelves, because nobody used them. So when the shelves collapsed the English records came down on top of them, and they protected them." Only one volume of Dutch records was lost, because it was on Van Laer's desk at the time the fire broke out.

The fire seems to have unsettled Van Laer. "After the fire, he came close to a nervous breakdown," Gehring said. "He gave up on the translation work." Meanwhile, the earlier, rushed, handwritten translation burned up. The Dutch records themselves survived, but, once again, were forgotten.

The practice of history changed dramatically in the 1970s. Before, history meant political history: the affairs of presidents and kings and armies. In the 1970s a gap was discovered: the rest of humanity. Slaves, carpenters, children, women: the new thinking was that the lives of ordinary people affected the course of events and were as worthy of historical interest as the deeds of the mighty. At the same time, Americans became interested in looking at their own history more broadly. Before, Americans had been proud to see their beginnings as English. For all its pride in its immigrant society, America had had Anglocentrism at its heart. This was expressed most pointedly in the reverence for the Puritans of New England as the progenitors of the American saga. The Puritans had traveled from England bringing with them their conviction that they were God's chosen people. As they began to succeed in their new home, they declared it the Promised Land. Over time, this came to be applied to the continent. As America spread westward and encountered native peoples with prior claims to the land, they clung to the Puritan conviction that it was theirs by sacred trust. In the nineteenth century this was given the name Manifest Destiny. One might argue that the concept continued to apply throughout the twentieth century as the United States spread its might around the globe. After World War I President Woodrow Wilson gave frank expression to the belief, declaring that America had "seen visions that other nations have not seen" and become "the light of the world."

By the 1970s—after Vietnam and Watergate, after the Civil Rights movement, after a revolution of thinking in history departments—many were ready to think about the country's origins in a new way. African American history became a burning topic. The contributions of Hispanics to the country were of interest. People wanted to correct the record. One offshoot of this interest in the role of minorities in American history was felt in Albany when a movement was begun to understand the Dutch roots of New York and other parts of the East Coast. A first step in this direction was to pick up where A. J. F. van Laer had left off. A small pool of money was made available, and a translator found to begin work anew on the archives of the colony of New Netherland. "I had recently gotten my PhD in Germanic linguistics, with an emphasis in seventeenth-century Dutch," Gehring told me. He seemed the right man for the job. He was hired for what was to be a one-year assignment. The year of the Hudson celebration—2009, the four hundredth anniversary of Henry Hudson's voyage—will also mark Gehring's thirty-fifth year as translator of the archives.

By the end of my second phone conversation with Charly Gehring, I had an idea about writing something on the topic of New Netherland. I had had a vague thought to write a magazine article about this search for the Dutch layer of New York history. I emailed an editor at *The New Yorker* with whom I'd worked. He suggested I write a "Talk of the Town" piece about Gehring and his work: something very short and pithy about the man and his solitary historical enterprise. I thought it over and couldn't imagine how to do it. The scope was too big. What I was considering, what Gehring and his colleagues had been telling me, not only encompassed the beginnings of New York—what made it so big, so fecund and vibrant, so impossibly rich—but was also a key to understanding American history, America's uniqueness. This, I began to feel, was a secret to appreciating the mad, staggering, contradictory, flawed genius of America.

My notes from those weeks tell me that I contacted and interviewed several historians: Martha Shattuck about Dutch legal systems in New Netherland, Cynthia Van Zandt about the Indians of the Delaware River Valley, and Firth Haring Fabend about the Reformed Dutch Church in New Netherland and in early New York and New Jersey. And I was reading others. One note runs as follows: "Reading O'Callaghan, Gehring, Van Laer, Huntington volume, Van der Donck, Huizinga, Goodfriend, Geyl, Ritchie, John Murrin, *de Halve Maen* and Bonomi; studying Dutch; planning trip: Bangs, others: Jaap Jacobs." I was deep into it now, immersing myself, committing myself. The subject had tentacles; it reached forward in time; it wove itself into the fabric of American history in a way that I had never imagined when I stood with my daughter in the churchyard where Peter Stuyvesant was buried. When I had been at the seminar in Albany, I had asked various scholars what they were working on. Their special subjects were fascinating, but I felt that there was something larger at stake. The broad story involved American beginnings, how the whole story had gotten started. It encompassed the saga of Europeans reaching the New World, encountering Natives, buying and selling slaves, exploiting and inhabiting and languishing and longing; it encompassed a dream, or a long set of dreams. It was a story that moved from Europe to Manhattan and from that fulcrum westward across the North American continent, all the way to the Pacific.

I placed a third call to Gehring. I asked about the archives again, and he began to talk about them in a way that made me want to see the actual documents. I knew by this time, near the end of 2000, that the New Netherland Project consisted of three people: Gehring, Dutch historian Janny Venema, and editor Martha Shattuck. "We work from the original documents," Gehring said. "We make a transcription, line by line, indicating what is lost, if an edge is broken, where there was fire damage. The documents were written on very high quality rag paper. The Dutch were one of the best paper producers in the seventeenth century. Because of the fire in 1911, the paper turned a brownish color, so there is now minimal contrast between the ink and paper. I've seen some examples of pages that didn't go through the fire, and they are snow white. Hillary Clinton sponsored a program to preserve our national heritage. We applied for funding and got money to preserve the manuscripts. So, after being neglected for much of American history, they are now considered a national treasure."

Eventually, with a bit of trepidation, I told him I was thinking about writing a book. Far from scoffing, he suggested I come to Albany for another chat. Thus it began. In the space of three phone conversations, a new path had opened up.

Soon after, I visited Gehring and Venema at their office in a corner of the State Library in Albany. I was taken, first, with the fact that while they were located on the eighth floor of the building, there was no button marked "8" in the elevator. The explanation was that the floor was off-limits to the general public, so that you had to ride to seven and then change to another elevator. I liked the symbolism: the history to which they had devoted themselves was similarly hidden from the general public. I soon discovered that over time seemingly all books and materials in the library's vast collection that were relevant to their work—on Dutch art, seventeenth-century shipbuilding, the Anglo-Dutch wars—had migrated to one vast wall that stood opposite their offices. Janny Venema's desk also caught my attention. The surface was a makeshift map. She was then working on her dissertation, on the city of Beverwijck, which would become Albany and which would be published as *Beverwijck: A Dutch Village on the American Frontier*. She had arranged on her work surface every house in the village and knew who lived in each and what they did.

I talked about what I proposed to do—write a book that told, in narrative form, the story of the New Netherland colony and tried to fit it into the overall story of American beginnings—and Charly Gehring said he would be happy to help. He offered me space to work. He gave me access to the files. We had already begun what would be, over the next three years, a friendship and collaboration. I was an outsider, with all the limitations of an outsider, but I hoped that position could also give me some perspective in retelling the history. I began making regular two-hour trips between my house—I was by then living in the Lower Hudson Valley—and Albany. In the morning Charly or Janny would point me in one direction or another, and I would begin reading. We would break for lunch. Then I would read all afternoon, pausing repeatedly to pose questions to my mentors.

Eventually I felt I had enough of a grasp on the subject that I wrote a book proposal. It sold at once. Bill Thomas, the editor-in-chief of Doubleday, saw in it what I had felt in those first conversations with Charly Gehring: that this was an entirely new way of understanding America's origins. Now that I had a publisher, I devoted myself full time to the project. My circle of acquaintances expanded to include many of the historians in the field. I traveled to the Netherlands and visited Texel Island, from which most of the settlers of New Netherland set out, the American Pilgrim Museum in Leiden, and the canals of Amsterdam. I took my daughters to the West India House in Amsterdam, from which the West India Company administered its colony; there is a statue of Peter Stuyvesant in the courtyard at its center, but my daughters were more interested in the playground at the back. I sat with Janny Venema as she pored over the original pages of the archives of the colony; she gave me a primer in how to read seventeenth-century Dutch handwriting. I attended seminars. And I read constantly. Charly and I had a lot of lunches together, in which we talked about the personality of Peter Minuit, the cultural differences between the Dutch provinces of Brabant and Friesland, currencies in use in New Amsterdam, slavery, piracy, log-cabin construction, childbirth in the era, orphanages, bricks, timber, salt, horses. Those were some of the happiest moments of my life. I felt a new world opening up inside me—or rather, I felt that my own appreciation of the world in which we live was being transformed. I had a teacher and guide, and I had a publisher who was ready and eager to promote the result.

The book I wrote, *The Island at the Center of the World*, focused on Manhattan, on the Dutch influence on its history, and in turn on its influence on American history. It became a bestseller, much to my surprise. It won awards, which surprised me even more. It sold in several countries, was adopted by schools and universities, was optioned for a feature film, and in many other ways achieved far more than I could have imagined. It has led to new avenues for me. I now live in Amsterdam, the city to which I was drawn as I began my work on the book, and I have become, in the eyes of the Dutch, something of a conduit between the two countries. The Dutch government asks me to attend meetings on relations between the Netherlands and the United States. I am now the director of the John Adams Institute, which is the American cultural center in Amsterdam. In what is almost a surreal case of things coming full circle, my office at the institute is in the West India House, the building where the colony of New Netherland began. Every day now, I park my bicycle alongside the playground where my daughters played those years ago while I marveled at the history that was laid out in stone before me and sit down to work in the same space where seventeenth-century administrators mulled over Peter Stuyvesant's letters about New World Indian skirmishes and slave transactions.

Those letters form part of the corpus of material that the New Netherland Project has devoted itself to translating and publishing. Through that organization, our understanding of our own history, our understanding of ourselves, has begun to change. History is never fixed, of course. It shifts with each generation, for each generation has its own needs, its own perspective. Once, Americans—self-conscious about their mixed society, perhaps with a bit of an inferiority complex vis-à-vis the Old Country, never mind the patriotic bravado—felt the need to extol the purity of their origins. They held up the Puritans and Pilgrims of New England as their progenitors. Times have changed. A mixed society—racially, culturally, religiously mixed—is the essence of modern society. Without being aware of it, the inhabitants of New Netherland helped to spawn something new. We are their heirs, their future. They are our fathers and mothers. I can't think of a grander achievement for a historical venture than to kindle the awareness of such a familial connection between the present and a forgotten moment of the past. That, to my mind, is the accomplishment of the New Netherland Project. A translation and research project housed in the corner of a library may be a small and modest thing, but its influence, like that of a long-ago colony, can go on and on.

Henry Hudson:

NEW WORLD, NEW WORLD VIEW

WILLIAM T. REYNOLDS

*E*ntering the Hudson River from sea and proceeding upstream is a dramatic experience, the first time and every time. A mariner leaves the exposure of the open ocean, passes the narrow neck between Brooklyn's Bay Ridge and Staten Island, and settles into the expansive but protected waters of New York Harbor. In short order, one passes the stark cliffs of the Palisades, then winds circuitously through the steep rise of the Highlands with its cragged peaks sloping sharply down right to the water's edge. The modern sailor cannot help but feel awed by the supersized contrast of the built skyline of urbanized New York and New Jersey, soon followed by the striking natural scenes little changed since the native people of Manahatta (Manhattan) met Henry Hudson and his little ship, the *Halve Maen* (*Half Moon*).

Hudson's vision was to find a route from northern Europe to the spice islands of the East Indies, the discovery of which would bring riches and fame. Entering this "River of the Mountains," every sign—the volume and depth of water, the significant tidal exchange, the steep cliffs so evocative of the Magellan Straits—reinforced the notion that it could be the way through America. Hudson had just come from Europe, where even in the early seventeenth century many problems we associate with the modern world were already having an impact. Near-shore fisheries produced fewer fish, and fishermen had to go farther to make their catch. The demand for timber thinned forest resources, and timbers had to be brought in from Baltic countries for shipbuilding. Rural people and those marginalized sought opportunity by moving into cities, which resulted in overcrowding and social problems.

Imagine the feelings that must have stirred within Henry Hudson upon entering this new world. His own words refer to "as pleasant a land as one need tread upon," and the log of the voyage marvels at the abundance of resources, from fish to mammals and from forests to minerals. More important, native people familiar with these resources appeared eager to trade.

Northbound from the Highlands the waters widen and turn, becoming the *Lange Rack*, or Long Reach, a straight stretch of water that serves as a counterpoint to the twisting Highlands with its craggy outcrops sloping into the water. In the Long Reach the river is a seemingly interminable length of unvarying course, width, and depth. Fighting a current or a headwind is tedious work; even with a fair wind or current, one's spirits flag compared with the surge of excitement that accompanied the quick sail maneuvers and constant course changes demanded in the Highlands. Sailors face hours of routine that becomes monotonous—taking soundings, recording speed and distances traveled, tending the set of the sails, pumping the bilges, constantly looking out for dangers that could destroy the ship and strand them—the sameness of the routine can dampen even the highest spirits.

Yet Hudson continued; having come this far he must have felt compelled to sail until they could go no farther. Finally, at a slight dogleg, the Catskills emerge and the call of the lookout jolts the crew. Even in mid-September there is often a dusting of white snow on the peaks, and spirits soar once again. A passage through these new mountains could lead to the ocean on the other side.

North of the mountains, above Saugerties, the river narrows, and more shoals obstruct the way. The signs of a passage through the continent have now passed, and the signs of a river reaching its upper course become more and more distinct. Eventually, the *Half Moon* must simply anchor and send its small boat ahead to verify what is already known—this water cannot carry ships. The river simply winds to its upper reaches. Little is left to do, except turn homeward.

The end of the voyage dashed Hudson's hopes, but marked the beginning of major change in the Hudson Valley. Within three years Dutch interests started the beaver trade between Europeans and the Indians of many different groups living in the Hudson Valley. Next was the rise of New Netherland that brought European settlement and distinctive Dutch customs to America. Over time followed changes in the ecology and geography of the Hudson River watershed, and in the people—native and Dutch alike—as colonization proceeded.

The purpose of this essay is to focus on the factual record from which we can gain better insight into Hudson, his endeavors, and his impact upon the world—and not to replicate interpretations of Hudson's life that have been repeated in many sources. Therefore, this essay will consider salient aspects of shipboard practice and life on the *Half Moon*, notable characteristics of his 1609 voyage with emphasis on experiences while on the River of the Mountains, and the intellectual context from which Hudson emerged.

Robert Juet's account of the *Half Moon's* voyage provides insightful and rare documentation of conditions in North America from a time when little written documentation exists. Reports about the geography of the Hudson Valley, the spread of forest resources, the extent of fisheries, the mineral deposits, the fur-bearing mammals, and the specific references to interactions with the resident Indians all serve to help illustrate what a bounty this valley provided in the early 1600s. These logs, with their detailed and objective reporting, provide value not only to historians but also to geographers, scientists, and planners considering how to manage the resources of the Hudson River Valley to this day.[1]

WHAT MAKES HENRY HUDSON DISTINCTIVE?

The epic voyages of the late fifteenth and early sixteenth centuries concentrated on the middle latitudes and Southern Hemisphere, with Spain and Portugal leading the explorations. Christopher Columbus crossed the Atlantic, Vasco da Gama rounded Africa, and Ferdinand Magellan's crew circled the globe. By the late sixteenth and early seventeenth centuries attention shifted to the Arctic as offering alternate routes to the riches of the spice trade from the East Indies. For a variety of reasons, including changing dynamics of world commerce, geopolitical influences, and the rise of mapmaking and the science of geography in Northern Europe, leadership in exploration of routes to the East Indies through the Arctic regions shifted to England and the Dutch Republic.[2]

Many notable explorers conducted voyages that pushed the envelope of exploration into some of the harshest sailing environments one could face. Martin Frobisher, John Davis, George Weymouth, and their colleagues sailed for English interests and focused their attentions on routes to the northwest over Canada. Willem Barentz, Jacob van Heemskerk, Olivier Brunel, and their colleagues sailed for Dutch interests and focused their attention on attempts to the northeast over Russia. Hudson had to have viewed the universe of possible Arctic routes to the Indies comprehensively and set out to test systematically each possible option.[3] Not only did Hudson pursue each of the four possible Arctic routes to the Indies; he did so by organizing and conducting four pioneering voyages in only four years. Even by modern standards, raising the funds, recruiting the crew, provisioning the ship, and planning the route and navigation for these voyages in such a short time is astounding. Although Hudson cannot be solely credited for the expansion of Arctic exploration, yet his voyages did help open three major European expansions: the development of the shore-based whaling industry in the Spitzbergen Islands, the opening up of the Canadian interior to English expansion, and the development of the Dutch colony of New Netherland.[4]

HUDSON'S ENCOUNTERS WITH INDIANS

The log of the *Half Moon* documents key interactions between the ship's crew and the Indians that ranged on both sides from warlike and hostile to friendly and mutually respectful. For example, at their landing in Maine, Hudson directed his crew to repair the foremast of the ship. As the *Half Moon* lay at anchor, the crew engaged in trade with the native people of the area, their attire and use of European tools indicating prior contact. This trade proceeded in a manner that was civil but cautious—not surprising as the crew of the *Half Moon* was small in number and had no other Europeans to provide assistance. After three days the work was done. As Hudson prepared to depart, however, a group of his crew stole one of the Indians' European-style boats, then went ashore and destroyed an Indian village. In the words of Robert Juet, the crew of the *Half Moon* "took the spoyle off them, as they would have done of us."[5]

Upon entering Raritan Bay, the first interactions between the *Half Moon* and native people in the Hudson Valley were civil but cautious as they engaged in trade, and the crew explored the resources of the area. Again, the Indians' knowledge of trade items that would interest the Europeans is consistent with prior contact and earlier trade. But, while exploring the area we know today as Kill Van Kull above Staten Island, a member of Hudson's crew was killed by an arrow through his neck, which intensified the tensions on the *Half Moon*. Soon thereafter Hudson captured two natives to take with him back to Europe (both escaped). Just days later, upon entering Mohican territory in the upper Hudson River, the log of the *Half Moon*, kept by Robert Juet, refers to meeting "the loving people," and Hudson personally visited one village where the leaders noticed Hudson's concern and broke their arrows in a sign of peace. In a later meeting the log refers to one of the local leaders bringing his wife to the ship; in the words of Robert Juet, she "sate so modestly, as any of our Countrey women would doe in a strange place."[6] Even with the "loving people" Hudson and his crew attempted to test for this treachery by plying one of the Indian leaders with alcohol aboard the *Half Moon*. The leader's fellow countrymen returned the next day, fearing for the worst, but were most pleased to find him unharmed. Days later, returning downstream out of Mohican country the *Half Moon* engaged in open warfare, firing cannon and muskets at a large group of Indians launching volleys of arrows from a highland.

This dramatic shift in the attitude of the crew in such a short span of time is notable and indicates a dynamic complexity that is difficult to interpret. No documentation exists to indicate the attitudes of the Indians Hudson encountered, but even filtered through the reports of Robert Juet, the Indians seem to have had the same range of responses.

THE CULTURAL AND INTELLECTUAL CONTEXT OF HUDSON

The voyaging of the modern replica of the *Half Moon* can help us gain insights, as it serves as a living experiment in the ways of a ship. These ways of a ship are easily understood to refer to specific methods of operation and sailing capability. Equally revealing are the human and cultural interactions aboard a ship that can help provide insight about aspects so difficult to document, as conflict and rapport, mutiny and harmony, behavior under stress and in times of ease. It is no easy task to understand the machinery and mechanical operations of a seventeenth-century ship, but those matters are trivial to comprehend compared to the human element of the crew, as Hudson's final tragic voyage so well illustrates. We can begin our assessment of Hudson and his circumstances by examining the larger cultural context in which he lived, and then move on into an examination of what we can learn about the operation of a ship.

Northern Europe during the late sixteenth and early seventeenth centuries presented a dynamic environment for intellectual and material advance. In science and engineering, advances ranged from astronomical to microscopic and crossed over disciplinary boundaries easily; the same instruments could be used for surveying, astronomy, navigation, and geography. Trade, travel, and communication expanded at a rapid pace. Business flourished, and even commoners could invest in and succeed with new enterprise. New technologies held great promise for the expansion of knowledge and the advance of humanity. And the horizon shifted, literally, with every voyage to unexplored parts of the globe. This was the world of Henry Hudson in the late 1500s—dynamic, ripe for those of an inquisitive mind, providing new opportunity for those of an entrepreneurial and ambitious character.[7]

Still, major incongruities coexisted on this intellectual watershed between the subjective, myth-based past and the rational, merit-based future. The very navigational charts so meticulously developed from hard factual reports also depicted the most fantastic giant serpents and mermaids. Ship captains who so dutifully reported speed and winds and water depth and positions would just as dutifully report imaginary sightings and encounters that could exist only in the imagination of the beholder. Cartographers could depict whole areas that had not been explored, but with a veracity conferred by the visual image—unfounded but compelling.

Henry Hudson illuminates the enigmatic nature of this time. On one hand, this major figure in the exploration of the North Atlantic exhibits a classic example of empiricism—the approach to gaining knowledge systematically by documenting and measuring the observed world. On the other hand, he is a mystery, with virtually nothing known or documented about his life prior to the undertaking of his four major voyages of 1607–1610. Indeed, the records from his four voyages provide the only evidence from which we can gain insight into Hudson, his methods, and his thinking. In spite of factual material documenting salient aspects of Hudson—his approach to his explorations—much of the interpretive record about him remains speculative.

If nothing else, the record shows that Henry Hudson was a disciplined practitioner of what today we would call the scientific method: (1) he developed a hypothesis based upon existing knowledge (that one could transit the North Polar region in an alternate route to the Indies); (2) he set about to test the hypothesis (by systematically sailing the four possible routes to the Orient); (3) he repeatedly measured the world around him (geographical position, courses sailed by speed and direction, winds and speeds, compass variation, depth of water, height of celestial objects, location of geographical objects, tidal changes, presence of oceanic and riverine currents); (4) he recorded his measurements and observations (pertaining to acquired data, interactions with native people, presence of natural resources—fur-bearing mammals, minerals, harbors, forest resources, fish and food sources); (5) he analyzed the data for repeatable patterns; and (6) he reported his findings to his financial backers and the academic community.

Hudson's approach was no accident. During Hudson's time a dramatic change in the acquisition and structure of knowledge swept through the learned world of Europe. Throughout the late 1500s to the mid-1600s, leading intellectuals began to advocate for and adopt a methodology of knowledge—empiricism—that holds primacy to this day. This change was not just academic; indeed, it became deeply and broadly ingrained, whether implicitly or explicitly, in such disparate fields as natural science, surveying, philosophy, business, and the world of global explorers.[8]

Oceanic navigators, such as Hudson, Willem Barentz, Jacob van Heemskerck, John Davis, Humphrey Gilbert, and others undertaking voyages during this time, had to be well-educated men. The very nature of their work required them to be literate, proficient in advanced mathematics, and thoroughly knowledgeable about the most recent advances in cosmography (world geography).[9]

The period from the mid-1500s into the mid-1600s saw a profusion of books and publications on navigational science and practice. Major contributions to these books came directly from, or were based upon, the work of leading mathematicians, astronomers, and cosmographers. In addition, practicing navigators made specific adaptations of these subjects to ocean navigation. Any competent ocean navigator would by necessity be familiar with these works, from the earliest prepared by the Portugese navigator and cosmographer Pedro Medina, up through English works by John Davis and John Dee and Dutch works by Willem Barentz, Lucas Janszoon Wagenaer, and Willem Janszoon Blaeu, among others.[10]

Through works such as these, ocean navigators like Henry Hudson would have had direct knowledge of the empirical methods being practiced by astronomers, such as Tycho Brahe, and leading mathematicians. It is more than plausible to conclude that these navigators would have been familiar with the work of other empirical scientists, such as Galileo in his studies of physics, and theoretical thinkers, such as Francis Bacon in his early writings on the advancement of learning. Helping to establish rapport between fields, the very tools of the navigator's trade were adapted from those used by many scientists, especially astronomers, surveyors, and mathematicians. Further, the educated world managed a level of communication and cross-fertilization that we can envy even today.[11]

Empirical methods may have had enlightening value in the advancement of scientific knowledge, but in the business world these methods could determine financial success or failure. More to the point, in the world of the oceanic explorer, repeatable and verifiable observations could mean the very difference between life and death. Oceanic voyagers may not have shared with the academic world the pure desire to advance human knowledge; they may not have even cared about the formality of using the terms *empirical* and *scientific*. However, they certainly did care about staying alive and being able to gain the riches that would come with a shorter route to the Spice Island trade. Thus, it should be of no surprise to find Henry Hudson a disciplined practitioner of scientific methods aboard ship and to see these empirical methods adopted universally amongst successful ocean-voyaging explorers and traders.

WORLD COSMOGRAPHY

Trade and commerce provided the engine for documentation of world geography, or cosmography, as it was known in early seventeenth-century Europe. Reports from trade expeditions, especially to South Asia and the East Indies, had well documented the coastlines and trade routes first through the Middle East and subsequently around Africa and across the Indian Ocean by the early 1500s. Portugese sailors rounded Africa and explored the sea routes to Indonesia and Brazil. Spanish explorers focused on the New World, especially in the Carribean and the west coast of South America. Basque fishermen exploited the abundant codfish banks between Cape Cod and Labrador. By the latter part of the sixteenth century, northern Europeans, noting the wealth to be gained from trade with the Spice Islands around Indonesia, initiated voyages around Africa and entered competition with the Portugese for dominance in the spice trade. Dutch and English voyages in the 1590s demonstrated the profits to be gained from the spice trade by completing the first successful trading voyages to the East Indies.[12]

At the same time, Dutch and English financial interests and explorers also began looking for more efficient routes that could avoid or minimize the difficult route around Africa, as well as direct confrontation with the Portugese. Central to this effort was the work of the innovative Flemish cartographer Gerardus Mercator. Synthesizing reports from a variety of sources and speculations, Mercator published in 1569 his world map including in it an insert showing an open sea at the North Pole with rivers bifurcating the ice.[13] This concept of an open North Polar sea route influenced later cosmographers and mapmakers well into the mid-1600s. In the 1590s and early 1600s Willem Barentz and Peter Plancius began to pursue such a route and influenced others to do so.

The prevailing idea was that the summer sun would melt the Arctic ice cap and open routes through the Arctic to the Pacific Ocean. Mercator's description of the North Polar regions highlighted three potential routes to the Spice Islands. First was the possibility of going due north, straight over the pole and down the other side into the Pacific. The second possibility was sailing to the northeast by Novaya Zemblya, over Russia, and into the Pacific. The third possibility was the prospect of sailing to the northwest and following one of two possible routes into the Pacific. A fourth possible route was through the North American continent.

Willem Barentz and expeditions organized by Balthasar de Moucheron explored to the north and northeast for the Dutch during the 1590s. These efforts added greatly to the base of information available about these routes. Attempts continued into the early 1600s to transit to the northeast; some stopped at

Novaya Zemblya but a few got as far as the Kara Sea. Whether the north and northeastern waterways could be passed remained inconclusive.

The eastern coastline of North and South America had been thoroughly vetted by the late 1500s, leaving two areas that could provide a northwestern passage.[14] From Tierra del Fuego to the mouth of the Chesapeake Bay there was no possibility of a sailing route from the Atlantic Ocean to the Pacific Ocean. The area between the mouth of the Chesapeake and Cape Cod was a different matter—in spite of voyages to the area by Verrazano in 1524, little was documented about the coast through this area, and nothing about the interior. The coast from Cape Cod north to Labrador was also very well known, having been fished and explored extensively by Basque fishermen for a century prior to Hudson. Dutch traders, French explorers, and even English sailors also visited the area in the late 1500s. Detailed charts from the last half of the sixteenth century were not fanciful in showing minute detail of small islands and inlets along this shore. Martin Frobisher, John Davis, George Weymouth, and others had all made voyages in the mouth of what we know today as the Davis Straits and along the Labrador coast. North of Labrador was a different matter.

The origin of Hudson's motivation is not known. Where he obtained his training and seafaring experience, how he obtained his geographic knowledge, and what bolstered his resumé to warrant subsidy by English and Dutch interests is not known. It is enough to conclude that the theoretical basis for his hypothesis was well known to educated Europeans. His sailing experience could have been obtained from any number of sources, including the voyages of Frobisher and Davis or from the Muscovy Company, amongst others. Given this background, it is the approach that Hudson took to his sailing that makes his explorations distinctive. He set out systematically testing each of the possible polar routes one by one, starting with the route least sailed—that of going due north.

HUDSON'S NAVIGATIONAL METHODS

To the modern observer—accustomed to satellite-navigational systems that can be found even in mobile telephones with accuracy to a few feet and internal clocks that can automatically measure nanoseconds (billionths of a second) to obtain this accuracy—the methods of Hudson and his contemporaries seem crude, giving the impression of just sailing blindly and luckily finding places. In reality nothing could be further from the truth—these navigators displayed excellent knowledge, skill, and discipline that modern sailors could emulate.

It was not always thus. As a notable example, Christopher Columbus did little more than sail by a compass course and dead reckoning; he had only the roughest approximation of his latitude and little sense of his longitude—yet his accomplishments rank among the most impressive in maritime history.[15] Columbus's stature is warranted not for his navigational skill but for crossing a conceptual and intellectual barrier that changed circumstances in Europe and the

Americas forever. One of the practical outcomes of Columbus's voyages was the recognition by European cosmographers and navigators that if they were to exploit the resources of the New World, they must have more sophisticated knowledge, skill, and practice of ocean navigation.

Systematic organization of navigational knowledge in Europe began in the mid-1400s as a result of the voyages Portuguese King Henry sponsored to the south seeking a route around Africa. The first formal presentation of such navigational knowledge was by the Portuguese authors Pedro Medina and Martin Cortes. Their treatments of the basic tenets of navigational astronomy, mathematics, and navigational discipline were soon translated into English and Dutch and led to further publications on navigational science by English and Dutch pilots, mathematicians, and astronomers. By the turn into the seventeenth century, such navigational publications included quite sophisticated descriptions of celestial motions, trigonometry, bathymetry, tables of declination of the sun, calculations to allow for the procession of Polaris in determining true north, magnetic variation, methods of constructing knot meters, tables to allow for the calculation of the length of a degree of longitude at different latitudes, methods of using trigonometry to determine distances (with both horizontal and vertical angles), systems of navigational marks, and more. These topics, with minor technical updating, could form a standard navigational text in the twenty-first century.[16]

The log from Hudson's voyage north by Spitzbergen Island in 1607 is the first indication of his systematic approach to navigational practice.[17] This voyage also provides the first evidence of the meticulous nature of Hudson's documentation of his sailing and observations. As was the norm with oceangoing navigators, Hudson maintained a formal discipline to his daily navigation—recording a noon sight when possible, tracking course and speed, comparing distance actually traveled to that predicted, noting magnetic variation and dip, and documenting astronomical events and weather conditions.

By the early 1600s ocean sailors had at their disposal a selection of navigational instruments of proven reliability. Some, such as the astrolabe and quadrant, had been in use for centuries; others, such as the cross staff, had been in use for many decades. The application of each of these instruments was the same: to take a measurement of the height of a celestial object (height being the vertical angular measurement from the horizon to object being measured). This might be the sun at noon or Polaris at night. The previous century had seen a significant improvement in the development of tables to aid in translating these measurements into latitude and in standardized methods for the mariner to follow. In addition to vertical angles, the cross staff and astrolabe could also be used to measure horizontal angles, a feature particularly useful for measuring distances off a visible shore, or in mapping coastal areas.[18]

At the time of Hudson's sailing the accuracy of readings taken with these instruments could place a competent navigator within thirty nautical miles of actual latitude. This accuracy might be as good as fifteen nautical miles in optimal conditions, but if weather deteriorated, even the best navigator could easily be more than one hundred miles off course. By comparison, in 1600 most astronomers working at fixed locations had repeatable accuracy consistent with a navigational range of about fifteen nautical miles. Tycho Brahe's highly sophisticated instruments, at the time the best in the world, provided an accuracy that would translate to approximately two nautical miles. Brahe used a quadrant nearly twenty feet in diameter that was permanently mounted—and he did not have to worry about his position when it was cloudy. A mariner's quadrant might be eight to ten inches in diameter, rocked and rolled with the ship and the wind, and mariners needed a position whether the sun was visible or not.[19]

Navigators and cosmographers knew the limitations of their instruments and commonly corrected for errors within their control. For example, owners of cross-staves might attempt to correct their instrument by shaving the end of the staff to correct for the error introduced by the distance from surface of the eye to the retina.

The daily noon sight to determine latitude formed the core of the sailor's practice. With the use of the astrolabe, quadrant, or cross-staff the mariner would begin taking observations well before the arrival of local noon. The objective of this noon sight was to measure the sun's highest position in the sky. At that moment of highest elevation, the sun was due south of the observer. This allowed the navigator to determine the compass deviation, or the difference between true north and magnetic north. By reference to tables of daily solar declination, the navigator could also calculate the latitude from the noon sight. By Hudson's time, oceangoing vessels had carried for nearly a century declination tables of ever-improving accuracy for calculation of latitude from the noon sight.

In addition to measuring and recording the latitude at noon whenever the sun was visible, transatlantic navigators also needed to track their dead-reckoned position. Dead reckoning consisted of keeping an accurate and continuous track of the vessel's compass heading and speed and plotting these as vectors. Speed was measured with the chip log, a navigational tool that was nothing more than a mechanical time-speed-distance calculator. The chip log was a reel of small line with a flat, weighted piece of wood attached at the end. On the line, small knots tied at standard distances indicated fractions of a nautical mile. When cast overboard, the log would trail behind the ship, and a thirty- or sixty-second sand glass would be started. Counting the number of knots that passed out during the timed interval would give the speed in nautical miles per hour, or knots. Plotting the compass heading and speed provided a series of vectors that in theory could locate the position of the ship. In practice the error of this dead-reckoned position was compounded with each reading; in a matter of days the error could be so great as to render the dead-reckoned position of little use. Even with the precision of modern instruments, maintaining the dead-reckoned position with high accuracy is a challenge. In Hudson's day the dead-reckoned position would be updated by observation of known geographic objects or by correlating a geographic feature with calculated latitude. In modern navigation the dead-reckoned position can be updated with precision using the Global Positioning System, a satellite-based method of calculating position by latitude and longitude to within a few feet.

It is difficult, even for those with experience in navigation, to appreciate the level of precision Hudson brought to his work. For example, while sailing in the open ocean of the North Atlantic in 1609, Hudson recorded the presence of an oceanic current that affected the forward progress of the *Half Moon*. To a modern reader it may seem inconceivable that he could actually measure this current. However, sailing experiments aboard the replica ship *Half Moon* demonstrate that a "foul" current of similar speed to that which Hudson measured can cause a difference in the ship's heading of several degrees between sailing a port and starboard tack. This is a difference easily detected by an observant mariner.

In addition to the measure of ship speed, compass course, magnetic variation, dead-reckoned position, distance made good, and latitude, the competent mariner would also record other observations. Of prime importance was the wind speed and direction, of immediate and obvious influence on a sailing vessel. Beyond the effect on navigation, mariners sought repeatable patterns in the winds and weather conditions. Knowing prevailing winds and weather would help them plan routes for sailing, such as following what we today call the trade winds—the very same wind pattern that Columbus followed. Two hundred fifty years after Hudson, Richard Maury, of the U.S. Naval Observatory and later the Chief of Confederate Sea Coast Defenses during the Civil War, was the first to compile wind and current charts of the North Atlantic. Maury used data taken from log entries of North Atlantic sailors—the very type of data that Hudson collected in hopes of observing repeatable patterns. Hudson knew what was needed to do this, but the information resources of the seventeenth century did not provide him with the tools to consolidate the mass of data needed to derive these subtle patterns. Maury's methodology (and Hudson's) is still in use to this day.[20]

HUDSON'S ROUTE OF SAILING

Far from sailing blindly and stumbling into discoveries, the track of Hudson's voyaging indicates a strategic plan and precision in sailing to the exact areas that warranted exploration. First, he made a systematic approach to his four voyages, testing each possible route indicated by Mercator and substantiated by later cosmographers with whom Hudson met and corresponded. Most prominent was Peter Plancius of the Dutch East India Company. In 1607 this approach took him from known areas northward along the coast of Greenland and thence to the north coast of Spitzbergen Island. On this voyage Hudson narrowly avoided disaster when sailing into icy fjords on the coast of Spitzbergen. He made planned observations or stops at Bear Island, Jan Mayen Island, and the Faroe Islands, all potentially important locations to confirm for future North Atlantic sailing. His 1608 voyage took the same strategic approach, voyaging from known areas. But in going to the northeast the principal issue was whether to pass Novaya Zemblya to the north or to the south. Again, Hudson tried going to the north, found ice blocking his way, then explored to the south along the coast before returning to England.

Hired by the Dutch East India Company in 1609, Hudson was to sail again to the northeast. He dutifully made the voyage towards Novaya Zemblya but found conditions blocking his way as in 1608. Rather than return to Amsterdam, he reprovisioned in the Faroe Islands and proceeded to sail to North America. This voyage could not have been made without significant prior navigational preparation. Van Meteren attributes the departure from Novaya Zemblya to a near mutiny, based upon arguments between the Dutch and English crew, and the unwillingness of the Dutch crew to sail in cold climates.[21] This is questionable, as carping amongst the crew is one of the most common daily occurrences aboard a ship, then and now, especially when facing tough times and setbacks. Further, both English and Dutch sailors had a long history of sailing in cold waters. Hudson's two previous voyages had ventured above the Arctic Circle and to Novaya Zemblya with some of the same crew. Dutch sailors had extensive experience in northern waters, from the fishing fleet in the North Sea to the Baltic trade to explorations and commercial voyages to the northeast above the Arctic Circle. Indeed, even as Hudson sailed to Novaya Zemblya, Dutch traders sailed to outposts in the Kara Sea north of Russia.

From the Faroe Islands, at about 62 degrees north latitude, Hudson proceeded southwesterly on a decreasing latitude until reaching the coast of Nova Scotia, where he encountered vessels of the cod-fishing fleet. From Nova Scotia he sailed to Maine at a north latitude of 44 degrees. At this latitude in Maine Hudson was well positioned to sail either north to the unexplored regions above Labrador or south to explore the area between the mouth of the Chesapeake Bay and Cape Cod. After a short layover in Maine the *Half Moon* headed south, making one brief landfall at Cape Cod and recording the shallows as they passed over the cod-fishing banks there. Hudson stayed offshore until he reached the latitude of the Chesapeake Bay and only then closed the shoreline. At the mouth of the Chesapeake Bay Hudson tarried for several days, riding out storms and easing into and out of the mouth of the bay while determining whether to enter the Chesapeake Bay or proceed north along the ocean shoreline. Once he determined not to explore the bay he headed deliberately north along the Virginia, Maryland, and Delaware coastal peninsula. Hudson recorded the coastal bays of Maryland and the entrance to Delaware Bay, which is noted as broad but blocked by shallow bars that prevented them from entering safely. He then proceeded along the New Jersey coast before entering Raritan Bay behind Sandy Hook.

From this position Hudson sent his shallop out for explorations to determine whether to enter the river and which of the possible entrances he should follow. He wasted no time pursuing entrances that held no prospect of a passage and proceeded straight up the only entrance that showed promise: the Hudson River. He followed the river to the limit of navigation, then sent his shallop and crew farther north to confirm whether indeed this was the end of navigation. Once this had been determined, he headed downstream and was back in the ocean by October 4. All told, Hudson spent ten days sailing up the Hudson (September 10–19), four days laying at the upriver point (September 19–23, between southern Albany and Rensselaer counties), and another eleven days sailing back downstream and into the Atlantic (September 23–October 4).[22]

On his fateful voyage of 1610, Hudson set forth in the English ship *Discovery* to explore the final option of sailing northwest over Canada. Again, he set forth following a known route, sailed to the extent of confirmed passage, and then began his systematic explorations. In this case Hudson coasted along the shoreline from Ungava Bay, thence into Hudson Bay and southward along the eastern shore into James Bay. Hudson overwintered in James Bay with the ship locked in ice and the crew miserable from the persistent cold, meager rations, and the inevitable onset of scurvy. By the spring, as Hudson was prepared to resume exploration, these extreme conditions led key crew members to mutiny. The mutineers put Hudson and his son John in the ship's boat, along with six other crew members debilitated from scurvy and malnutrition. The first mate, Philip Staffe, joined Hudson voluntarily.[23]

It is at this point that Hudson is most often depicted having given up, recognizing his failure. The most notable representation of this event is John Collier's famous painting showing a despondent Hudson with his son in his lap. In contrast, the deposition of Edward Wilson, the ship's surgeon, paints an entirely different picture of his last view of Hudson: he describes Hudson in the ship's boat having set all sail, chasing down the mutineers as they sailed away in the *Discovery*.[24] This depiction is more in keeping with the drive exhibited by a man who had made the incredible voyages we know.

Hudson's logs of the 1609 voyage eventually made their way to the Dutch East India Company and into the hands of a circle of influential cosmographers and businessmen. The first tangible response to Hudson's reports included trading voyages between about 1610 and 1614 to the Hudson River by Adriaen Block, Hendrick Christiaensen, Thijs Mossel, and other Dutch captains interested in the beaver trade. Soon came the establishment of the New Netherland Company, an attempt to set a monopoly on the beaver trade in the fecund area that Hudson explored.[25] These trading voyages set the routes of sailing, expanded the knowledge of the area around Manhattan and into what we know as Long Island Sound and led to the establishment of Fort Nassau, a trading post located on Castle Island about at the modern-day location of the Port of Albany. Expanded interest in the area resulted in the formation of the Dutch West India Company and the settlement of New Netherland.

Hudson's impact on world geography remains today. Major geographic features known worldwide are named after him, and he remains known for his precedent-setting arctic voyages. Although exploration of the Arctic followed Hudson's voyages, it was not until 1878–1879 that Nils Nordenskjold, sailing in his steamship *Vega*, completed the Northeast Passage over Russia. Roald Amundsen was the first to complete the Northwest Passage over Canada, sailing in his small schooner *Gjoa* east to west from 1903 to 1905. Neither route proved commercially successful, but in recent years the retreating Arctic ice cap may make both routes possible. The log of the *Half Moon* from 1609 continues to inform ecologists, geographers, and historians to this day with its accounts of natural resources and interactions with the Indians. Hudson's methods can still serve as an example for educational studies of the natural world. He remains an icon of early New York history and the determination that was required for European explorers and traders to settle the Hudson River Valley. It is fitting, then, that we reflect upon the final image of Henry Hudson, all sail set in his small boat, determined to forge ahead and recapture his ship and the mutineers that had so rudely cast him adrift.

NOTES

1. Above and throughout this essay the principal source of information about the voyage of the *Half Moon* is the log of Robert Juet, one of the sailors (often erroneously identified as the mate) on the voyage. Hudson's logs of the voyage are not known to exist and are assumed to have been lost in the purging of Dutch East India Company records in the early nineteenth century. Samuel Purchas, *Purchas His Pilgrimes, In Five Books* (London: Henrie Fetherstone, 1625), Third Part, chapter XVI, 581–595, is Robert Juet's account of the voyage of the *Half Moon*; preceeding and following chapters in *Purchas* describe the other known voyages of Henry Hudson. A facsimile of Chapter XVI is available on-line at www.halfmoon.mus.ny.us. *Henry Hudson's Voyages by Samuel Purchas*, March of America Facsimile Series, Number 19 (Ann Arbor: University Microfilms, Inc., 1966) contains the accounts of all four voyages. Nineteenth-century sources of English translations of documents related to the voyage of the *Half Moon* are Henry Cruse Murphy, *Henry Hudson in Holland: An Inquiry into the Origin and Objects of the Voyage which Led to the Discovery of the Hudson River* (1859; repr., New York: Burt Franklin, 1972); G. M. Asher, *Henry Hudson the Navigator: the Original Documents in which his Career is recorded* (London: Hakluyt Society, 1860). Two early twentieth-century compilations provide additional related documents and comparative translations. Thomas A. Janvier, *Henry Hudson: A Brief Statement of His Aims and His Achievements* (New York and London: Harper and Brothers Publishers, 1909) addresses the final voyage of Henry Hudson and trial of the mutineers. J. F. Jameson, ed., *Narratives of New Netherland 1609–1664* (1909; repr., New York: Barnes & Noble, 1937) includes excerpts from several authorities who reference Hudson, especially Emanuel van Meteren, 1610, and Johan de Laet, 1625. As Jameson noted in 1909, so must we today: earlier translations need to be considered with care as to their accuracy. A comprehensive popular source with modernized accounts of the logs is Donald S. Johnson, *Charting the Sea of Darkness: The Four Voyages of Henry Hudson* (Camden, Me.: International Marine, 1993).

2. Jonathan I. Israel, *Dutch Primacy in World Trade, 1585–1740* (Oxford and New York: Clarendon Press/Oxford University Press, 1990) provides a good treatment of the rise, eventual dominance, and decline of Dutch shipping and trade.

3. Documentation of Hudson's thinking does not exist, but given the timeline of Hudson's voyages it would have been necessary to hold a comprehensive view at the outset; it would have been a near impossibility both to develop the geographic concept of each voyage and also to mount each voyage in four years. Exposure to the geographic concepts related to any one of the possible routes would also expose one to the concept of the other routes.

4. The shore-based whaling industry was in its time the equivalent of finding a major new oil reserve. The demand for whale oil was so economically beneficial that by the latter 1600s the shore-based whale fishery of Spitzbergen was depleted and abandoned. In Canada early English settlement had been eclipsed by the French and their explorations up the St. Lawrence River; Hudson's entry into the Hudson Bay and subsequent English explorations into the region provided the opening that led to the Hudson Bay Company and competition against the French in the fur trade and political control of Canada. Hudson's voyage also led directly to Dutch trade in beaver skins and subsequently to the establishment of New Netherland, the Dutch West India Company enterprise, and its unique role in the American colonies. A comprehensive review of these matters, with sections on the Netherlands and New Netherland and with access to comprehensive original sources, is John F. Richards, *The Unending Frontier: An Environmental History of the Early Modern World* (Berkeley: University of California Press, 2003). Specific to the Netherlands is Audrey M. Lambert, *The Making of the Dutch Landscape: An Historical Geography of the Netherlands* (New York: Seminar Press, 1971). Somewhat dated but still useful is Elspeth M. Veale, *The English Fur Trade in the Later Middle Ages* (Oxford: Clarendon Press, 1966). Carl O. Sauer, *Seventeenth Century North America* (Berkeley: Turtle Island Press, 1977) provides general insight about the environment of North America immediately post contact but suffers from minimal attention to the Dutch sources from the Hudson River Valley.

5. Purchas, *Purchas His Pilgrimes*, Third Part, p. 586, line 34.

6. Ibid., p. 593, line 58.

7. See Harold J. Cook, *Matters of Exchange: Commerce, Medicine, and Science in the Dutch Golden Age* (New Haven: Yale University Press, 2007); Jaap R. Bruijn and Femme S. Gaastra, *Ships, Sailors and Spices: East India Companies and Their Shipping in the 16th, 17th, and 18th Century* (Amsterdam: NEHA-Series III, 1993). Hugh Kearney, *Science and Change, 1500–1700* (New York: McGraw-Hill, 1971), provides an older but still standard review of the development of science at this time.

8. See H. Floris Cohen, *The Scientific Revolution: A Historiographical Inquiry* (Chicago: University of Chicago Press, 1994), for an academic but thorough review of the scientific revolution with sections on seventeenth-century voyages of discovery and the role of society.

9. Many masters of near-coastal traders could function very well even though illiterate. Rules of thumb and routes could be memorized, tides and currents observed purely by eye, and sailing could rely entirely upon experience. While it was possible for a captain to make an oceanic crossing without being literate, he would have been severely limited; by the turn of the seventeenth century, syndicates financed most voyages, and the backers of these voyages would not have risked their money on an illiterate captain.

10. One of the earliest publications in this field is Martin Waldseemüller, *Cosmographiae Introductio*, 1507, in modern translation by Joseph Fischer and Franz von Wieser, *Cosmographiae Introductio* (Readex: Microprint Corporation, 1966). Waldseemüller describes a theory of the sphere, outlining latitude and longitude, defining the polar circles, the Tropics of Cancer and Capricon,

basics of spherical geometry, and the use of a quadrant. In 1538 Pedro de Medina further advanced navigational science by addressing fundamental navigational theory and practice in the form of a dialogue between a cosmographer (theoretician) and a pilot (practitioner) in straightforward terms, well presented by Ursula Lamb in *A Navigator's Universe: The Libro de Cosmographia of 1538 by Pedro de Medina, translated and with an introduction by Ursula Lamb* (Chicago: University of Chicago Press, 1972). Medina followed his *Libro de Cosmographia* with *Arte de navegar* in 1545. It is notable that Willem Barentz carried this book on his 1596 voyage to Novaya Zemblya in a Dutch translation by Michiel Coignet, *De Zeevaert oft Conste van ter Zee te varen. Extended: met noch een ander nieuwe Onderwijsinghe op de principaelste puncten der Navigatien* (Antwerp, 1580). Barentz also had published his own navigation manual, *Nieuwe Beschryvinghe ende Caertboeck van de Middellandtsche Zee* (Amsterdam: Cornelis Claesz., 1595). Medina further improved his work with *Regimiento de navegación* in 1552 and a second edition in 1563. In the United Provinces, Lucas Janszoon Waghenaer, an experienced pilot and mariner, published *De Spieghel Der Zeevaerdt* in 1586 and *Den Nieuwen Spieghel der Zeevaert* in 1596. Willem Janszoon Blaeu published *Het Licht der Zeevaert* in 1608. The number of texts available to Hudson or any oceanic navigator is impressive. At least twenty-eight manuals and instructions on marine navigation and an additional twenty-eight books on navigational mathematics and astronomy were published in English from 1560 to 1609; see citations by Thomas R. Adams and David W. Waters, *English Maritime Books Printed Before 1801* (Greenwich, England: The National Maritime Museum, 1995).

11. Thomas Blundeville, *The Theoriques of the Seven Planets, shewing all their diuerse motions...* (London: A. Islip, 1602), goes into planetary astronomy with special emphasis for pilots and seamen and descriptions of special instruments for determining latitude. Thomas Hill, *The Schoole of Skil containing two bookes: the first of the sphere of heauen... the second of the sphericall elements, of the celestial circles* (London: T. Iudson f. W. Iaggard, 1599), is a textbook that specifically identifies mariners as a target audience. Georg. Henisch, *The Principles of geometrie, astronomie and geographie...* (London: I. Windet, 1591), is also available for the mariner as an English translation of the original printed in Latin. John Dee, *General and rare memorials pertaining to the perfect Arte of navigation* (London: I. Daye, 1577), was written specifically to encourage English navigation and includes a description of Dutch hydrographic work. Thomas Hood lectured publicly on mathematics and published some of his speeches and translated into English other documents, such as Pierre de la Ramée, *The Elements of Geometrie* (London: I. Windet f. T. Hood, 1590).

12. Little narrative documentation exists regarding the Newfoundland fisheries, but evidence that Dutch ships traded in the area exists from petitions to the States General for assistance in protecting against piracy. Simon Hart, *The Prehistory of the New Netherland Colony* (City of Amsterdam Press, 1959) treats the Newfoundland fishery and related voyages in pages 7 through 17.

13. Gerard Mercator, *Nova et Aucta Orbis Terrae Descriptio* (Duisburg, 1569), held by Bibliothéque Nationale, Paris, was his first map publication using what we now call the Mercator Projection and showed the polar regions; Gerard Mercator, *Atlas sive Cosmographicae Meditationes de Fabrica Mudni et Fabricati Figura* (Duisburg, 1595), held by the United States Library of Congress, shows much the same features and indicates Mercator's continued influence. The Willem Barentz map of the North Polar regions was published after his death and shows more accurately the shorelines that Barentz and others had explored but still shows the potential for the routes Hudson followed.

14. In addition to Mercator, see others such as Edward Wright's chart of the world from 1599, held by The Newberry Library in Chicago.

15. Even Samuel Eliot Morison, the unabashed Columbus champion, acknowledges Columbus's lack of navigational ability; *Admiral of the Ocean Sea* (New York: MJF Books, 1942, 1970), chapter XIII. For those who would like to keep current with the various Columbus controversies, see http://www.columbusnavigation.com, active as of March 2008.

16. Morison, 183–196.

17. Purchas, *Purchas His Pilgrimes*, Third Part, chapter 24.

18. Illustrations of these instruments can be found in many sixteenth- and seventeenth-century sources, such as Govaert Willemsen van Hollesloot, *Die Caerte vande Oost ende West Zee* (Harlingen, 1588), as well as the texts cited in 10–11.

19. Victor E. Thoren, *The Lord of Uraniborg: A Biography of Tycho Brahe* (Cambridge: Cambridge University Press, 1990); W. F. J. Morzer Bruyns, *The Cross-Staff: History and Development of a Navigational Instrument* (Zutphen: Uitgeversmaatschappij Walburg Pers, 1994); A. Stimson, *The Mariner's Astrolabe. A survey of known, surviving sea astrolabes* (Hes & De Graff Pub B V, 1988); Maurice Daumas, *Scientific Instruments of the Seventeenth and Eighteenth Centuries and Their Makers* (London: Portman Books, 1989); personal experience with replica instruments and examination of original instruments.

20. Chester G. Hearn, *Tracks in the Sea, Matthew Fontaine Maury and the Mapping of the Oceans* (Camden: International Marine, 2003), provides a good overview of Maury's life and the accomplishment of combining thousands of mariner's readings over many years.

21. Jameson, *Narratives*, 6.

22. Purchas, *Purchas His Pilgrimes*, Third Part, 591–595.

23. Janvier, *Henry Hudson*, 135, 136, 141.

24. Ibid., 139.

25. Hart, *Prehistory*, 17–21, 33–38.

The Native-Dutch Experience

IN THE MOHAWK VALLEY

WILLIAM A. STARNA

In his now-classic *Indian Affairs in Colonial New York* (1960), Allen Trelease placed the native people resident within and adjacent to the colony of New Netherland into two camps. The first was comprised mainly of Munsee (Eastern Algonquian) speakers who occupied the mid- to lower Hudson Valley and the environs of western Long Island, Manhattan, and New Jersey. These natives were, in Trelease's words, the "'expendable' Indians, whose economic value as consumers of European trading goods failed to outweigh their destructive capacity." The other camp embraced the "'valuable' Indians, who controlled the peltry supply."[1] For the most part these were Iroquoians, in particular the Mohawks, whose densely populated villages could be found west of Schoharie Creek in the valley that bears their name. Occupying the important literal and metaphorical intervening ground were the Mahicans (also Eastern Algonquian speakers) of the upper Hudson Valley, situated close by the important Dutch posts of, first, Fort Nassau, and, then, several years after its abandonment in 1617, Fort Orange.

Trelease's categories, of course, were shaped by historical hindsight. It is true that soon after the Dutch arrival in 1609 and the commencement of trade, the most sought-after fur-bearing animals were all but extirpated from coastal regions and much of the Hudson Valley, rendering the Indians there at least economically "expendable."[2] But many of these same natives quickly turned to exchanging two equally valuable commodities—their lands and the wampum they produced—for the myriad trade goods the Dutch could supply them. This shift in focus, however, did not diminish in any way the ensuing violence and devastation Trelease pointed to, as Kieft's War of the 1640s and the Esopus Wars that began the following decade, along with numerous other clashes in the region, so well attest.[3]

At the same time, contacts between the Dutch and the Mohawks took place in a considerably more pacific environment, a circumstance that stemmed largely from the obvious need to ensure the continued flow of furs from Iroquoians and Algonquians in the interior. Moreover, historians have since modified Trelease's views, holding that it was much less a matter of who "controlled" the supply of furs as it was where, from whom, and how furs could most readily be obtained.[4] It is equally apparent, fully acknowledging the primacy of the trade in furs, that the economic rationale Trelease and others postulated to sustain the "expendable" and "valuable" dichotomy of native people, framed as it has often been in capitalistic terms, is neither sufficient nor complete. That is to say, there undoubtedly were other factors at play that might shed further light on the historical reality Trelease described, especially in terms of the differing levels of belligerency and conflict that for a half century characterized Dutch-Munsee and Dutch-Mohawk relations.

That native people did not respond in the same way to the Dutch presence has long been recognized, initially, of course, by the original interlopers from the Low Countries and subsequently by modern historians. Emanuel van Meteren, in 1610, was the first to describe the dissimilarities: "In the lower part of the river they [Henry Hudson's crew] found strong and warlike people; but in the upper part they found friendly and polite people...who had an abundance of provisions, skins, and furs...[that] they traded amicably with the people."[5] Anthropologist Jack Campisi has suggested that this perceived demarcation corresponded to the geographical and cultural boundary separating the Mahicans in the upper Hudson Valley from the Munsees farther down. At the same time, unlike their brethren upriver, Munsee groups may have previously weathered more extensive and less cordial meetings with Europeans probing New York Bay and the river's mouth in their search for a passage to Asia, experiences that perhaps were contributing factors to their several unhappy encounters with Hudson and his men.[6]

The first years of contact between Dutch traders and the Mohawks, which coincided with the establishment of Fort Nassau at the mouth of the Normanskill in 1614, appear to have been uneventful. At least there is little in the admittedly thin record to suggest otherwise. In 1622, however, in obscure circumstances related to an alleged dispute with the Mohawks, Hans Jorisz Hontom, a Dutch ship's captain, took a Mohawk headman prisoner. After receiving the ransom he had demanded, Hontom brutally "cut out the male organs of the aforesaid chief." Nothing is known of the Mohawks' immediate reaction to this murder. A decade later, however, after Hontom had been appointed commissary at Fort Orange, the Mohawks made it clear to everyone that they would kill him "wherever they first would be able to find him alone" and, perhaps as a warning, may have been responsible for torching the Dutch yacht *De Bever* and dispatching numbers of cattle near Fort Orange.[7] Hontom managed to survive this threat only to be fatally stabbed the following year in an altercation with Cornelis van Vorst, the commissary of Pavonia, a Dutch post in New Jersey.[8]

An even more serious clash between the Mohawks and Dutch occurred at the onset of what has been called the Mohawk-Mahican War. Sometime in early to mid-July 1626, Mahican warriors, accompanied by several Dutchmen led by Daniel van Crieckenbeeck, the commander at Fort Orange, marched against the Mohawks. A short distance from the fort, most likely somewhere in the lower Normanskill drainage, they were overwhelmed by what apparently was a waiting party of Mohawks. Van Crieckenbeeck, three of his men, and an unknown number of Mahicans were killed. As a contemporary reported it, Van Crieckenbeeck's breach of West India Company policies and his "reckless" actions—to have entangled the Dutch in what was a dispute between the Mohawks and the Mahicans—badly disrupted the trade at Fort Orange. The Dutch were so concerned about the fallout from this encounter that they speedily dispatched Pieter Barentsz, a company trader well known to the Indians, to meet with the Mohawks and defuse the crisis, which was done.[9] Absent from the record is any sign that, in spite of their losses, the Dutch considered military action to punish their attackers. Given their few numbers and assuming that they had some inkling that there was a healthy number of Indians just to their west, such a move would have been foolhardy in the extreme. But this inaction introduces the factor of demographic disparities that may have acted, in part, to dampen either the potential or reality of warfare between the Mohawks and Dutch at the level of the bloody struggles that took place in the Hudson Valley through the middle decades of the seventeenth century.

In his "*Historisch Verhael*," pamphleteer Nicolaes van Wassenaer reported that, at its establishment in 1624, Fort Orange was occupied by eight families and ten or twelve seamen of the West India Company. Following the Van Crieckenbeeck incident, no matter that amends had been made with the Mohawks, the colony's director, Pieter Minuit, ordered a withdrawal from Fort Orange to Manhattan Island. A garrison of sixteen men, "without women," was left to maintain a presence and also to continue the trade.[10] At the same time, beginning just thirty-five miles west of Fort Orange was Mohawk territory, the home of more than 7,000 natives.[11] With little effort, these culturally unified, geographically advantaged, and politically skilled and resourceful people could put hundreds of warriors in the field, something they nonetheless never did do against the Dutch. And what of the Dutch population? In 1630 there were a reported 300 colonists in New Netherland, 270 of whom were on Manhattan Island. The Jesuit Father Isaac Jogues claimed in 1643 that about 100 persons lived within the bounds of the patroonship of Rensselaerswijck surrounding Fort Orange. In 1653 there were 230 men capable of bearing arms there, suggesting a population around 700 or 800. Finally, near the end of the Dutch period (1664), the same area was home to some 1,000 colonists, who were still outnumbered by the Mohawks by a factor of two.[12] By this time, however, the Mohawks had their hands full, engaged as they were in an ongoing war with the Mahicans and their Algonquian allies to the north and east and in another with French-allied Indians in the Richelieu River region, both conflicts made difficult by their having lost a formerly held advantage of out-gunning their foes. Moreover, economic (and other) conditions in Beverwijck had turned chaotic as merchants could not find sufficient quantities of goods to trade while also having to deal with stiff competition from the increasingly aggressive English operating out of the

Connecticut Valley. None of this was helped by an ongoing and precipitous slide in the value of wampum, that critical exchange commodity used by colonist and Indian alike throughout New Netherland and New England, a financial crisis that anthropologist Lynn Ceci argued worked to defeat the Dutch "before the Duke of York's ships ever entered New York Bay."[13]

The Indians of the Hudson Valley stood in a different light from the Mohawks in several important respects. Neither the Munsees nor the Mahicans lived in large, often fortified, towns containing hundreds of residents set within a relatively circumscribed landscape; nor were they as heavily invested as the Mohawks in horticulture, a subsistence base supplemented by hunting and foraging.[14] Instead, the most recent work on these Algonquians describes them as forming small communities, comprised of one or more extended families, that tended to shift location with the seasons. Rather than a strong emphasis on farming—a labor-intensive activity that required a more sedentary way of life, greater numbers and concentrations of people, and a distinct form of social organization—Munsees and Mahicans were primarily foragers and fishermen who balanced these activities with hunting and the planting of corn, beans, and squash.[15]

The divergences in population size, density, and distribution, in addition to settlement area—that is, the landscape on which dwellings and towns were sited—between these three groups of natives were significant. Population estimates for the Mahicans, who were located within the large geographic area encompassing both sides of the Hudson stretching from about Schuylerville in Saratoga County south to above Rhinebeck, a distance of some eighty miles, range from 2,000 to 3,000. There may have been as many as 12,000 Munsees occupying a much more expansive region east and west of the Hudson River from near Rhinebeck south to Manhattan, including western Long Island and New Jersey.[16] In comparison, Mohawk towns were confined to a territory that extended just under forty miles along a narrow east-to-west axis.[17] The contradiction, it seems, is that the small, dispersed, and unconsolidated Mahican and Munsee settlements, indicators of highly mobile and, in terms of subsistence strategies, opportunistic native people, were able to raise such havoc with Dutch colonists, while the politically confederated and militarily powerful Mohawks remained largely detached. But there is perhaps a partial explanation—the matter of land.

With the rapid depletion of furs on the coast and in the lower Hudson Valley, numbers of Munsees, along with some Mahicans farther upriver, turned to selling their lands in exchange for trade goods, beginning, of course, with the well-known purchase of Manhattan Island by the Dutch in 1626. Then, during the 1630s, additional Munsee lands were ceded in New Jersey and on western Long Island, and by the late 1640s, in Westchester County. In 1646 the first lands were patented to colonists at Catskill in the mid-Hudson Valley, and in 1652 at Esopus.[18]

These and numerous other land purchases were regulated initially under the Freedoms and Exemptions of 1629, essentially a charter upon which the patroonship plan of colonization in New Netherland was based. Article XXI stipulated that "private persons…may with the approbation of the director and council there, choose and take possession of as much land as they can properly cultivate and hold the same in full ownership either for themselves or for their masters."[19] This policy of permitting private persons to possess and own land, all of which would obviously be acquired from native people, remained in effect, substantially unchanged, for the duration of the Dutch period.[20] Notwithstanding, Dutch authorities in 1652 were forced to acknowledge that "many and extensive tracts of lands" had nonetheless been bartered or purchased from Indians by colonists in New Netherland, and often conveyed to fellow countrymen, in direct violation of the Freedoms and Exemptions, as well as other orders and regulations. After due consideration, the director general and council intervened, declaring once again that no lands could be either purchased or resold without the approval of the company or its deputy.[21]

The 1652 ordinance in respect to the alienation of Indian lands points to a clear and pressing need to restate all previous regulations in the face of their contravention; that is, various colonists had been dealing directly with native people to acquire their lands without seeking authorization or approval by sitting Dutch officials. Although the intent of the ordinance was to ensure that lands would be put to their best use, that is, for the benefit of the colony, concerns were also expressed by the director general and council about the high price of lands and certain "irregularities" in their transfer. It is safe to assume, therefore, that such private, surreptitious exchanges had led to misunderstandings and disputes, some of which undoubtedly resulting in violence between the parties—Indian and Dutch—that required the immediate attention of these same officials.[22] The situation in the Mohawk Valley was decidedly different.

There is no record of the Dutch visiting the Mohawk homeland before 1634, when a party led by Harmen Meyndertsz van den Bogaert traveled there to learn why the trade at Fort Orange had fallen off. And although they obviously were aware of the Mohawks' economic potency and relative strength, they had no knowledge of how their communities were organized or functioned.[23] This, of course, was not the case with the Algonquians of the Hudson Valley. Fort Orange was founded in 1624 and New Amsterdam in 1626, settlements that stood at the northern and southern extremes of the valley. The lands that would constitute the patroonship of Rensselaerswijck, that one-million-acre holding on both sides of the upper Hudson, were acquired from several Mahicans in 1630.[24] Soon a few farmsteads were in operation there although life was difficult, reliable tenants were in short supply, and to make matters worse, trade in the colony was in general going badly. The viability of both Fort Orange and the patroonship was in question.[25] Despite this situation, which would begin to improve beginning about 1640, the Dutch had learned a great deal about the Indians of the Hudson Valley, certainly enough to negotiate with them for the purchase of their lands and to conduct a lucrative face-to-face exchange of goods. Furthermore, their frequent travels up and down the Hudson, in addition to the everyday interactions with Indians living in the vicinity of New Amsterdam, resulted in the Dutch producing a number of informative, relatively sophisticated ethnographic treatises on native people.[26]

Nothing similar occurred between the Dutch and the Mohawks before mid-century, although, setting Van den Bogaert aside, the earliest description of distinctively Mohawk culture dates to 1644.[27] What is significant, however, is that the first acquisition and thus "settlement" of Mohawk lands by the Dutch did not take place until the summer of 1661, fully three decades after the establishment of the patroonship of Rensselaerswijck, just a day's walk east. Having to contend with the English expanding outwards from their colonies in New England, the increasing demands of Dutch farmers for agricultural lands outside the boundaries of Rensselaerswijck, and the continued growth of Beverwijck, the Dutch looked to the west and the rich lands of the Mohawk Valley. There the first deed was signed between three Mohawk headmen and Arent van Curler, representing a group of Dutch proprietors, for a large parcel of land at Schenectady (from the Mohawk *skahnéhtati*, "it is beyond the pines"). The transfer had the approval of Petrus Stuyvesant, the colony's director.[28] A short three years later the Dutch would lose New Netherland to the English, leaving little time for disputes over land to arise; nonetheless, the late acquisition of Mohawk land by the Dutch most certainly acted to forestall and perhaps avoid altogether the violent clashes that marked Dutch-Algonquian relations in the Hudson Valley.

Ongoing quarrels and hostilities between the Mohawks and their Iroquois neighbors to the west were also factors influencing Dutch-Mohawk relations. In meetings with the Dutch in mid-June 1657, Mohawk headmen asked for horses to drag logs out of the woods so that they could repair their palisades. This required doing, they explained, "in case they should be involved in war with the *Sinnekes*." And in the event of such a war they wanted permission to send their women and children to Fort Orange for protection, an arrangement that would help to explain the détente that, over the long term, characterized relations between themselves and the Dutch.[29] A historic enmity between the Onondagas and Mohawks is well documented, one that was exacerbated by the arrival of Europeans and the fur trade. For example, a year earlier, a party of what were presumably Onondagas showed up in the neighborhood of Manhattan with bundles of furs. Their more than two-week journey to trade had been necessary, they reported, because they previously had been harassed by Mohawks when they attempted to take the short route east from their villages to the Dutch at Fort Orange. To avoid any such trouble in the future, they petitioned Stuyvesant for a trading post on the lower Hudson.[30] It is likely that entanglements such as these were one of a number of distractions that worked to mitigate the possibility of hostilities between the Mohawks and their Dutch neighbors.

What may have been another source of potentially dangerous friction between the Dutch and native people—although the record is silent on this matter—is the practice of hunting and control over hunting territories. Under essentially all circumstances, Dutch colonists enjoyed free hunting, fowling, and fishing in the colony. This right is traceable to article XXII of the 1629 Freedoms and Exemptions, which states that private persons "also have rights of hunting, as well by water as by land, in common with others in public woods and rivers and exclusively within the limits of their colonies, either for themselves or their masters."[31] What constituted "public woods" and whether they might have been bounded is unclear. And there remains the central question of Indians either recognizing or respecting these "rights" or, if they had existed, any such boundaries. Regardless, this manifestly unilateral prerogative for colonists to hunt in the woods and to fish in all waters and rivers of the colony "not heretofore owned by other persons" was reaffirmed in 1656.[32] As a nonetheless-important aside, discord, often leading to violence, ensued when Dutch livestock—cows and pigs—wandered into the Indians' unfenced fields, trampling on and eating their crops, especially corn; however, unlike the situation in the Hudson Valley, there is no record of problems such as these arising in Mohawk country.[33] Again, this is due to the Dutch having acquired Mohawk land so late in their administration of the colony.

In the early fall of 1650 reports began to surface about a situation that, on its face, should have been good cause for the Mohawks to respond in kind. It concerned the activities of *boslopers*, or "woods runners." Increased competition, in part stemming from a falloff in the numbers of pelts, had led to attempts by private traders to convince Indians to trade with them in the woods much before they reached the merchants in Beverwijck. Over time, however, this approach turned violent. Indians with their packs following inland trails leading to Beverwijck or on the road from Schenectady often were intercepted and forced to exchange their furs for what was offered them. Many found themselves robbed of their pelts or, in extreme cases, assaulted and beaten. When officials in Beverwijck moved to prohibit such activities, merchants went around the edict by sending brokers, both Indian and Dutch, into the woods to conduct business in their stead. By June 1660 the situation had reached such a stage of lawlessness that the Mohawks appeared before officials at Fort Orange warning that any continuation might well "develop into the same trouble as between the Dutch and the Indians in the Esopus."[34] It never did. Indeed, there is no evidence that, notwithstanding the abuse they suffered, the Mohawks retaliated with force. But by the early 1650s the Beaver Wars, which had heavily taxed the Mohawks and other Iroquois, were winding down; moreover, all of the Iroquois had suffered greatly from a series of epidemics, thereby reducing their numbers. Thus weakened, the Mohawks may not have had the strength or the will to fight yet another enemy, one which, ironically, furnished them with the weapons to continue their warring and also the trade goods they now depended on for survival.[35]

Throughout the period there were times when the Dutch and the Mohawks seem to have been of a similar mind or, as historian Francis Jennings put it, where "Dutch dependence on the Mohawks grew in much the same measure as Mohawk dependence on the Dutch."[36] A perfect example of this interdependence is the important role the Mohawks played in the fur trade, both in delivering valued pelts to the Dutch and, in the exchange, acquiring the trade goods they both valued and wanted. On several occasions, however, the Mohawks collaborated with the Dutch in either rebuking Munsees of the Hudson Valley, with the intent to keep them in line, or actively working to restrain these Indians when they became restive or belligerent toward the now firmly entrenched Dutch colonists.[37] The Mohawks, then, were party to seeing the "expendable" Indians "subjugated" and "submerged," these also being Trelease's words.[38] Yet, it must be said, none of these groups faired well in the face of the presence of Dutch, English, and, to their north, French colonial powers. Mahicans found themselves pushed off their traditional lands by the ever-acquisitive Dutch, forcing the relocation of settlements and a realignment of alliances, while they and their Mohawk neighbors remained locked in their timeworn struggle. The Mohawks remained engaged in several wars to their west and south, as well as with the French and their native allies, and, as did Indians throughout the region, suffered from recurring epidemics, which together decimated their towns. Compounding matters was the ruin of alcohol and increasing difficulties finding enough food for themselves. By the end of the Dutch period the Munsees in the mid- to lower Hudson Valley had sold off a significant portion of their lands and had begun a withdrawal from the coast, slowly making their way into the upper Delaware drainage and other, even more remote locations.

A final matter. An attractive though ultimately unsatisfactory explanation for the relative absence of conflict between the Mohawks and Dutch revolves around wampum. Some years ago it was concluded that the Mohawks were directly involved in obtaining wampum from coastal groups in southern New England, specifically the Narragansetts and Pequots, and carrying it back home, where it would be distributed among other Iroquois. In exchange for the wampum, it was argued, the Mohawks provided these New England natives with furs that been taken as spoils in the Beaver Wars, which were then traded to the English for goods.[39] Thus, it might be suggested that the Dutch tolerated this exchange to ensure a supply of wampum that could then be used in trade at Fort Orange, a move that kept their relations with the Mohawks peaceable. Unfortunately, there is virtually no evidence that the Mohawks were obtaining quantities of wampum from the Narragansetts or Pequots to be used in such a manner. Furthermore, recent research unequivocally demonstrates that the Mohawks did not fight the Beaver Wars to plunder furs, following from the claim that they lacked their own or a sufficient supply of furs.[40]

Throughout the seventeenth century, then, with the exception of the few clashes mentioned, the Mohawks and the Dutch remained on generally good if cautious terms with each other. Other than the Van Crieckenbeeck episode at the outset of the Mohawk-Mahican War, their half century of increasingly intimate interaction produced a few quarrels but no serious fights or wars. As long as it lasted, theirs was a relationship characterized by a practiced mutual advantage.

NOTES

1. Allen W. Trelease, *Indian Affairs in Colonial New York: The Seventeenth Century* (Ithaca: Cornell University Press, 1960), xii–xiii.

2. The beaver, never abundant in coastal regions, had largely been hunted out of the lower Hudson Valley and the environs of New York Bay and Long Island Sound by about 1625. See Kevin A. McBride, "Fort Island: Conflict and Trade in Long Island Sound," in Gaynell Stone, ed., *Native Forts of the Long Island Sound Area, Readings in Archaeology and Ethnohistory*, vol. 3 (Stony Brook, N.Y.: Suffolk County Archaeological Association, 2007), 256; William Cronon, *Changes in the Land: Indians, Colonists, and the Ecology of New England* (New York: Hill & Wang, 1983), 99.

3. The best work on the Indian-Dutch wars in the Hudson Valley, western Long Island, and eastern New Jersey remains Trelease's *Indian Affairs*, but see also Oliver A. Rink, *Holland on the Hudson: An Economic and Social History of Dutch New York* (Ithaca: Cornell University Press, 1986); Jaap Jacobs, *New Netherland: A Dutch Colony in Seventeenth-Century America* (Leiden and Boston: Brill, 2005). A more narrowly focused treatment is Evan Haefeli, "Kieft's War and the Cultures of Violence in Colonial America," in *Lethal Imagination: Violence and Brutality in American History*, ed. Michael A. Bellesiles (New York: New York University Press, 1999), 17–40.

4. See José António Brandão, *"Your fyre shall burn no more": Iroquois Policy toward New France and Its Native Allies to 1701* (Lincoln: University of Nebraska Press, 1997); William A. Starna and José António Brandão, "From the Mohawk-Mahican War to the Beaver Wars: Questioning the Pattern," *Ethnohistory* 51, no. 4 (2004): 725–750.

5. J. Franklin Jameson, ed., *Narratives of New Netherland: 1609–1664* (New York: Charles Scribner's Sons, 1909), 7.

6. Jack Campisi, "The Hudson Valley Indians Through Dutch Eyes," in *Neighbors and Intruders: An Ethnohistorical Exploration of the Indians of Hudson's River*, ed. Laurence M. Hauptman and Jack Campisi (Ottawa: National Museum of Man, Mercury Series, Canadian Ethnological Services, Paper no. 39 1978), 169; Charles T. Gehring and William A. Starna, "Dutch and Indians in the Hudson Valley: The Early Period," *The Hudson Valley Regional Review* 9, no. 2 (1992): 8; Jameson, *Narratives*, 16–28.

7. The Dutch text, translated by Charles Gehring and quoted in Gehring and Starna, "Dutch and Indians," 15-16, was taken from A. Eekhof's *Bastien Jansz Krol* ('s-Gravenhage, M. Nijhoff, 1910). A. J. F. van Laer, trans. and ed., *Van Rensselaer Bowier Manuscripts: Being the Letters of Kiliaen van Rensselaer, 1630–1643, and Other Documents Relating to the Colony of Rensselaerswyck* (Albany: University of the State of New York, 1908), 303. (Hereafter cited as *VRBM*.)

8. Jacobs, *New Netherland*, 455.

9. Starna and Brandão, "Mohawk-Mahican War."

10. Jameson, *Narratives*, 85.

11. Dean R. Snow, "Mohawk Demography and the Effects of Exogenous Epidemics on American Indian Populations," *Journal of Anthropological Archaeology* 15 (1996): 164. The Mohawks did not suffer the effects of European-introduced disease, notably smallpox, thereby sharply reducing their numbers, until 1633.

12. Rink, *Holland on the Hudson*, 144; Jameson, *Narratives*, 262; Martha Dickinson Shattuck, "A Civil Society: Court and Community in Beverwijck, New Netherland, 1652–1664" (Ph.D. diss., Boston University, 1993), 9–11; Snow, "Mohawk Demography," 164.

13. On events affecting the Mohawks during the mid-1600s, see Daniel K. Richter, *The Ordeal of the Longhouse: The Peoples of the Iroquois League in the Era of European Colonization* (Chapel Hill: University of North Carolina Press, 1992), 96–104 and *passim*; see also Brandão, *Iroquois Policy*. On wampum see Lynn Ceci, "The First Fiscal Crisis in New York," *Economic Development and Cultural Change* 28, no. 4 (1980): 839–847.

14. For works describing Iroquois life and settlements, see Dean R. Snow, *The Iroquois* (Cambridge: Blackwell Publishers, 1994); William N. Fenton, *The Great Tree and the Longhouse: A Political History of the Iroquois Confederacy* (Norman: University of Oklahoma Press, 1998); William Engelbrecht, *Iroquoia: The Development of a Native World* (Syracuse: Syracuse University Press, 2003).

15. On Mahican and Munsee life, see James W. Bradley, *Before Albany: An Archaeology of Native-Dutch Relations in the Capital Region, 1600–1664* (Albany, N.Y.: New York State Museum Bulletin 509, 2007), 8–12.

16. Ibid., 12; Robert S. Grumet, *Historic Contact: Indian People and Colonists in Today's Northeastern United States in the Sixteenth Through Eighteenth Centuries* (Norman: University of Oklahoma Press, 1995), 215.

17. Dean R. Snow, *Mohawk Valley Archaeology: The Sites* (Albany: The Institute for Archaelogical Studies, University at Albany, SUNY, 1995), "A.D. 1614–1626," chap. 6 and "A.D. 1626–1635," chap. 7.

18. Charles T. Gehring, "Peter Minuit's Purchase of Manhattan Island—New Evidence," *de Halve Maen* 55, no. 1 (Spring 1980): 6–7, 17; E. B. O'Callaghan and Berthold Fernow, ed., *Documents Relative to the Colonial History of New York; Procured in Holland, England, and France by John R. Brodhead*, 15 vols. (Albany: Weed, Parsons and Company, 1853–87), 13:1–3, 5, 20. (Hereafter cited as *NYCD.*) Dingman Versteg, trans., Peter R. Christoph, Kenneth Scott, and Kenn Stryker-Rodda, ed., *Kingston Papers*, 2 vols. (Baltimore: Genealogical Publishing Company, Inc.,1976), 1: ix.

19. *VRBM*, 149.

20. The so-called "proposed" Freedoms and Exemptions of 1640 has no similar stipulation regarding land ownership, and there remains a question whether it was formally approved. See O'Callaghan, *Documents Relative*, 1:119–123; Jacobs, *New Netherland*, 121n59. However, the 1650 Freedoms and Exemptions states: "And if any one be disposed to settle on a spot not as yet the property of the Company but belonging to the natives of the country, he shall be obliged to satisfy them for the soil, which can be effected very reasonably and for a few trifles, in presence of some person representing the Company." O'Callaghan, *Documents Relative*, 1: 401.

21. Charles T. Gehring, trans. and ed., *Laws & Writs of Appeal, 1647–1663* (Syracuse: Syracuse University Press, 1991), 29–31.

22. The most complete analyses of land sales in New Netherland, including their cultural dynamics

and implications, are Robert S. Grumet, "'We Are Not So Great Fools': Changes in Upper Delawaran Socio-Political Life, 1630–1758" (Ph.D. diss., Rutgers, The State University of New Jersey, 1979); Robert S. Grumet, "The Selling of Lenapehoking," *Bulletin of the Archaeological Society of New Jersey* 44 (1989): 1–6; Robert S. Grumet, "An Analysis of Upper Delawaran Land Sales in Northern New Jersey, 1630–1758," in *Papers of the Ninth Algonquian Conference*, ed. William Cowan (Ottawa: Carlton University, 1978), 25–35.

23. See Charles T. Gehring and William A. Starna, trans. and ed., *A Journey Into Mohawk and Oneida Country, 1634–1635: The Journal of Harmen Meyndertsz van den Bogaert* (Syracuse: Syracuse University Press, 1988).

24. *VRBM*, 166–169.

25. Bradley, *Before Albany*, 58–62.

26. See, for example, Jameson, *Narratives*, 57–60, 67–73, 85–87, 105–109, 126–129, 216–225; Diederik Willem Goedhuys, trans., Charles T. Gehring and William A. Starna, ed., *A Description of New Netherland by Adriaen van der Donck* (Lincoln: University of Nebraska Press, 2008).

27. Jameson, *Narratives*, 168–180.

28. See Thomas E. Burke, Jr., *Mohawk Frontier: The Dutch Community of Schenectady, New York, 1661–1710* (Ithaca: Cornell University Press, 1991), 16–21.

29. See Charles T. Gehring, trans. and ed., *Fort Orange Court Minutes, 1652–1660* (Syracuse: Syracuse University Press, 1990), 304–306; *NYCD*, 13:72–73. "Sinnekes" ("Sinnekens" and various other forms) was used by the Dutch as a collective for the Iroquois nations living west of the Mohawks, but here meant the Onondagas. Only later was it applied and restricted to the westernmost group, the Senecas. See Ives Goddard's synonymy in Thomas S. Abler and Elisabeth Tooker, "Seneca," in *Handbook of North American Indians, Volume 15, Northeast*, ed. Bruce G. Trigger (Washington D.C.: Smithsonian Institution, 1978), 51.

30. William A. Starna, "Seventeenth Century Dutch-Indian Trade: A Perspective from Iroquoia," *de Halve Maen* 59, no. 3 (1986): 8, 21; Charles T. Gehring, trans. and ed., *Correspondence 1654–1658* (Syracuse: Syracuse University Press, 2003), 107. According to Jesuits in Canada, such ill treatment at the hands of the Mohawks had sent the Onondagas north to trade with the French. Reuben Gold Thwaites, ed., *The Jesuit Relations and Allied Documents: Travels and Explorations of the Jesuit Missionaries in New France, 1610–1791*, 73 vols. (Cleveland: Burrows Bros., 1896–1901), 44: 151.

31. See corresponding statements on hunting and fishing in the Freedoms and Exemptions of 1640 and 1650. *NYCD*, 1: 122, 401.

32. *VRBM*, 149; E. B. O'Callaghan, trans. and ed., *Laws and Ordinances of New Netherland, 1638–1674* (Albany: Weed, Parsons and Company, 1868), 244–245.

33. See James Homer Williams, "Great Doggs and Mischievous Cattle: Domesticated Animals and Indian-European Relations in New Netherland and New York," *New York History* 76 (1995): 245–264.

34. Gehring, *Fort Orange Court Minutes*, 503. On "woods runners" see Donna Merwick, *Possessing Albany, 1630–1710: The Dutch and English Experiences* (New York: Cambridge University Press, 1990), 88–94; Jacobs, *New Netherland*, 211–214.

35. On the Beaver Wars, see generally Brandão, *Iroquois Policy*; Richter, *Ordeal*.

36. Francis Jennings, *The Ambiguous Iroquois Empire: The Covenant Chain Confederation of Indian Tribes with English Colonies from its beginnings to the Lancaster Treaty of 1744* (New York: W. W. Norton & Company, 1984), 57.

37. Ibid., 55–57, 110–110, 123–125; Trelease, *Indian Affairs*.

38. Trelease, "The Subjugation of the Algonquian," chap. VI, and "The Submergence of the Algonquian, chap. VII, in *Indian Affairs*.

39. Neal Salisbury, "Indians and Colonists in Southern New England after the Pequot War," in *The Pequots in Southern New England: The Fall and Rise of an American Indian Nation*, ed. Laurence M. Hauptman and James D. Wherry (Norman: University of Oklahoma Press, 1990), 86–89.

40. See Brandão, *Iroquois Policy*.

Jews in New Netherland:
AN ATLANTIC PERSPECTIVE

NOAH L. GELFAND

ixteen fifty-four was a pivotal year for the Dutch empire in the Atlantic world. On January 26 the West India Company capitulated to Portuguese-Brazilian liberation forces in Pernambuco, marking an end to twenty-four years of Dutch rule in the sugar-rich province. In May of that same year a peace treaty was signed between the Netherlands and England, officially ending the First Anglo-Dutch War but leaving tensions over commercial rights and territorial holdings in the Atlantic unresolved. Meanwhile, in the aftermath of the Peace of Westphalia, the West India Company began to envision the small and previously marginal island of Curaçao as a suitable place from which to engage in the Caribbean trade. From 1654 onwards the company would devote great energy and resources to making Curaçao the hub of its commercial empire in the Atlantic world. Sixteen fifty-four also marked the beginning of the final decade of New Netherland—a period that saw unprecedented growth for the colony.

For Atlantic-world Jews, 1654 was also a pivotal year of transition. The fall of Dutch Brazil meant that the few remaining Jews in the once-thriving community at Recife had to finally evacuate Pernambuco.[1] Some fled to English Surinam, a colony that would later be conquered by Zeelanders during the Second Anglo-Dutch War. Others returned to Amsterdam. A number of these Jews who had lived in Pernambuco eventually remigrated to fledgling colonies on the Wild Coast of South America or to Curaçao, which would become a principal destination for Jews emigrating from the Netherlands and Europe during the next seventy-five years. Significantly, the Jewish settlers of Curaçao were especially important in helping the West India Company realize its goal of turning the island into a commercial emporium. Additionally, in September 1654 a very small group of Brazilian Jewish refugees—twenty-three to be exact—arrived in New Netherland aboard the *St. Catrina*.

The story of the twenty-three Jewish refugees from Brazil has often been recounted and celebrated.[2] Although we know very little about them individually, collectively they have become quite famous. Indeed, the twenty-three Sephardic

Jews who disembarked in New Amsterdam have been mythologized as the founding mothers and fathers of what would later become the greatest Jewish community in the world.[3] Yet, a closer look at the experiences of Jews in New Netherland within the context of Jewish activities in the greater Atlantic world of the era complicates this foundation narrative and suggests a more complex history of community formation. Moreover, compared to other locations in the Dutch Atlantic world, the movement of Jews to New Netherland and then New York was slow, transitory in nature, and modest in number. This essay seeks to understand Jewish colonization to New Netherland and New York within this larger context.

While most historians have focused on the twenty-three Sephardic refugees from Brazil, three Ashkenazi Jews from Europe actually preceded them in the colony. Jacob Barsimon, along with Solomon Pietersen and Asser Levy, reached New Amsterdam on the *Peereboom* from Amsterdam via London on August 22, 1654, more than two weeks ahead of the refugees from Brazil.[4] Of course, in the scheme of 350 years of history, that Barsimon, Pietersen, and Levy established themselves in New Amsterdam before the twenty-three is not the most important or even interesting point. What is important, however, is to recognize that these individuals were separate and distinct from the Brazilian refugees. Acknowledging this fact allows for a comparison between the two groups and leads to an understanding that each had very different reasons for being in the colony—the former came on their own accord and deliberately to New Amsterdam to engage in commercial opportunities, while the latter arrived somewhat involuntarily after a long and circuitous journey in which they probably had originally intended to go to the Netherlands, not its small, struggling outpost in North America.

Thus, the issue of intent becomes a key to understanding New Netherland's initial Jewish inhabitants. The twenty-three Sephardic refugees were among the last Jews to flee Recife following the fall of Dutch Brazil. Beyond this detail, little else is clear. We are not even certain of all of their names.[5] We do know, however, that they arrived in New Amsterdam indebted to the ship's captain for their passage. Yet, the fact that they waited so long to leave Brazil suggests that the Portuguese-Brazilian rebellion had already left these Jews impoverished and unable to pay the West India Company the departure fees required of all settlers leaving their colony.[6] This is a crucial point. Rather than comprising a cohesive group determined to reestablish a Jewish community elsewhere in the Dutch Atlantic, the twenty-three were most likely a diverse group of families— the remnants of a once-thriving population—united only in their poverty and desire to avoid Portuguese rule. There is nothing in the evidence to suggest that— like Barsimon, Pietersen, and Levy, who came to New Amsterdam individually to engage in trade—the twenty-three were anything other than a collection of individual families.

Once in New Netherland, the Sephardic Jews faced opposition and hostility from the colonial leadership. On September 22, 1654, for example, the director general of New Netherland wrote a letter to his superiors at the Amsterdam Chamber of the Dutch West India Company regarding the recent arrival of the Jewish refugees from Brazil. Claiming that the Jews were "very repugnant" to nearly everyone in the community, Petrus Stuyvesant told the directors of the West India Company that he had "deemed it useful to require them in a friendly way to depart," adding that such a "deceitful race…be not allowed further to infect and trouble this new colony."[7] For Stuyvesant, a staunch Calvinist who was already having trouble maintaining order in the pluralistic religious culture of New Netherland that included Lutherans, Puritans, Mennonites, and Catholics, the addition of these particular Jews was not a welcomed development.[8]

When news of Stuyvesant's letter reached the Sephardic community in Amsterdam, the Jews there responded swiftly with an appeal to the West India Company to ensure the rights of their kin to live and conduct business in New Netherland. In a politically shrewd petition of January 1655, the Jews reminded the directors of the West India Company of their faithful service in Brazil, the subsequent losses and poverty they suffered as a result of the Dutch defeat there, the benefits of adding a loyal and taxable population to a spacious and underpopulated colony, and the increase in trade that would surely result from their being allowed to reside in New Netherland. Moreover, and suggestive of a threatened withdrawal of capital if they were not "permitted, together with other inhabitants, to travel, live and traffic there, and with them enjoy liberty on condition of contribution like others," the Jews mentioned their investments in the company and the fact that the French allowed them to trade and settle in Martinique and that the English welcomed them in Barbados.[9]

Accordingly, the West India Company responded favorably to the petition of the Amsterdam Sephardic community. Writing to Stuyvesant on April 26, 1655, the directors of the Amsterdam Chamber of the West India Company declared that the Jews "may travel and trade to and in New Netherland and live and remain there, provided the poor among them shall not become a burden to the company or to the community, but be supported by their own nation."[10] The last part of the company's statement was critical. Stuyvesant's original decision to ask the twenty-three Jews to leave the colony had much to do with their impoverished status. In contrast, Barsimon, Pietersen, and Levy, who all presumably had sufficient resources, were never asked to depart. The company was most concerned with making sure that the twenty-three did not become a financial drain on the colony. If they could support themselves, they were as welcome to stay as any other group. An additional motive of the directors in allowing these Jews to remain in New Netherland, though this seems to have been wishful thinking on their part, was the West India Company's effort to recover "the large sums of money for which they are still indebted to the Company."[11]

While the April 1655 statement by the West India Company should theoretically have been the last word on the Jewish question in New Netherland, in practice a number of issues involving privileges and rights continued to arise.

Included among these issues was a decision by Petrus Stuyvesant and the New Amsterdam Council to exclude Jews from militia service and instead tax them for defense, curtailments on trade by Jewish merchants at Fort Orange and on the Delaware River, and a decision to prohibit the purchase of a house by a Jew in a certain area of Manhattan.[12] Significantly, Stuyvesant and the council wished to have all the Jews live together in the same area of New Amsterdam, though a formal ghetto was not attempted.[13] In the end, the directors of the West India Company sent a stern rebuke to Stuyvesant in which they admonished him to obey and execute their orders punctually and with more respect.[14]

Nevertheless, despite the West India Company's support for Jewish settlement, a permanent Jewish community was slow to develop in New Netherland and New York. Abraham de Lucena brought a Torah to New Amsterdam from the Netherlands in 1655, but Jews were initially denied the right to build a synagogue. Instead, they worshiped privately in their homes.[15] Some of the leading members of the colony, including the aforementioned Abraham de Lucena, did succeed in gaining the right to purchase a plot of land for a cemetery—an important consideration for Jews, who needed to bury their dead separately in consecrated ground.[16] Still, by 1663, de Lucena's Torah had been returned to Amsterdam, apparently because a minyan (prayer quorum of ten males over the age of thirteen) could not be maintained in the city.[17] The following year, Asser Levy and his wife appear to have been the only Jews present in the Dutch colony when it fell to English invaders.[18]

The fact that Asser and Miriam Levy were the only known Jews in New Netherland when it became New York demands explanation, though oddly the celebratory histories of the twenty-three supposed founding mothers and fathers of North American Jewry largely ignore this inconvenient truth. The early, accidental Jewish inhabitants of New Netherland disappear from the mid-1660s colonial records because some probably died, while the rest departed the colony. Indeed, the twenty-three Sephardic Jews had no intention of staying in New Netherland. They were not pioneers or founders but rather displaced persons who preferred to return to Europe or the Caribbean. Furthermore, the explanation as to why most of the other Jewish inhabitants of New Netherland—those who actually came of their own accord—did not persist in their settlement of the colony lies, in part, in the diffuse nature of the Jewish diaspora in the Atlantic world during the early modern period.

The mid-seventeenth century offered Jews willing to migrate to the New World a myriad of possibilities. Barbados, Jamaica, Martinique, Surinam, and Curaçao all developed settlements where Jews could pursue economic opportunities and worship relatively freely during this period.[19] Moreover, on the European side of the Atlantic, London became a promising destination for Jews after their readmission to England in 1656. Comparatively speaking, in both religious and economic matters, New Netherland was a much less attractive option for Jews.

Exploring seventeenth-century Jewish commercial activities helps shed light on Jewish settlement patterns and makes it easier to understand why New Netherland and early New York did not figure as a major destination for Jews during this period. In the Netherlands, Amsterdam's Sephardic Jewish merchants were able to develop family networks involving New Christian kin[20] along Portuguese trade routes to create an economic niche for themselves and essentially corner the market in the transatlantic trafficking of sugar during the first half of the century. The special language skills and family connections that Jews possessed, which enabled them to bring sugar into the Dutch Republic, even through indirect continental routes during times of war between the Netherlands and Spain, were not applicable in the North American colony. New Christians were not present in any numerically significant number in New Netherland, and the initial cash commodity—furs—was not something that Jews specialized in trading. In fact, after the West India Company abandoned its trade monopoly on furs in 1639-1640, anyone in the colony could participate in the exchange.[21] While Jews had the advantage of being the main importers of sugar in the Netherlands and essentially competed amongst themselves for shares in the traffic, most did not embrace the opportunity to take part in the trade of a commodity that was open to all competition.

In considering Sephardic economic patterns as central to an understanding of why Jews did not migrate to New Netherland before 1654 or stay after this date, we can see how these factors began to change (slowly) after 1654. As Jews started forming communities in London, Barbados, Jamaica, Curaçao, Surinam, and other Atlantic locations, new economic opportunities arose. Chief among these was the provisioning trade that supplied the cash-crop plantation colonies (and Curaçao, which, though not a plantation colony, was unable to produce enough to be self-sufficient) with food and supplies.[22] Moreover, after the English conquest of New Netherland, New York City became an important port from which merchants could legally engage with the developing English Atlantic, while still managing to traffic illegally with Dutch, French, and Spanish partners, in spite of the Navigation Acts. These developments contributed to New York becoming a more attractive location for Jewish settlers.

In the liminal second half of the seventeenth century, a period of imperial wars, territorial conquests and exchanges, and reconfigured trade routes, Jewish merchants moved throughout the Atlantic world to find the most advantageous locations in which to live, conduct business, and worship.[23] Some maintained individual residencies in multiple Atlantic locations. Indeed, many of the Jewish merchants who came to New York in the second half of the seventeenth century were transient—seemingly living in the colony on a part-time basis while moving throughout the Atlantic world, much like the goods they were trading.[24] Isaac Pinheiro, a leading Sephardic businessman of both New York and Nevis at the end of the seventeenth century, was one such merchant who moved back and forth and took advantage of the city's position as a significant port in both the

English and Dutch empires.[25] In Nevis, Pinheiro had an estate, mill, slaves, and at least two sons in residence to oversee production and commercial operations of sugar. In New York he lived with his wife, Ester, in a house that he owned, and he capitalized on New York City's position as a burgeoning slave depot.[26] He also had trade connections with planters in South Carolina and network ties to family members in both the Amsterdam and Curaçao communities. These diverse ties undoubtedly helped him to maneuver between the empires and contributed to his success as a merchant.[27]

The link between the Jewish merchants of latter seventeenth-century English New York City and the earlier period of Dutch New Amsterdam is Asser Levy. His business career as the only member of the 1654 migrants to make New Amsterdam his permanent home and the only Jew to live continuously in the town as it transitioned from Dutch to English rule illustrates how New York City eventually became a viable option for Jewish settlers. An Ashkenazi Jew originally from Vilna, Lithuania, Levy pursued a diversified commercial strategy in New Amsterdam that in many ways would become typical of the later Jewish residents of New York City. As an Ashkenazi, Levy lacked the familial ties with and economic orientation towards Portugal and Portuguese colonial routes that were characteristic of the commercial activities of his Sephardic brethren. Accordingly, his lack of connections among the Spanish and Portuguese Jews and New Christians of the Atlantic mercantile system may have made his foray into commercial trade all the more daunting and his subsequent success all the more surprising and remarkable. Yet these same circumstances may have also worked to his advantage in the sense that at a time when routes, goods, and networks were being reconfigured, he was not tied to historic patterns and traditional Sephardic familial associations. Levy was able to transcend this history to take advantage of the specific opportunities that existed in New Netherland and New York and the changing Atlantic world of the second half of the seventeenth century. In this way, though he was a unique figure in his own era, he set the tone for those Jews who came to New York after him.

One of the most significant points about Asser Levy's entrepreneurial career in New Amsterdam and New York City was that he was involved in a myriad of business activities. He is probably best remembered for being one of the town's few licensed butchers and for owning a slaughterhouse.[28] Yet this occupation was only a small component in his overall effort to support himself.[29] A few years after his arrival in the colony, the director general and the Council of New Netherland authorized the burgomasters of the city to grant the leading Jewish merchants the burgher right. Acquiring this right guaranteed that Levy would be able to participate on a level of equality with other settlers in the economic affairs of the colony.[30] Moreover, after the English assumed governance of the colony, Levy made sure to obtain endenization status, with privileges to trade in both New York City and at Albany.[31]

Asser Levy also maintained economic ties with his coreligionists in Amsterdam, where he had resided prior to his move to New Netherland. In 1659, for example, Levy acted as attorney for powerful Sephardic Amsterdam merchant Abraham Cohen Henriques in a case involving the repayment of a loan.[32] The following year, like many other Jewish merchants in the Atlantic world, Levy returned to Amsterdam to cement his trade connections with associates there, before continuing his travels in Germany to conduct business.[33] Significantly, in Germany, his trading partners would have been Ashkenazi rather than Sephardic Jews. Thus, Levy's commercial ventures bridged economic boundaries between the two distinct groups of Jews and foreshadowed eighteenth-century trade patterns as larger numbers of Ashkenazim migrated to North America and participated in transatlantic exchange.

In contrast to his predecessors in Dutch Brazil who specialized in financing sugar production and the trafficking of sugar to Europe, the types of business dealings in which Asser Levy was involved were quite varied in New York. Among the bulk items that Levy traded in were grains, flour, salt, peas, and tobacco.[34] He also carried an array of finished products for exchange, including linens, clothing, hats, jewelry, and silver containers.[35] Furthermore, those he traded with were dispersed throughout the colony, from Albany and Esopus to Long Island and New York City. For payment, Levy accepted specie, wampum, furs, tobacco, and other goods.[36] He was also involved in buying and selling real estate in New Netherland and New York. In one real-estate transaction of note, he sold a house to Christian Pieters for the use of the Lutheran Congregation.[37]

Levy's diversified business portfolio was the key to his success. By involving himself in so many different aspects of the colony's economic life, he made himself an invaluable broker of goods and provider of provisions to all segments of New York society. At the time of his death in 1682, over 400 people owed money to Asser Levy.[38] Those Jews who migrated to New York after him followed his lead in varying the commodities that they traded and in developing the provisioning market. Indeed, by the turn of the century, New York's Jewish merchants were taking advantage of multiple trade routes and a dispersed Atlantic diaspora to provision Jews in Curaçao, Surinam, Barbados, Jamaica, Nevis, and other Caribbean locations.[39]

In the end, the story of Jewish settlement in New Netherland and New York is really one of fits and starts rather than one of continuity and steady growth. After the fall of Dutch Brazil, rather than chance relocation in North America, Sephardic Jews chose the Caribbean as a center from which they could take advantage of an existing system of commercial networks and their knowledge and experience in handling traditional trade goods to establish a viable economic base and religious communities. The rise of England and the development of an English Atlantic in the second half of the seventeenth century eventually led to the establishment of a Jewish community in New York. The dispersal of Jewish merchants from Brazil to English colonies, such as Barbados, Jamaica, and Nevis, and the readmission of Jews to England in 1656 all contributed to a reconfiguration of trade routes and a partial reorientation of Jewish commerce. In English New York, new opportunities opened to legally trade and provision kin within the English Atlantic, while illicit avenues remained for commerce with relatives and associates in the Dutch Atlantic. By the end of the 1680s, a core group of Jewish settlers actualized these potential opportunities and made New York their home. According to my calculations from colonial records, eighteen Jewish families consistently resided in the city by the end of the decade.[40] By the turn of the century, at least twenty families called New York their home, and a public congregation with a building designated as a synagogue did form.[41] Thus, it was at that moment, and not earlier, that Jews established the formal communal framework in New York that was a hallmark of their experiences in the Netherlands, Dutch Brazil, and Curaçao.

Asser Levy, the Ashkenazi Jew who migrated to New Netherland by choice and succeeded in making the colony his permanent home, should be considered the forerunner of this 1680s New York community, rather than the twenty-three Sephardic refugees whose stay in the colony was fleeting. Levy persevered and provided future generations of Jews with a shining example of the limitless possibilities settlement in New York offered.

NOTES

1. Jews were an important population in Dutch Brazil. Through their language skills they helped the West India Company communicate with Catholic Portuguese planters, while they also played a leading role in financing sugar production and handling that trade with Europe. Though population figures are inexact for this period, the consensus among historians is that Jews comprised between one-third and one-half of the total white civilian population in Dutch Brazil—a figure that exceeded 1,000 during the 1640s. The reassertion of Portuguese rule in Pernambuco meant that Jews who had formerly been baptized as Catholics would again be subject to prosecution by the Inquisition, thus necessitating their need to depart from the colony. For more on Jewish activities in Dutch Brazil, see Noah L. Gelfand, "A Caribbean Wind: An Overview of the Jewish Dispersal from Dutch Brazil," *de Halve Maen* 78 (Fall 2005): 49–56.

2. The 350th anniversary of their arrival occurred in 2004. That year saw an enormous outpouring of celebratory media commemorating the first Jews in the future United States. Everything from newspaper editorials and magazine articles to short films, dedicated Web sites, books, museum exhibits, and a congressional mandate all marked the anniversary.

3. Drawing a direct line to the twenty-three refugees, New York City's Congregation Shearith Israel has long claimed these Jews as the founders of the first Jewish community in North America. See Congregation Shearith Israel's Web site, http://www.shearithisrael.org/folder/main_frames_new .html (accessed December 12, 2007).

4. Leo Hershkowitz makes the case for Barsimon, Pietersen, and Levy all arriving on the *Peereboom*. See Hershkowitz, "By Chance or Choice: Jews in New Amsterdam, 1654," *de Halve Maen* 77 (Summer 2004): 23.

5. Leo Hershkowitz has identified some of the Brazilian refugees, as well as other early Jewish migrants to New Netherland. In addition to Barsimon, Pieterson, and Levy, Hershkowitz claims Riche Nunes, Judith de Mereda, Abraham Israel, David Israel, Moses Ambrosius, and Jacob Lucena were in the colony by autumn 1654. Jacob Cohen Henriques, Salvador d'Andrada, Abraham de Lucena, Joseph de Costa, Benjamin Cardozo, Isaac Israel, and David de Ferera appear by the beginning of 1655, and Elias Silva and Moses de Silva by 1656. See Leo Hershkowitz, "Asser Levy and the Inventories of Early New York Jews," *American Jewish History* 80 (1990): 26.

6. The Portuguese-Brazilian rebellion against West India Company rule destroyed the economy of Dutch Brazil. As financiers and creditors, Jews were especially hurt by the precipitous drop in sugar production during the war. In addition to their poverty, Jewish efforts to leave Dutch Brazil may have been hampered by a shortage of ships in the region due to the First Anglo-Dutch War (1652–1654).

7. Extract from "Letter of Petrus Stuyvesant to the Amsterdam Chamber of the Dutch West India Company, Manhattan, September 22, 1654," in *A Documentary History of the Jews in the United States, 1654–1875* (hereafter cited as *DHJUS*), ed. Morris U. Schappes (New York: The Citadel Press, 1950), 1–2.

8. Stuyvesant's views and comments about the Jewish refugees should be understood within the context of his preference for a monoreligious society and his similar treatment of other religious minorities in New Netherland, such as Lutherans and Quakers. In other words, Petrus Stuyvesant's attempt to rid New Netherland of Jews was not simply a manifestation of his anti-Semitism (though he certainly harbored prejudices against Jews that were typical of the age) but rather consistent with his larger attempt to limit the practices of dissenting denominations in the colony. Instructions from the directors of the Amsterdam Chamber of the West India Company to Stuyvesant help shed light on his attitude toward Lutherans and highlight the company's policy regarding religious minorities in the colony. See "Letter from the Directors to Stuyvesant, June 14, 1656," in which they state, "We would also have been better pleased, if you had not posted the placard against the Lutherans—a copy of which you sent us—and committed them to prison, for it has always been our intention, to deal with them quietly and peacefully. Hereafter you will therefore not post such or similar placards without our knowledge, but you must pass it over and let them have free religious exercises in their homes," in *Correspondence, 1654–1658*, New Netherland Documents Series, vol. 12, trans. and ed. Charles T. Gehring (Syracuse: Syracuse University Press, 2003), 93.

9. Petition of the Amsterdam Jews "To the Honorable Lords, Directors of the Chartered West India Company, Chamber of the City of Amsterdam, January 1655," in *DHJUS*, 2–4.

10. Extract from "Reply by the Amsterdam Chamber of the West India Company to Stuyvesant's letter, April 26, 1655," in *DHJUS*, 4–5.

11. Ibid, 4. Jaap Jacobs has recently completed an important retranslation of this document. According to Jacobs, the phrasing in the last part of the letter from the Amsterdam directors—*de groote capitalen die sij alsnoch inde compagnie sijn heriderende*—was originally mistranslated by nineteenth-century historian Berthold Fernow, and subsequent translators have followed suit. Jacobs makes a compelling argument that instead of "the large amount of capital which they *still have invested* in the shares of this Company," the directors actually meant "the large sums of money for which they are *still indebted* to the Company" (italics added). Thus, by allowing Jews to settle and trade in New Netherland, the company envisioned the possibility of recovering some of the debt owed to them. See Jaap Jacobs, *New Netherland: A Dutch Colony in Seventeenth-Century America* (Leiden: Brill, 2005), 374–377.

12. *DHJUS*, 5–9.

13. William Pencak, *Jews and Gentiles in Early America, 1654–1800* (Ann Arbor: The University of Michigan Press, 2005), 32.

14. Extract from "Letter of Directors of the Dutch West India Company to Stuyvesant, June 14, 1656," in *DHJUS*, 11–12.

15. In contrast, Jews had two synagogues in Dutch Brazil.

16. On February 22, 1656, Abraham de Lucena, Salvador d'Andrada, and Jacob Cohen Henriques were granted the right to purchase a plot of land to bury the dead. The exact location of the original burial plot is not known. In 1682 Joseph Bueno de Mesquita purchased land for a cemetery near Oliver and Madison streets. See David De Sola Pool, *Portraits Etched in Stone: Early Jewish Settlers, 1682–1831* (New York: Columbia University Press, 1952), 8, 10–11. The Babylonian Talmud, Tractate Sanhedrin 47a, mentions the rule that a pious and a wicked person must not be buried side by side.

17. Jonathan D. Sarna, *American Judaism: A History* (New Haven: Yale University Press, 2004), 10.

18. Departure dates for the twenty-three Sephardic refugees are not known. Records indicate that Jacob Barsimon, one of the three merchants who migrated to New Netherland of his own accord, was still in New Amsterdam as late as February 1659, when he appeared in court regarding a dispute with Warnaer Wessels over tobacco owed to him. "February 27, 1659," *Laws and Writs of Appeal, 1647–1663*, New Netherland Document Series, vol. 16, part one, trans. and ed. Charles T. Gehring (Syracuse: Syracuse University Press, 1991), 110.

19. The legal Jewish involvement with the French Atlantic ended in 1685 with the institution of the Black Codes, which banned Jews from French colonies.

20. "New Christian" was the term used to identify Spanish and Portuguese Jews who converted to Catholicism. Their descendents were also identified as New Christians. The term was introduced in the Iberian Peninsula so that Old Christians could distinguish themselves from these conversos.

21. For more on the Dutch West India Company and the fur trade, see Oliver A. Rink, *Holland on the Hudson: An Economic and Social History of Dutch New York* (Ithaca: Cornell University Press, 1986), 134–135.

22. In the late seventeenth and eighteenth centuries, Jews in New York sent flour, bread, butter, meat, and other provisions from Manhattan to Curaçao. See Wim Klooster, "Jews in Surinam and Curaçao," in *Jews and the Expansion of Europe to the West*, ed. Paolo Bernardini and Norman Fering (New York: Berghahn Books, 2004), 354.

23. For example, the Netherlands and England fought three wars during the seventeenth century (1652–1654; 1665–1667; 1672–1674), and New Netherland/New York passed between Dutch and English authority three times between 1664 and 1674.

24. Isaac Rodriguez Marques, for example, seems to have split his time between New York and Jamaica. See his will, dated October 5, 1707, in Leo Hershkowitz, *Wills of Early New York Jews, 1704–1799* (New York: American Jewish Historical Society, 1967), 8–10.

25. According to Leo Hershkowitz, Isaac Pinheiro was naturalized in New York on February 2, 1695. Hershkowitz, *Wills of Early New York Jews*, 21–24.

26. Ester Pinheiro in fact purchased a slave from New York's governor, Edward Hyde, for £40 in 1706. See "Isaac and Esther Pinheiro File," in Oppenheim Collection, box 15, American Jewish Historical Society, New York, New York.

27. It is clear from his will that Pinheiro was quite wealthy. A number of slaves, horses, and other property are listed in his will, while he distributed a significant amount of money to a number of relations.

28. Berthold Fernow, ed., *The Records of New Amsterdam*, 7 vols. (New York: Knickerbocker Press, 1897), 5: 312.

29. Levy may have taken the job as butcher for religious reasons, as well. During the period when he was the only Jew in the colony, he may have felt the need to personally slaughter his own meat according Jewish kosher laws. Additionally, as more Jews arrived in New York in the 1670s, he may have seized on the opportunity, for both economic and communal reasons, to provide kosher meat for the growing group of Jewish inhabitants.

30. Salvador D'Andrada, Jacob Cohen Henriques, Abraham de Lucena, and Joseph D'Acosta petitioned the director general and the Council of New Netherland to secure the burgher right for their coreligionists after Asser Levy had initially been denied by the burgomasters. On April 20, 1657, Stuyvesant and the council authorized the burgomasters to admit the petitioners "and their Nation to the Burghership." See New York Colonial MSS, vol. 8, 531, reprinted in Samuel Oppenheim, "Early History of the Jews in New York," *Publications of the American Jewish Historical Society* 18 (1909): 1–91.

31. Peter R. Christoph and Florence A. Christoph, eds., "March 31, 1665," in *Books of General Entries of the Colony of New York, 1664–1673,* New York Historical Manuscripts: English, 2 vols. (Baltimore: Genealogical Publishing Co., Inc., 1982), 1:105.

32. Gemeentearchief Amsterdam (hereafter GAA), N.A. 2443, fol. 479–480, January 27, 1659, nots. Jan Molengraeff.

33. GAA, N.A. 2443, fol. 761, May 24, 1660, nots. Jan Molengraeff.

34. List of commodities derived from "May 14, 1675," Ordinary Court Session held at Kingston, in the Samuel Oppenheim Collection, box 9, American Jewish Historical Society, New York.

35. Hershkowitz, "Asser Levy and the Inventories of Early New York Jews," 35–55.

36. On April 12, 1658, for example, it was found that Dirckje Harmens, wife of Jan Mertens, residing at Fort Orange in Beverwijck, was indebted to Asser Levy for 176 guilders in beavers, payable in 22 skins (eight guilders per beaver). Record in Oppenheim Collection, box 9, American Jewish Historical Society, New York.

37. "June 29, 1671," *Books of General Entries of the Colony of New York, 1664–1673*, 2: 438.

38. The list of those indebted to Levy reads like a Who's Who of late seventeenth-century New York and includes Stephen Van Cortlandt, Jacob Kip, Peter Delanoy, Nicholas Bayard, and Jacob Leisler. Asser Levy's Estate, Liber 19B of Wills, New York Surrogate's Office, 33–45, in Oppenheim Collection, box 9, American Jewish Historical Society, New York.

39. For examples of this trade, see shipping transactions in GAA, N.A. 3777, fol. 279–281, June 14, 1674 (New York – Curaçao – Surinam); GAA, N.A. 5889/1161, August 31, 1703 (New York – Curaçao); GAA, N.A. 6121, December 13, 1719 (New York – Curaçao); Liber 26 of Cons., 89, April 2, 1706, in the Samuel Oppenheim Collection, box 2 (New York – Jamaica), American Jewish Historical Society, New York.

40. This calculation is from my review of 42 boxes of files in the Samuel Oppenheim Collection, American Jewish Historical Society, New York.

41. Jonathan Sarna claims the renting of a space for a public synagogue occurred between 1695 and 1704. See Sarna, *American Judaism*, 9–10.

Fortune in the New World:

JAN JANSZ DAMEN IN AMERICA

JAAP JACOBS

TRANSLATED BY ELISABETH PALING FUNK

Why did a farmer's son from Bunnik, a small community in the province of Utrecht, leave for the New World? Jan Jansz Damen left no documents that provide an answer to this question. In 1655, four years after his death, several old inhabitants of Bunnik declared that they had known him well. They stated that about twenty-five years earlier he had "traveled to New Netherland and established his domicile there to make his fortune."[1] But that was an explanation after the fact. Did Jan Jansz Damen really plan to settle definitively in New Netherland when he left the Dutch Republic in 1630?

New Netherland, the territory including present-day New York and surrounding areas, did not amount to much at that time. After the New Netherland Company had traded with the local Indians for several years, the colony was taken over by the recently established West India Company (WIC). Not until 1624 did the WIC send the first groups of colonists to Manhattan, where Fort Amsterdam was constructed. These colonists were mainly Walloons, religious refugees from the Southern Netherlands. Damen almost certainly did not belong to this first group, although a few of its members were connected with Utrecht in some way. Pieter Minuit and his wife, Geertruijt Raedts, for example, lived in Utrecht in 1615 and 1616. Minuit, who was born in Cleves to parents who were refugees from the Southern Netherlands, served from 1626 to 1632 as director of New Netherland. Similarly, a connection exists between some other early colonists and the city of Utrecht. Most Walloons were not content in the New World, however. After a few years, a large number of them had left New Netherland.[2]

Although New Netherland remained a marginal part of the WIC's interests, the colony's population began to increase somewhat after 1629 when the WIC established the patroon system, which to some extent privatized colonization. The patroon system enabled individual merchants to acquire a large territory in New Netherland where they were allowed to govern and administer justice, on the condition that they would send at least fifty colonists there within a period of four years. Some merchants in Amsterdam were interested, but most of them withdrew quickly when the required investments proved rather high. The only patroon to remain was Kiliaen van Rensselaer, an Amsterdam jeweler from a family in Nijkerk. He owned land in Nijkerk and the estate Crailo, near Hilversum, among other properties. For his patroonship Rensselaerswijck, a vast area around present-day Albany on the Hudson River, he recruited a large number of the required colonists from towns that were situated by and large between the city of Utrecht and the village of Nijkerk to the northeast, such as Westbroek, Maartensdijk, and Amersfoort, or to the south and east of Utrecht, like Bunnik and Houten.[3]

At least seventeen of the farmers and farm workers who were hired by Van Rensselaer came from Bunnik and Houten. Most of them were part of the first group of Rensselaerswijck's settlers; labor contracts for some of them are located in the notarial archives of Amsterdam. Jan Jansz Damen's contract is not among them, but it is possible that he was hired to go to New Netherland when he was in his early twenties. He is listed in a 1635 document as being in the colony as a company servant, perhaps, considering his background, as an overseer. Farm workers were usually hired for three years and were paid about 125 guilders. In addition they received room, board, and free passage to the New World.[4]

Some of the early immigrants returned to Holland when their contract expired, but Jan Jansz Damen remained in New Netherland. In 1638 he leased two parcels of land on Manhattan from the West India Company. He had a six-year lease, and his rent was agreed to be half of the land's yield. The WIC undertook to keep the fences around the property in good repair and to lend Damen two laborers during harvest time. In turn, Jan Jansz Damen was obligated to cultivate and fertilize the land.[5]

Shortly after the lease had been signed, Damen decided to marry. His choice was Adriaentje Cuvilje, also written as Cuvilly or Cuvilier, widow of Guillaume Vigne. She came from Valenciennes, in the north of France, and probably arrived in New Netherland with the early Walloon colonists, along with her first husband. Jan Jansz Damen was about thirty-one when he married, but Adriaentje must have been considerably older. She had four children from her first marriage—Maria, Rachel, Jan, and Christina—two of whom were married already. Christina's husband was Dirck Volckertz de Noorman, a colonist from Scandinavia, who did not get along well with his stepfather-in-law. Adriaentje's daughter Rachel was the wife of Cornelis van Tienhoven, secretary of New Netherland. To have such an influential person in colonial society within his family circle must have been beneficial to Damen in his rise on the social and economic ladder. Jan Jansz Damen prospered nicely in the following years. He did have to appear before the court in Fort Amsterdam on several occasions. Once he was condemned to pay ten guilders in compensation because his cattle had damaged his neighbor's vegetable garden, a fairly common occurrence. More noteworthy is a minor incident concerning his stepson-in-law, Dirck Volckertsz de Noorman, who owed him money. When Volckertsz denied his indebtedness,

Damen became furious and tried to throw him and his wife, Christina, who were visiting him, out of the house. A scuffle ensued, during which Dirck threw a tin jug at Jan Damen's head. The fight escalated to the point that Damen threatened his stepson-in-law with a knife, causing several tears in his clothing. The court probably arranged an amicable resolution to the conflict, but the incident reveals that Damen had a rather hot-tempered disposition.[6]

The dispute may have been generated by Jan Jansz Damen's attempt to collect all outstanding debts because he was about to travel back to Holland. Why he undertook that journey is unknown. It is clear, however, that in July 1638 he empowered Cornelis van Tienhoven to act for him in all his affairs in New Netherland. Less than a year later, in May 1639, Jan Damen was back in Amsterdam, making a declaration at the request of New Netherland's former director Wouter van Twiller. Van Twiller had just been replaced as the top man in New Netherland by Willem Kieft and was required to account for his administration. Damen's declaration, which concerns primarily the prices of different kinds of horses and cows, indicates that Van Twiller's financial management, among other things, had drawn criticism.[7] But between the lines there is information about Damen himself. He declares that he is thirty-two years old and had left the colony in July 1638, after having occupied himself for about ten years with agriculture. Jan Damen made his declaration jointly with Jacques Bentin, a Walloon with whom Damen maintained close connections. They said they were about to return to New Netherland aboard the ship *Haring*.[8]

Two months later Damen was back in the colony. In the following years, he occupied a prominent position in the young colony's society. He was repeatedly asked, for example, to function as arbiter when compensation had to be assessed in judicial cases or when conflicts had to be settled in an informal way. Together with David Provoost, the WIC's keeper of provisions, he served as guardian of Jan van Vorst, whose father Cornelis van Vorst had lost his life some years earlier during an unfortunate brawl. This guardianship required quite a few organizational chores, which entailed Damen's regular appearance in court to collect debt payments on behalf of the heirs. His function as church warden and his appointment to the board of Twelve Men, whose duty it was to advise director Willem Kieft, also signify his standing in New Netherland.[9]

Jan Damen's farm prospered, as well. As early as 1639 he employed at least one laborer. He engaged a second in 1641, Hendrick Harmensz van Utrecht, under a four-year contract. In the same year Jan Damen bought a parcel of land on Manhattan from Marijn Adriaensz. The purchase price of 1,000 guilders, payable in installments over three years, indicates that he was probably quite affluent by that time.[10]

But dark clouds began to gather. The purpose behind the creation of the board of Twelve Men in August 1641, of which Jan Damen was one, was to advise director Kieft in a thorny problem: how to react to the murder of Claes Cornelisz Swits. The old man had been shot to death by a young Indian of the

Wechquaesgeek tribe while he was replacing the reeds on the roof of his house. This incident was not the first between colonists and Indians. Since a decision in 1639 to have the Indians pay some kind of contribution, several skirmishes had occurred, with casualties on both sides. The situation seemed somewhat calmer during the summer of 1641, but Swits's murder had made clear that this calm had been in appearance only.[11]

The response from the Twelve Men was simple. They advised first to reinforce the colony with provisions, ammunition, guns, and armament and to postpone taking revenge until a good opportunity presented itself. It was deemed best to wait until the winter, when the Indian men were hunting in small groups that were separated from each other in the forests. With only women and children left, the villages would be unprotected. Not until February 1643 did the opportunity to retaliate present itself. A group of 400 to 500 Wechquaesgeek and Tappan Indians were fleeing before another tribe and were temporarily camping on the west shore of the Hudson, opposite Manhattan. The colonists regarded their sudden presence as a providential opportunity to exact retribution. The pamphlet *Breeden-Raedt* gives a rather biased account of the manner in which the decision had been taken:

> Around this time there was a dinner at the home of Jan Jansz Damen set for Shrove Tuesday or Mardi Gras, at which dinner the director [Willem Kieft], under the pretense of a toast, announced his intent to attack the Indians to three hotheaded farmers. These were Marijn Adriaensz, Jan Jansz Damen and Abraham Blancq, who presented the director with a request, ostensibly submitted by the secretary Tienhoven, pleading . . . for permission to avenge [this murder] to maintain the reputation of our nation.[12]

Then a glass was raised to a good outcome. The story itself is somewhat peculiar but not implausible: those involved all belonged to Damen's circle of acquaintances. The result was that Kieft granted permission to attack the Indians. Some days later, on the night of February 25, 1643, a group of colonists and soldiers crossed the river and surprised the Indians in their sleep, causing a horrific bloodbath. Although Jan Jansz Damen's presence during the attack is not recorded, as one of the instigators he was likely to have been one of the participants. A reaction on the part of the Indians was unavoidable, a consequence that had already been predicted by some colonists who had counseled Kieft against the attack. During the entire summer of 1643 several Indian groups united in attacking isolated farms and homes of the colonists. They did not dare to attack Fort Amsterdam, which is why Damen, whose house was close to the fort, did not suffer damage to his property.

Other colonists were not as fortunate. Hence, the rash, murderous raid created great dissatisfaction. Many colonists, supported by Everardus Bogardus, minister of the Dutch Reformed Church, turned against Kieft's policies and blamed the director for the colony's problems with the Indians. He was primarily reproached for his attempt to collect a contribution from the Indians, although general criticism was leveled as well at the policies of the WIC, and for his lack of strong leadership during the events of February 1643. Because of his role in the attack, Jan Jansz Damen himself became identified with the side of Kieft and the WIC. Significantly, when late in 1643 a new advisory body of Eight Men was appointed to replace the Twelve Men, Damen was elected at first, but the other members excluded him, "for certain reasons moving them [to act] this way," as the sources relate.[13] These reasons obviously pertained to his signature on the petition to attack the Indians earlier that year.

There are no signs that Damen suffered much disadvantage from his exclusion, although for a number of years he focused more on his own affairs than on administrative activities. His business affairs went quite well. He sold grain and cattle to a number of people, some of it intended for ships that took in fresh provisions in New Netherland. With Jan Evertsz Bout, who had replaced him in the Twelve Men, Damen owned a ship, *St. Pieter*, which was sold in 1645 for 4,050 guilders. A year later he owned one-eighth of the privateer *La Garce*, which operated in the Caribbean from New Amsterdam. He also acted as middleman in the grain trade for Cornelis Maesz van Buren, who lived in Rensselaerswijck. And Kieft granted him property rights to the lands that he had earlier leased from the West India Company.[14]

Not until 1647 do we encounter Damen again in a public position, when he was appointed as one of the guardians of the property and the minor children of a deceased colonist. By this time, the conflict within New Netherland society had abated a little, in part because there was peace again with the Indians. Besides, it was already known that Kieft would be relieved by Petrus Stuyvesant. During Stuyvesant's administration, Damen was appointed church warden and took a seat on the board of Nine Men, the advisory body established by the new director-general a few months after his arrival in the colony.[15] Interestingly, while the *Breeden-Raedt* called Damen a farmer, the description of him in the ordinance that established the Nine Men names him one of its three members who are designated as burgher. The other two categories were those of merchants and farmers. Evidently Damen, his commercial activities and ownership of a farm notwithstanding, had so many diverse occupations and had been a resident for so long that he was included among the burghers.

That designation does not take away from the fact that agricultural products continued to be his main sources of income. In 1647 he sold provisions to Stuyvesant and Kieft for 1,350 guilders. Damen tried to have the WIC chamber in Amsterdam pay this amount via his stepson Jan Vigne, by this time a merchant in Amsterdam, but as the WIC promissory notes were not accepted in Amsterdam, he received payment later, in New Netherland. Shortly afterwards, Damen bought a property in New Amsterdam with a house and a garden, slightly north of the fort. This may have been the location of the new house that, in October 1648, he undertook to have constructed. The house was to be 60 feet long and to be built

with three aisles. The front room was to be twenty-four feet square and provided
with three built-in bedsteads. A unique feature was the spiral staircase, "to enable
one to go from the cellar to the attic." The costs were to be 425 guilders, but Jan
Jansz Damen also had to provide carpenter Jeuriaen Hendricksz with "food and
drink" during construction.[16]

Hence, Jan Jansz Damen appeared to prosper, but the problems of the
past had not been entirely forgiven and forgotten. Opponents of the WIC and
their representatives in the colony had put their case before the States General in
the Republic and found a ready audience there. An important part of this case
consisted of the attack on the Indians, and Jan Jansz Damen as one of the key
figures was obligated to give testimony before the States General. This required a
voyage home to *patria*. Before his departure Damen fell ill, and in December 1649
he made his last will. His primary heirs were his brothers and sisters in the Dutch
Republic. Jan Cornelisz Buys, also known as Jan Damen but, in fact, the son of his
deceased sister Hendrickje, had joined his uncle in New Netherland. He shared in
Jan Jansz Damen's bequest to the amount of 600 guilders, a considerable sum. The
poor of the town of Bunnik were remembered with 400 guilders. This testament
gives first proof of the fact that Damen was a slave owner. In case his widow, who
would have the farm at her disposal, would sell or rent this property, Damen's
"Indian servant girl from the West Indies named Cicilje shall be completely . . .
emancipated and released from her slavery and otherwise not." [17]

Damen seems to have recovered quickly enough to undertake the
journey. He was not the only New Netherlander who had to appear before the
States General. Secretary Cornelis van Tienhoven also returned to the Dutch
Republic, acting as Stuyvesant's representative. Both men would be questioned by
a committee of the States General about their role in the wars with the Indians.
Internal complications within the Dutch Republic impeded a rapid resolution
of the matter and, furthermore, caused a loss of influence on the part of the
opponents of the WIC. These circumstances forced Jan Jansz Damen to remain
in the Republic for some time. How he spent his time is not clear, but some of
it may have been taken up with visits to his relatives in Bunnik and Utrecht. In
early 1651 he was in Amsterdam to arrange some affairs. Among other matters, he
engaged Hendrick Jansz van Schalkwijk and Andries Pietersz van Putten as farm
laborers to serve him in New Netherland.[18] These transactions indicate that he
wanted shortly to return to the colony. Damen also acted for others. For example,
he was Stuyvesant's authorized representative in managing the purchase of land
on Manhattan from the WIC. This purchase concerned the director's farm, which
later would be called the Bowery. Damen might be making arrangements for
his departure, but he still had not appeared before the States General. When the
States General requested the WIC chamber in Amsterdam to send him to The
Hague as soon as possible, it was too late. The directors had to reply that Damen
had already left for New Netherland.[19]

On June 18, 1651, shortly after his return to New Netherland, Jan Jansz Damen died. The interior of his new house can be reconstructed from an extensive inventory of possessions that was taken some weeks later.[20] Damen and his wife probably slept in the front room. Here we find "a single bed with an old bolster, a double bed with a bolster, four pillows, two green blankets, a white woolen blanket" and "two white linen sheets," all flanked by a "pewter chamber pot." The wall displayed "seven paintings on paper in wooden frames." Damen was not a well-read man and possessed only a few books: a folio-size Bible, an old quarto Bible, and a "chronicle." Further, we find some arms, two flintlocks, a fire lock, a sword, and a large powder horn. The linens were stored in a few chests. Here, next to the bed linens, was also Damen's clothing, such as a new, carmine-red long-sleeved garment to be worn between the undershirt and upper clothing, a suit of colored fustian (a sturdy, twilled fabric of cotton or cotton and wool), a colored worsted suit with piping, and a red night cap. There were only a wooden bench and a small table, but that is unremarkable as furniture was rare in New Netherland. The china and other tableware consisted, among other items, of earthenware pots, fifteen tin plates, small tin bowls, a tin drinking vessel with a hinged lid, six copper kettles and five wooden plates. Damen also possessed eight silver-plated spoons, a silver-plated beaker, a silver-plated wine bowl, and fourteen black-handled knives.

The back section of the house was used for storage of farm implements and functioned as a barn. Here were two hay forks, two new plow shears, two whips, a wooden rake, a few scythes and a flail, among other things. The inventory contains an extensive list of cattle. With four horses, six cows, a steer, an ox, four calves, and fourteen pigs, Damen had considerable livestock at his disposal.

The brewery supplies were kept in the attic: $154\,^1/_3$ bushels of malted barley, $30\,^1/_2$ bushels of wheat, 136 bushels of rye, and 4 bushels of oats. The malt was intended for the brewery, which held a brewing kettle with a capacity of 500 cubic meters, a cooling vessel, a pouring vat, and assorted other containers. This inventory is sole proof that Damen also worked as a brewer, an occupation that explains in part his affluence. In the Dutch Republic, brewers belonged among the wealthier burghers, as did those in New Netherland.

The settlement of Jan Jansz Damen's estate took several years, because the assets were in New Netherland while most of his heirs lived in the Dutch Republic. And, before there could be a definitive settlement, all existing debts had to be paid. Correspondence between New Netherland and the Republic was seriously impeded by the First English War, which erupted in 1652. The administrators of Damen's property wrote to his three brothers as early as September 1652, but their letter was not received until 1655. The administrators reported that they had already executed some testamentary directives. For example, they had paid 600 guilders to Jan Cornelisz Buys and had transmitted, via Cornelis van Werckhoven, 400 guilders to the magistrate of Bunnik for the benefit of the poor. A complete accounting of the estate would follow, but the estimated residual amounted to more than 5,000 guilders. This was an important sum for the heirs, and it is understandable that they looked forward to receiving it soon. To that end, they gave an authorization to act on their behalf to captain Adriaen Blommaert, who regularly traveled to New Netherland. But for their authorization to be lawful, a declaration had to be included that they were the rightful heirs. This is why a number of old inhabitants of Bunnik declared in March 1655 that Jan Jansz Damen and his three brothers had been well known to them. He had "more than 25 years or so ago traveled to New Netherland to seek his fortune, where (as they understood) he had died without leaving children."[21] Whether Jan Jansz Damen, when he left the Dutch Republic, truly intended to establish himself permanently in New Netherland cannot be determined, but considering the size of his estate he had certainly made his fortune.

This article was previously published in Dutch as "Fortuin in de Nieuwe Wereld: Jan Jansz. Damen in Amerika" in Nederland aan de Hudson: Utrechters in New York in de 17e eeuw [The Netherlands on the Hudson: Inhabitants of Utrecht in Seventeenth-Century New York]. *It is being published again with the permission of the author.*

NOTES

1. Utrechts Archief, Notarial Archives, City of Utrecht (34-4), UO17a008 fol. 239, 239v (10 March 1655). (Hereafter cited as UA, NAU.)

2. Jaap Jacobs, *New Netherland: A Dutch Colony in Seventeenth-Century America* (Leiden: Brill, 2005), 31–44, 108.

3. Jaap Jacobs, "Dutch Proprietary Manors in America: The Patroonships in New Netherland," in *Constructing Early Modern Empires: Proprietary Ventures in the Atlantic World,* ed. Lou Roper and Bertrand Van Ruymbeke (Leiden: Brill, 2007), 301–326.

4. M. S. F. Kemp, "Krommerijners in de nieuwe wereld. Een onderzoek naar de achtergrond en onderlinge verwantschap van vroege kolonisten in Nieuw Nederland (voornamelijk Rensselaerswijck), afkomstig uit het Utrechtse Krommerijngebied," *De Nederlandsche Leeuw* 109 (1992): 405–433.

5. A. J. F. van Laer, trans. and ed., *New York Historical Manuscripts,* 4 vols. (Baltimore: Genealogical Publishing, Inc. Co.,1974), 1:2–3. (Hereafter cited as *NYHM*).

6. *NYHM* 4:17, 4:18, 1:38–40.

7. Jaap Jacobs, "A Troubled Man: Director Wouter van Twiller and the Affairs of New Netherland in 1635," *New York History* 85 (2004): 213–232.

8. *NYHM* 1:45. Gemeentearchief Amsterdam, inv.nr. 1280, fol. 60v-61 (5 May 1639). (Hereafter cited as GAA NA.)

9. For example, *NYHM* 4: 60. David Pietersz De Vries, *Werken Linschoten-Vereeniging*, vol. 3, *Korte Historiael ende Journaels Aenteykeninge van verscheyden voyagiens in de vier delen des werelts-ronde, als Europa, Africa, Asia ende America gedaen*, H. T. Colenbrander, ed. ('s-Gravenhage: M. Nijhoff, 1911), 250. See also De Vries's translated journal entries pertaining to New Netherland in

Narratives of New Netherland, 1609-1664 ed. J. Franklin Jameson (New York: Charles Scribner's Sons 1909), 183–234. Nationaal Archief, archief Staten Generaal [National Archives, Archives of the States General], hereafter cited as NA SG, inv. nr. 12564-25 (29 August 1641); E. B. O'Callaghan and B. Fernow, eds. *Documents Relative to the Colonial History of the State of New York*, 15 vols. (Albany: 1853-1885), 1: 414-15. (Hereafter cited as *DRCHNY.*)

10. *NYHM* 4:9; GAA NA inv. nr. 1625, fol. 340 (20 April 1641); *NYHM* 1: 359-360.

11. Jacobs, *New Netherland: A Dutch Colony*, 133–138.

12. *Breeden-Raedt aende Vereenichde Nederlandsche Provintien: Gelreland, Holland, Zeeland, Utrecht, Vriesland, Over-Yssel, Groeningen, gemaeckt ende gestelt uyt diverse ware en waerachtige memorien door I.A.G.W.C.* (Antwerpen, 1649), C1 (a pamphlet purporting to give comprehensive advice to the United Dutch Provinces; extracts in English, to be used with caution, are in E. B. O'Callaghan's *Documents Relative to the Colonial History of the State of New York*, 4:99–112).

13. NA SG inv. nr. 12564.25 "Stucken raeckende den staet van Nieu Nederlandt ende de proceduren tegen Cornelis Melijn ende den aencleve van dien" ["Documents relating to the condition of New Netherland and the procedures against Cornelis Melijn and everything connected with them"], letter D (September 1643; *DRCHNY* 1:192-93); *NYHM* 4:203.

14. *NYHM* 2:172–173; 2:182; 2:263; 2:289; 2:296; 2:374–375; 3:114; 2:226–227; 2:274–275. New York Colonial Manuscripts Land Papers GG: 91 (25 April 1643), 137a (15 March 1646).

15. *NYHM* 4: 362, 411, 438–442.

16. GAA NA inv. nr. 1083, fol. 116–116v (12 November 1647), inv. nr. 1087, fol. 6v (3 January 1648), inv. nr. 1088, fol. 241–241v (12 March 1649); *NYHM* 4: 557, 3: 8–9, 3: 63–64; H. Zantkuyl, "Reconstructie van enkele Nederlandse huizen in Nieuw-Nederland uit de zeventiende eeuw." ["Reconstruction of some seventeenth-century Netherlandish houses in New Netherland"], *Bulletin KNOB* 84, no. 2/3, *Nieuwnederlandse studien. Een inventarisatie van recent onderzoek. [New Netherland Studies. An inventory of current research and approaches.]* (1985): 166–179, specifically 175–176.

17. *DRCHNY* 1:357; *NYHM* 3:208–210.

18. NA SG inv. nr. 12564.25 "Pointen en articulen waermede de Ho: Mo: Heeren Staten Generael offte derselver Heeren Gecommitteerde den secretaris Cornelis van Tienhoven souden konnen belasten en vervolgens ordineeren ende beveelen, dat hij daerop categorice sal hebben beantwoorden." ["Points and articles with which the High Mightinesses Lords States General or the Gentlemen of their committee could charge the secretary Cornelis van Tienhoven and subsequently instruct and command him to reply unconditionally to the same."] 21 July 1650; *DRCHNY* 1: 409–414. See Jaap Jacobs, "A Hitherto Unknown Letter of Adriaen van der Donck," *de Halve Maen* 71 (1998): 1–6; GAA NA inv. nr. 1346, fol. 14 (10 March 1651), inv. nr. 1346, fol. 18 (14 March 1651).

19. *NYHM* 3:216; *DRCHNY* 1:434–435.

20. *NYHM* 3:267–276.

21. UA NAU (34-4), UO17a008 fol. 240, 241, 241v, 242 (10 March 1655), fol. 239, 239v (10 March 1655).

Barber-Surgeons

IN NEW NETHERLAND AND EARLY NEW YORK

PETER R. CHRISTOPH

In popular lore, the barber-surgeon of colonial days was an ignorant bumbler whose bizarre potions often produced results worse than the disease, while his surgical practices supposedly produced much suffering but little in the way of cure. This view is always contrasted with the wonders of modern medicine, although the skeptical observer might point out the frequency with which today's prescription drugs are recalled because of unanticipated side effects, while surgery still involves some degree of risk. So it might behoove us to be less judgmental of the practices of the past, at least without first finding out what they really were. My goal is to show that medicine as practiced by Dutch physicians in the seventeenth century was an improvement over earlier times, more scientific and effective than might be credited in modern lore, and that the barber-surgeon was a skilled healer with years of training. There had long been antagonism among physicians, surgeons, and barbers as to areas of competence.[1] Certainly there were distinct differences in their training.

The Dutch physician was university trained (one introductory year and two years of instruction in medicine, anatomy, and botany) and held the degree of doctor of medicine. He treated the sick, not the injured, as dressing wounds was beneath his dignity, and an examination consisted of taking the pulse and perhaps examining the tongue and urine. Ailments were treated by prescribing drugs, herbs, and elixirs.[2]

By contrast, the surgeon, called a *chirurgeon*[3] in Dutch, began as an apprentice, learning by assisting the master, by study, and by attending demonstrations, such as autopsies. After an apprenticeship of anywhere from three to six years, he became an assistant to a surgeon. When he had at least five years of experience as an assistant, he could take the master's examination, and if he passed, he became a full-fledged surgeon or master (*meester*, abbreviated *Mr.*, or *heelmeester*, master of healing), entitled to open a shop for surgery and barbering. In the Netherlands the surgeon belonged to a guild that advanced the interests of the profession by conducting the master's examination, including a practical examination in the infirmary, and by petitioning government to restrict competition from barbers and others.[4]

The chirurgeon, then, was a skilled healer with years of training. He treated wounds, sores, contusions, growths, and abscesses, using damp cloths, plasters, and poultices. He also pulled teeth, mended fractures, administered douches and enemas, and, of course, performed surgery, including cauterization, trepanning, removing tumors, and amputation.[5]

The barber cut hair and shaved and might trim off corns and other surface blemishes, dress wounds, and bleed the patient, a practice that was regarded as a cure for fever and for various diseases and as necessary to maintain a proper balance of fluids in the patient. The barber also had to serve an apprenticeship and pass a test before setting up shop.

All these practitioners, and midwives as well, had to obtain a license from the local government before they could set up a practice. Midwives, who apprenticed under other midwives, were forbidden to use instruments and (in Amsterdam, at least) had to send for a chirurgeon if there were complications.

Despite these separate titles, in the colonial records the same man may be called a barber, a chirurgeon, and, in the case of Jacob de Hinsse, a doctor as well,[6] which makes it challenging (but not impossible) to determine which, in fact, he really was. Writers of later centuries are even more careless, labeling everybody as doctor, particularly those who had attained some status in society, and of course one's own ancestors are always doctors, not barbers or chirurgeons.

Beyond the physicians, chirurgeons, barbers, and midwives there were the unlicensed quacks, practicing folk medicine or their own curious inventions, despite the government's efforts to suppress this sort of thing. They removed cataracts, cut stones from bladders, pulled teeth, and even treated fractures.[7] The Dutch *kwakzalver*, "quack anointer," was a popular subject for Dutch and Flemish artists who often sought their subjects in ordinary life, even at its more grotesque.[8] We should not scoff overmuch at the people of the seventeenth century for being taken in by quacks: we are not rid of unlicensed healers today.

Folk medicine was dispensed by family members, often the oldest woman. Jacob de Hinsse once treated a patient who had lost considerable blood from a wound, but his efforts were judged insufficient by friends and family, and they therefore gave the patient some buck's blood to drink, which did not prevent his death the next day.[9]

Medicine as practiced by Dutch physicians and chirurgeons in the seventeenth century could actually be scientific and effective, although advanced healers had by no means displaced all the advocates of such ancient writers as Galen and Aristotle. Both physicians and chirurgeons consulted medical literature in the seventeenth century: a Dutch practitioner could read groundbreaking works by Hendrik van Roonhuyse on gynecology, including Caesarian section; Job Janszoon van Meekeren on bone grafting; Franciscus de la Böe concerning the tubercles in tuberculosis; Adriaan van den Spieghel on the treatment of malaria; Gerard Blaes on the spinal cord; and Willem Piso's differentiation of yaws from syphilis.[10]

Interesting evidence that the chirurgeon could be well informed on matters of medicine, and not on surgery alone, comes from the estate of a Kingston chirurgeon, Gysbert van Imbroch. A lengthy inventory of his property, taken on September 1, 1665, shows an extensive personal library, including a number of medical texts.[11] One was Christopher Wirtsung's *Medecyn-Boec* (medicine book), which treats all parts of the human body and their illnesses, together with cures, mainly by means of herbs. Another was identified as Andreas Vesalius's *Anatomy*, presumably his *De humani corporis fabrica libri septem*, or *The Seven Books on the Structure of the Human Body*, which encouraged anatomists to trust only their own observations, not Galen's. Vesalius's discovery of the important differences between species also helped usher in the science of comparative anatomy.

A book identified in the inventory as "Medical remarks by Nicolaes Tulp" was, presumably, his *Observationes Medicae*, published in 1641 and again in 1652 and so a fairly recent work. Tulp wrote in Latin, which the public could not read, to prevent people from treating their own illnesses. The book comprises minute descriptions of his work, including 231 cases of disease and death. Tulp is best known today from Rembrandt's painting *The Anatomy Lesson of Dr. Nicolaes Tulp*, reproduced on the Dutch Masters cigar box (minus the scalpel and cadaver).

Among the older works in Van Imbroch's collection was a work by the sixteenth-century chirurgeon Cornelis Herls, called in the inventory an "Examen der Chyrurgie" (examination of surgery). This would be Herls' *Exam tractatus medici de moscho a Davide Ultralaeo in lucem od*. Several other works were not identified by title: a medicine book of Ambrosius Paree (Ambrose Parée) and one by Johannes De Viga, as well as a German medical manual by Q. Apollinaren. Others included a book on surgery, a German work on "medicine and products of art," and three books identified only as "written" medicine books, as well as a written medicine and student book. Among the authors were at least three identifiable as chirurgeons because of the title *Mr.*: Herls, Paree, and Wirtsung. Obviously chirurgeon Gysbert van Imbroch had an extensive medical library. One might suppose that at least part of this collection came from his physician father-in-law, Dr. Johannes La Montagne, who had studied at the University of Louvain.

Also in Van Imbroch's inventory were various tools and equipment for surgery and for medicine generally. There was a medicine chest; copper scales and weights; a bottle of tragacanth vinegar and another with perfumery and fumigating matter; a glass with juniper oil and one with yellow medicine (the men taking the inventory were not practitioners and thus imprecise in some of their descriptions); an enema syringe and three other medical syringes; and a bleeding bowl.

While the use of medicines was more the preserve of the physician, Van Imbroch had various potions in his home and three books on gardening. Adriaen van der Donck wrote that "a certain chirurgeon who was also a botanist had a beautiful garden there, wherein a great variety of medicinal wild plants were collected."[12] Van der Donck then proceeded to name more than forty native plants of medicinal value, a list perhaps supplied to him by the botanist.

Van Imbroch also had barbering equipment, including razors, a barber's grindstone, shaving towels, one barber's case, and a barber's chair. While chirurgeons held themselves above barbers, as did the law and the general public, that does not mean that the chirurgeons separated themselves from barbering. Rather, it provided a significant part of their income. Among supposed surgeons in New Netherland, Sybrandt Cornelissen van Flensburgh in 1664 was appointed assistant surgeon, probably meaning he was not yet a master, to be employed in shaving, bleeding, and administering medicines to the soldiers, duties which sound very much like those of a barber. Jan Pieterson van Essendelft was sent to the South (Delaware) River settlements in 1638, but as a barber, and his salary of ten guilders a month was far below the twenty-five guilders that the West India Company was paying chirurgeons.

In this regard, it is interesting to note that the chirurgeons of New Amsterdam (much like their guild in Amsterdam) in 1652 petitioned New Netherland's Director-General Stuyvesant and the council that they alone be allowed to shave.[13] The director and council responded that "shaving is actually not in the domain of surgery, but is only an appendix to it" and that friends cannot be prevented from cutting each other's hair, as long as they are not paid for it and do not keep a shop.

While they were on the subject, Stuyvesant and the council ordered what is, perhaps, the earliest instance on record of a medical regulation in New Netherland: "Whereas last summer two or three serious mistakes were made by the inexperience of some ships' barbers, therefore, the director and council hereby order that such ships' barbers shall not dress any wounds, bleed, or prescribe any drinks for anyone on land without the knowledge or special consent of the petitioners or, at least, of Doctor La Montagne."[14] Ships' chirurgeons had a shorter apprenticeship and in the Netherlands were prohibited from opening a surgery on shore, but on shipboard they were both surgeon and physician.[15] This case demonstrates the prerogative of civil government to qualify and license medical practitioners.

Court records relating to an early malpractice suit provide an example of the sort of operation that was considered to be within the chirurgeons' competence. Chirurgeons were required to report any woundings and if possible to inquire of the victim the name of his attacker. One such case occurred in 1639, with one soldier stabbing another. Chirurgeon Hans Kierstede testified that he had been called to attend to Jacob Jeuriaensen from Dansick (Danzig), who was wounded by Jochem Beeckman. Kierstede found the wound to be in the buttock and that "the great artery and nerve had been cut." He does not describe how he treated it but notes that the wound progressed favorably up to the eighth or ninth day. "But as the patient did not follow the surgeon's orders and did not observe a proper diet according to the instructions of the surgeon, who found him standing up and bleeding in front of his bunk." Kierstede asked Jacob Jeuriaensen, "Why did you come out of the bunk?" He answered, "I wanted to get a pot." He bled so profusely at the time that Kierstede had great difficulty in stopping it, and thereafter the wound continued to reopen once or twice a day, Jacob becoming weaker and weaker. Kierstede concluded his deposition by declaring "that the patient himself is to blame for the bursting open of the wound."[16]

The wounded man died ten days after his relapse, and Beeckman was brought up on a charge of manslaughter. The court noted that according to the chirurgeon, "deceased did not die of his wounds, but through his own negligence and excesses." Additional testimony from four other men noted that two or three days after he had been wounded Jacob Jeuriaensen, among other things, "kindled a fire, made an omelet, and then drank an entire pint of wine at one draft." The council acquitted Beeckman of the charge of manslaughter.[17]

COMFORTERS AND PHYSICIANS

At first there were no medical personnel in New Netherland at all. The Reformed Church did supply "comforters of the sick" (called *sieckentroosters* or *krankebesoeckers*), who included Evert Pietersen, Arent Evertsen, Sebastian Jansen Krol, and Jan Huyck, among others. They practiced a little medicine but mostly visited the sick and prayed with them. In the absence of an ordained minister, they led Sunday services, reading from a book of approved sermons. They served in New Amsterdam, Breuckelen, Esopus, and Fort Orange.

In time there would be physicians, a few actual doctors of medicine. Harmen Mynderts van den Bogaert sailed for America in 1630, when he was only nineteen. He was not mentioned again by name in the records until 1638, so he may have returned to the Netherlands for a time to complete his education. Johannes la Montagne arrived in 1637, but he and Van den Bogaert are seldom mentioned in connection with medical practice. Instead they were quickly recruited into government leadership positions.

The sons of the Rev. Johannes Megapolensis, Samuel and Johannes Jr., who had come over with their father in 1637, returned to the Netherlands to study medicine, after which they returned to America. Johannes practiced at Beverwyck in 1654 and New Amsterdam in 1655 but returned to Holland around 1656. Samuel left for the Netherlands in 1656, returning in about 1662. Two years later he participated in the surrender of New Netherland to the English. He had also attended Harvard College, where he studied religion, and is better known as a clergyman.

Johannes Kerkbyle was a graduate of Leyden and served in New York from 1664 to about 1693. In 1687 he was appointed to attend the poor in New York City. Aided by five chirurgeons, he conducted an autopsy on the body of Gov. Henry Sloughter, who died suddenly in 1691. There may have been a few other physicians, but most of the practitioners in New Netherland and early New York were chirurgeons, not doctors of medicine.

THE COLONY'S CHIRURGEONS

The medical practitioners of whatever degree were sent, for the most part, by the West India Company, some as ships' surgeons and others to minister to the settlers. The usual port of entry was at Manhattan, the largest community of New Netherland. They received a salary from the company to attend its employees, supplemented by treating other settlers on an individual basis. Often an annual fee was arranged with a family (including servants), but payment could also be made on a case-by-case basis. We know of both types of arrangements from court records when the chirurgeon had to sue for payment. As with everyone else, chirurgeons found that collecting debts could be an arduous process in a society where income was often cyclical and payment was in kind rather than coin. Thus, Aldart Swartwout sued for delivery of a kettle as promised payment for healing Jacob Schellinger's leg. The defendant claimed it was less than a perfect cure. Following normal Dutch practice in a civil suit, the court referred the matter to referees, appointing to that role Hans Kierstede and Jacob Hendricksz Varrevanger, who the court called "old and experienced surgeons." The status of surgeons is suggested in another court order for the settlement of the estate of Salomon La Chair: "Mr. Hans [Kierstede] is to be preferred before the other creditors as the same is for surgeon's service."

An early chirurgeon was Jacob Mollenaer, perhaps one of the ships' surgeons. When he left the West India Company's service in 1637, two men were sent in his place: Hans Kierstede and Gerrit Schutt, who seem to have arrived with Director Willem Kieft in 1638. Mr. (meester) Hans and Mr. Gerrit, as they were often called, in 1638 performed the earliest recorded coroner's inquest in New Amsterdam, determining that Gerrit Jansen, gunner at Fort Amsterdam, had been stabbed to death.

Jacob Hendricksz Varrevanger entered the company's service in 1646. In 1654 he told the council he had considerable expense in importing medicines, and it was ordered that he be paid twelve guilders per month starting retroactively in 1652 and that his salary be increased. The company's sick soldiers had been billeted on private families, and Varrevanger thought there was a need for a company hospital, which he established in December 1658. Patients included not only the company's soldiers and slaves but also the poor of the city. Among the chirurgeons on staff was Lucas Pieters, whose father, Pieter Santome, had been a slave freed by the company for his years of good service. It seems reasonable to assume that Lucas apprenticed under Varrevanger.

SOCIAL STATUS

Three of the ways in which we can judge someone's status in the seventeenth century are by wealth, family, and public service. Certainly chirurgeons were among the few well-educated persons in New Netherland and therefore often called upon to take leadership positions in municipal government. This does not mean that the medical-professional-turned-public-official was a colonial invention. A notable example in the old country, but hardly the only one, was the aforementioned Dr. Nicolaes Tulp, four-term burgomaster of Amsterdam and long-time city council member. In his capacity of councillor he administered the oath of allegiance to the refugee Walloons who became the first permanent settlers of New Netherland.[18]

Chirurgeons often served in public office in New Netherland and New York. For example, Roelof Kierstede, the son of Mr. Hans, was a chirurgeon at Kingston beginning around 1668. He served on the board of magistrates there in the 1670s. Jacob de Hinsse, mentioned earlier on Manhattan, was identified in 1661 as "Mr. Jacob de Hinsse, chirurgeon in the village of Beverwyck near Fort Orange." He owned several parcels there and was a magistrate during the later 1660s. His clients included the deacons of the Reformed Church, probably in their capacity of overseers of the poor.

Another public-spirited practitioner was Abraham Staets, who served the colony of Rensselaerswyck from 1642 (when he was aged twenty-four) to 1648 as chirurgeon, his contract specifying "to the exclusion of all others." He served on Rensselaerswyck's council from 1643 to 1648 and as its president from April 10, 1644, on. He was a magistrate of the court of Fort Orange and Beverwyck from 1652 to 1659. Staets was also a fur trader and boat owner, and he possessed large tracts of land. His training in Amsterdam is on record: he served his apprenticeship with Jan Eckius, then served six years as assistant to Johan Dircsz Brim, who recommended him to Kiliaen van Rensselaer.[19] Other chirurgeons served in public office. Abraham van Tricht was one of the first members of the Albany city council in 1686 but had only a brief political career, as he died in October 1687. Hendrick van Dyck served as assistant alderman in the first ward of Albany from 1690 to 1694. Reynier Schaets, son of a minister at Albany, served the village of Schenectady as a justice of the peace during the Leisler administration and in 1690 was among the many killed by French and Indians in the Schenectady massacre. Peter van der Linde, from Belle in Flanders, settled on Manhattan in 1638 and served as tobacco inspector in 1640, schoolmaster, and clerk of the church in 1648. Lewis Giton, chirurgeon, was made a freeman of the city of New York on December 24, 1695. He would seem to be the same person as Louis Gitton, constable of the West Division of Staten Island in April 1699.[20]

Chirurgeon Gysbert van Imbroch served Esopus[21] as commis, schepen, and delegate to the colonial assembly. Kingston town records show that he also augmented his income as a tapster. The inventory of his library, in addition to the already-mentioned medical books, includes a number of histories and religious works—not the sort of reading matter one would find in a barber shop. Apparently Van Imbroch was involved in primary education as well: the inventory mentions multiple copies of schoolbooks and catechisms.[22]

Chirurgeons tended to be among the wealthier residents of the colony. The inventory of Van Imbroch's estate listed hundreds of items that were sold at auction for a total of over 2,600 guilders. Jacob Varrevanger, the chirurgeon who established a hospital on Manhattan, also did very well for himself: an inventory of his estate in 1674 valued his property at 8,000 guilders. By way of comparison, a common laborer might make 150 guilders a year.

The will of chirurgeon Jacob Staets, written in 1734, showed that he had a house and lot in Albany, another lot "near the creek," and two pastures in the city, as well as his share of his father's estate. Jacob had been an assessor and alderman like his father (chirurgeon Abraham).

Jacob De Lange was also wealthy, although not entirely through his surgical practice. An inventory of his estate in 1685 included 136 teapots, and one can only imagine that he was dealing in them and perhaps other wares as well. It is hard to know which were personal effects and which were sale items, but he had sixty-one paintings, including six banquet scenes, two still lifes, several Scriptural scenes, a genre scene of a cobbler, two rustic views, and a picture of a "plucked cock." Included in the estate were porcelain items and numerous boxes, cabinets, and trunks from the East Indies. And as a reminder of the more humble but remunerative part of his work was an "iron stick to put out to hang the barber's bason," apparently the seventeenth-century equivalent of a striped barber pole. The estate was valued at £740-17-7 (equal to about 4,500 Dutch guilders).

West India Company records show clergy among the highest paid of employees (35 guilders per month). Although the chirurgeons were a step below that (25 guilders), there were soon family interrelationships between the two groups. After the death of the Rev. Johannes Lydius at Albany, his widow married chirurgeon Jacob Staets. The aforementioned sons of the Rev. Johannes Megapolensis were doctors of medicine, Samuel a clergyman as well. Reynier Schaets, son of another Albany minister (Gideon Schaets), was trained as a chirurgeon.

MISCELLANEOUS NAMES

The chirurgeons above were mentioned because they either served as good examples or had interesting stories connected to them. In order that the reader not be misled into thinking that there were only these few, others that appear in the records are mentioned briefly below.

Paulus van der Beeck from Bremen settled in Brooklyn in 1644 after having served the West India Company in Curaçao and as a ship's surgeon. William Hays of Barry's Court, Ireland, arrived in 1644, having served since 1641 as chief surgeon in Curaçao. Alexander Carolus Curtius (Curtis) arrived at Manhattan in 1659, practiced surgery and conducted a Latin school. Jan du Parck, an army surgeon, was among the wounded at Wiltwyck during the war with the Esopus Indians in 1662.

Peter Vreucht was in New Netherland in 1647; Cornelis Clock, Jan Hervey, and Jacobus Hughes in 1652; Peter Jansen van den Bergh and Jacob l'Orange in 1658; William Leverich in 1663. Others in the colony of New Netherland included Hermann Wessels, John Newberry, Jacob Provoost, Hugh Farquhar, John Miller, Jan Croon, and several ships' surgeons, including Isaac Jansen, Jan Pauw, and William Nobel (he of the ship *La Garce*). On Long Island, James Clark was at Maspeth during the Dutch period, while Robert Reade was in Jamaica in 1699.

There were also chirurgeons in the Delaware region. Jacob Krap went there from New Amsterdam in 1656. Jacob de Commer did the same after 1660, settling at Newcastle; in August 1662 he was called to testify as to the deathbed statement of Hermen Hendricksen van Deventeer, a cadet who was shot by Schout Gerrit van Sweeringen.[23] Michiel de Marco Chertser was sent out from the Netherlands in November 1661 to serve as company surgeon at New Amstel.[24]

Chirurgeons in the colony after the English takeover included twenty-year-old John de Foreest, who was given a certificate of denization by Gov. Francis Lovelace prior to sailing for Europe in 1670, and Henry Taylor in 1673. Henry Pichet was named as executor in a will of November 1700. The New York City estate of Peter Bassett and his daughter was inventoried in 1707.

APPRENTICES

Since one learned to become a chirurgeon by serving an apprenticeship, it was not at all unusual for one or more of a chirurgeon's sons to learn the trade from their father. Roeliff Kierstede was born in 1647 on Manhattan, the son of Master Hans. Trained by his father, he set up practice in Kingston, where he served until his death in 1691. Besides the original Hans and his son Roelof, there was a Jochem Kierstede, late of Maryland, chirurgeon; since he died intestate, letters of administration were granted to Hans Kierstede Sr., his nephew, on July 5, 1710.[25]

Jacob and Samuel Staets were sons of Abraham of Rensselaerswyck and Albany. Samuel also studied in the Netherlands, where training included classes on the theory of anatomy two or three times a week, a luxury not available in New Netherland. Jacob's first wife was Ryckie van Dyck, widow of Jacob de Hinsse and sister of Cornelis van Dyck, de Hinsse's former assistant.

Surgery was also the family trade for the Van Dyck family: Cornelis studied for four years, through June 1661, with de Hinsse, in whose footsteps he followed as chirurgeon: his clients included the Albany almshouse and the church deacons. Two of Cornelis's sons, Hendrick and Jacob (who moved to Schenectady), were chirurgeons, as was Jacob's son Cornelis. This last Cornelis's son Henry, born 1726, was a chirurgeon in Albany and among the wealthiest citizens, practicing there until the outbreak of the American Revolution, when he was banished from the city because of his loyalist sympathies. He was allowed to return in 1783, three years before his death.[26]

Youth from various walks of life sought to become chirurgeon's apprentices. Cornelis, the first of the Van Dyck chirurgeons, was the son of Hendrick van Dyck, the colony's former *schout-fiscaal* (the senior officer for finance and law enforcement, the judge in civil suits, and the criminal prosecutor in civil, military, and naval courts). Gerrett Strudle, whose father was an innkeeper, was apprenticed for five years to Cornelis Viele in New York, beginning in 1700. Hartman Wessels in 1677 accepted John, the son of John Archer, lord of the manor of Fordham, as an apprentice for six years. This arrangement did not work out, with Wessels claiming that the father "hath enticed the said apprentice away," while the senior Archer accused Wessels of maltreating his son.

Two Notable Surgeries

One of the most famous of surgical operations occurred in 1644 on the island of Curaçao. Petrus Stuyvesant, at that time the West India Company's director of Aruba, Bonaire, and Curaçao, led an expedition against the Spanish on the island of St. Martin. During the final siege on April 16, Stuyvesant was struck in the right leg by a cannonball. He was taken back to headquarters in Curaçao, where the company surgeon amputated the crushed limb below the knee. The leg failed to heal and after several months Stuyvesant went home to the Netherlands, where additional surgery was performed. After the wound healed, he was fitted with a prosthesis. Three years later he was in Manhattan as director-general of the West India Company's possessions in the Western Hemisphere: New Netherland and his former charge in the Caribbean.

An instructive case as to the state of medical practice in the seventeenth century is provided by the medical history of Maria van Rensselaer,[27] which includes the use of various massages and balms, of both the useful and useless varieties, and some first-rate surgery.

In August 1663, following the birth of her first child, Maria developed a pain in her hip, which affected her walking. By the following April the situation had so deteriorated that the pain prevented her from walking or even standing. Neither salves nor hot treatments helped. The diagnosis as of August 1664 was a weakening of the nerves, since the leg was not injured, yet Maria required both a crutch and a cane to walk. Her husband Jeremias wrote to his mother in the Netherlands, asking her to send "the red salve or balm of Joost de Coge" and some bottles of oil of sulphur, "as this has been recommended to her here as a good remedy." Another interesting remedy that was proposed by a number of people was that Maria would recover if she had another baby, which, in fact, soon occurred.

The various salves, ointments, and childbearing did not have the desired effect. In fact, modern physicians believe that Maria was suffering from septic arthritis, accompanied by osteomyelitis of the femur. Septic arthritis most often strikes one of the large, weight-bearing joints, in this case the hip. Although swelling is common in some joints, it is usually not seen in infection of the hip, so the attending chirurgeon may have missed the symptoms during a critical period of time. Bacteria eating away cartilage and other tissue in the joint may develop within as little as two weeks, and attending chirurgeon Jacob de Hinsse waited two years before deciding that surgery was necessitated by Maria's deteriorating condition. An incision was made in the leg, just below the hip, and then and for several days thereafter there was a considerable drainage of matter, including pieces of bone and cartilage. The corruption is evidence of serious deterioration: osteomyelitis can occur with inadequate or delayed treatment, and dead tissue, usually bone, can become separated from the surrounding healthy tissue.

This surgery was, in fact, exactly the right course to take, albeit exceedingly late in the day. Of course, the fact that de Hinsse did not have antibiotics meant that the infection remained in Maria's system. That she survived is amazing, considering that even today, "five to ten percent of patients with an infected joint die, chiefly from respiratory complications."[28] But her problems were hardly over. The next spring three fistulas developed in the hip, indicating the presence of draining abscesses. These would recur throughout her life, often after a bump and at times when Maria was under stress. She would suffer from her condition for the rest of her life, and she died at the young age of forty-three. The various medicines, folk remedies, and multiple pregnancies (seven in all) would not have been the least help, but Jacob de Hinsse's surgery certainly saved her life.

A visitor in 1680 recorded that after her last child she was having pain in both legs and needed two canes or crutches to get around. This may indicate that the infection had migrated to the other side via the circulating blood (blood poisoning) to infect other joints. But, with various salves to at least ease the pain (in 1681 her son Kiliaen sent her a package from Boston) Maria carried on in her widowhood as manager of Rensselaerswyck, eventually acquiring majority interest so that her children could inherit it all, almost one million acres. She died on January 24, 1689, having survived with her illness for twenty-five years.

Conclusion

The healing arts in the seventeenth century were much improved over previous times, and new techniques were being adopted throughout the century. Doctors of medicine had the best educations, at least on paper, but their schoolwork was theoretical, and practical training was not part of their scholastic experience. The chirurgeons, on the other hand, had apprenticed with master chirurgeons, learning the craft by observation and practical instruction. The years thereafter serving as an assistant provided further practical training. While some ideas, such as trying to establish a proper balance of fluids in the patient by draining some of his blood, were less than helpful, the chirurgeon was nonetheless often skilled and knowledgeable in his craft. The barbers, too, while not as rigorously trained, had their areas of competence. Licensing regulations gave the community the means to establish standards, such as requiring a master's certificate and recommendations from previous communities of residence. The residents of New Netherland and colonial New York were served by trained medical professionals and benefitted from their skill and knowledge.

NOTES

1. Fielding H. Garrison, *An Introduction to the History of Medicine*, 4th ed. (Philadelphia and London: W. B. Saunders Co., 1929), 94.

2. Annet Mooy, *Doctors of Amsterdam: Patient Care, Medical Training and Research (1650–2000)*, trans. Beverly Jackson (Amsterdam: Amsterdam University, 2002), 36.

3. Both words, *surgeon* and *chirurgeon*, were used in English, even though they meant exactly the same thing. In modern Dutch we find the terms *chirurg* (surgeon) and *chirurgie* (surgery).

4. Mooy, 39.

5. Ibid., 62.

6. Janny Venema, *Beverwyck: A Dutch Village on the American Frontier* (Albany: State University of New York Press, 2003), 129.

7. Mooy, 45.

8. Garrison, 300.

9. Venema, 130.

10. Ibid., 282–283; Leslie T. Morton and Robert J. Moore, *A Chronology of Medicine and Related Sciences* (Cambridge: Cambridge University Press, Scolar Press, 1977), 39–56, and passim.

11. Peter R. Christoph, et al., eds. *Kingston Papers*, 2 vols. (Baltimore: Genealogical Publishing Co., Inc., 1976), 2: 568–569

12. Adriaen van der Donck, *A Description of the New Netherlands* (Syracuse: Syracuse University Press, 1968), 28.

13. Charles T. Gehring, trans. and ed., *New York Historical Manuscripts, Dutch*, vol. 9, *Council Minutes, 1652–1654* (Baltimore: Genealogical Publishing Co., Inc. 1983), 13.

14. It is worth noting the reference to La Montagne, who was a member of the council and one of the few physicians in the colony.

15. Mooy, 41–42.

16. A. J. F. van Laer, trans., *New York Historical Manuscripts, Dutch*, vol. 1, *Register of the Provincial Secretary, 1638–1642* (Baltimore: Genealogical Publishing Co., Inc., 1974), 151–152.

17. A. J. F. van Laer, trans., *New York Historical Manuscripts, Dutch*, vol. 4, *Council Minutes 1638–1649* (Baltimore: Genealogical Publishing Co., Inc. 1974), 51.

18. Russell Shorto, *The Island at the Center of the World* (New York: Doubleday, 2004), 40.

19. Venema, 128.

20. *The Burghers of New Amsterdam and The Freemen of New York, 1675–1876* (Collections of the New-York Historical Society for the Year 1885) (New York: The Society, 1886), 58–59; John E. Stillwell, comp., *Historical and Genealogical Miscellany; Data Relating to the Settlement and Settlers of New York and New Jersey* (Baltimore: Genealogical Publishing Co., Inc., 1970), 1:22, 47.

21. Later called Wiltwyck and eventually Kingston.

22. The inventory and auction records appear in *Kingston Papers*, 2: 566–575.

23. Charles T. Gehring, trans. and ed., *Delaware Papers* (*Dutch Period*) (Baltimore, Genealogical Publishing Co., Inc., 1981), 281, 287–289.

24. E. B. O'Callaghan and B. Fernow, trans. and eds., *Documents Relative to the Colonial History of the State of New York*, 15 vols. (Albany: Weed, Parsons, 1853–1887), 2:191.

25. Roeliff and Roelof Kierstede are presumably the same person; however, there is no known family genealogy to definitively settle the question.

26. Stefan Bielinski, The People of Colonial Albany Live Here, http://www.nysm.nysed.gov/albany.

27. The following is based upon my article "Worthy, Virtuous Juffrouw Maria van Rensselaer" in *de Halve Maen*, summer 1997. My source for the quotations was A. J. F. van Laer, *Correspondence of Jeremias van Rensselaer, 1651–1674* (Albany: University of the State of New York, 1932). The physicians I consulted were Cajsa J. Schumacher, MD, and Ian H. Porter, MD, Professor of Pediatrics/Medical Genetics at Albany Medical College.

28. *Current Medical Diagnosis and Treatment* (Los Altos, Calif.: Lange Medical, 2007), 759.

Glimpses of Childhood

IN THE COLONY OF NEW NETHERLAND

ADRIANA E. VAN ZWIETEN

INTRODUCTION

Within two decades of Henry Hudson's exploration of the river that would later carry his name, children from Europe had crossed the Atlantic to a new home in New Netherland. Upon arrival, they worked alongside their parents to build settlements. They were present when the walls of Fort New Amsterdam (now New York City) were erected. Imagine their excitement when a whale swam up the North (Hudson) River beyond Beverwijck (now Albany) in 1647 and their sense of wonder when comets were observed in the heavens in 1665.[1] Children were rocked in their cradles, learned to walk on New Netherland's soil, ran and skipped on the roads, dashed through the fields, and sometimes caused mischief. Many grew to adulthood; many died in infancy; many others became orphans. Filled with youthful exuberance, the healthy and capable went to school and worked, learning the skills that would see them through adulthood. Yet children left no written record describing their experiences; consequently, it is through the writings of adults that their activities are exposed. The numerous pages of extant colonial manuscripts reveal how important children were to their parents and the community.[2]

According to Nicasius de Sille, who was a prominent member of New Netherland's society, children and pigs were abundant in New Amsterdam by 1654. Both multiplied, he wrote, "rapidly and more than anything else."[3] Little did De Sille realize that his oft-quoted words would be difficult to verify. The data required to corroborate his statement have, for the most part, been lost. The baptismal registers of the Dutch Reformed churches in New Amsterdam and Breuckelen (now Brooklyn) do chronicle the presence of over 2,600 children from 1639 through 1674,[4] but such evidence is lacking for the colony's other villages and towns and for other religious denominations for this period. Furthermore, the birth of some children was simply never recorded. Many were born elsewhere, then immigrated to the colony with their parents but remained nameless on ships' registers or in various accounts. Furthermore, the total number of all children was greatly decreased by infant-mortality rates, which were high in the seventeenth century.

BIRTH AND BAPTISM

It is possible, nevertheless, to begin with birth and baptism to tell the story of childhood in New Netherland, for the records reveal that babies of European heritage generally were born at home, their mothers attended by midwives and surrounded by female family members and friends.[5] Immediately after birth, a newborn was wrapped in warm diapers and laid in the arms of his or her grandmother or godmother. Lightly swaddled, the babe was then offered to its father, who, by his acceptance, acknowledged the infant to be legally his. The birth of a child was usually a joyous occasion and was celebrated in the Netherlands, and probably also in the colony, with sweets, pastries, and caudle (a drink made from wine, egg yolks, sugar, cinnamon, and cloves).[6]

The Dutch customs associated with the birth of a child can be contrasted with the birthing rituals of Native Americans as they were recorded by two seventeenth-century commentators of Dutch origin. Adriaen van der Donck noted in 1653 that Native American babies were born in a simple hut or behind a screen of matting set up in "a quiet, sheltered spot [in the woods] near running water." Their mothers gave birth "unaided," he wrote. In 1644 Johannes Megapolensis observed that newborns of the Mohawk nation were washed by their mothers in the river or the snow. Van der Donck, on the other hand, asserted that if the child was a boy, he was immediately immersed in a nearby stream and left there for some time, so that he would be "hardened from the first…so as to grow up a brave man and a good hunter." The infant was then dressed and wrapped in fur clothing, his mother watching him closely for fear that he might "die accidentally." Mother and newborn returned to their home and friends within a few days.[7]

Far different was the birth of a baby born to Dutch Reformed communicants. The infant was carried to church by a godparent within the first few days of life and presented to the minister for baptism by his or her father, the babe's mother still confined to her bed after childbirth.[8] During this religious ritual, a child was admitted into the congregation of believers. Godparents or baptismal witnesses assisted in this process and were chosen from among the nearest relatives or closest friends. They promised to ensure a godchild's Christian upbringing, especially if the child became orphaned. Some presented the child with a christening gift. Kiliaen van Rensselaer, for example, who was baptized in Beverwijck in 1663, received two silver salt cellars from his grandmother Anna van Rensselaer, who was also his godmother.[9]

During baptism a child also received his or her first name, which was carefully recorded in the church's baptismal register, along with the names of the parents and witnesses. Dutch naming customs usually followed a distinctive pattern: first- and second-born daughters and first- and second-born sons were given the names of their paternal and maternal grandparents. Children were also named for parents, aunts, uncles, godparents, and friends. The pattern varied by alternately choosing from the paternal then the maternal line with the birth of each child. When a child died young, his or her name was given, at times, to the next child born of the same sex, thereby preserving the name that the dead child had carried.[10] Of the six sons born to Cornelis Steenwijck and Margareta de Riemer, two were named Jacob, one Isaacq, two Cornelis, and one Jacobus. Beginning in 1659 Steenwijck had recorded their births in the family Bible, along with that of their sister Margariet. By 1684 all the children had been buried in the church in New York.[11]

INFANT AND CHILDHOOD MORTALITY

How the Steenwijck children died is unknown. Disease and the lack of effective medical treatment certainly took many lives in the seventeenth century. Even a chest cold could be fatal. When five-year-old Maria Ebbingh caught a cold in October 1665, her parents called in two of New Amsterdam's medical experts to treat her for congestion, but a fever developed and her body weakened.[12] The last few days of her life were vividly described by her father, Jeronimus Ebbingh. During the day she played by the fire and sat at the table to eat the midday meal, although she had little appetite. During the night she tossed and turned in her bed and asked to sleep with her parents. Just an hour before her death she arose, and her stepbrothers were called in to see her. Shortly thereafter, surrounded by her family, she gave two little sobs, and with the last, her little mouth remained half open. The tragic death of one child from the complications of a cold can be contrasted to the devastating effects of a smallpox epidemic that affected children and adults alike in Beverwijck in 1662. The disease, wrote Jeremias van Rensselaer, the director of Rensselaerswijck (now part of Albany), was so severe that "hardly any one escaped who had not had it in the fatherland."[13] The frequent rental of the pall, both small and large, from the deacons of Beverwijck's Dutch Reformed Church from September to December of that year supports Van Rensselaer's claim. These special cloths, which covered the coffins of children and adults during burial rites, were rented fifteen (the small pall) and fourteen (large) times during that period. Before and after the epidemic, they were rented regularly but much less often.[14]

While many youngsters died at birth or from childhood and contagious diseases, other potential hazards also threatened their lives. Toddlers wandered around in homes with open fireplaces and boiling pots and in yards with open wells. Danger also loomed on the crowded streets of New Amsterdam in 1665 (by then renamed New York), where a child was killed by a runaway horse belonging to Jan Smedes. The youngster was not identified, but it could have been five-year-old Lysbeth van Hooghten or her two-year-old brother, Johannes, both of whom had been baptized in the city's Dutch Reformed Church. Frans van Hooghten, the dead child's father, sued Smedes in the municipal court, where the magistrates concluded that the horse be "forfeited" and its owner ordered to pay the court costs and to satisfy Van Hooghten for the loss of his deceased child.[15]

The perilous consequences of life in the seventeenth century resulted in high infant-mortality rates in New Netherland, as well as in other North American colonies and in Europe. Although mortality studies have not been done for the period under consideration in this paper, a study of the Haring family in Tappan, New Jersey, from 1688 to 1743 revealed that the first generations produced on average 9.3 children, with thirty percent dying in infancy or youth. In colonial Maryland forty to fifty-five percent of children never turned twenty, and only fifty percent of infants in the Netherlands lived to reach their twenty-fifth birthdays. Of those who survived, half would lose one or both parents, for, as the rental of the large pall in Beverwijck suggests, parents were as susceptible to contagious diseases as their children.[16] Surviving spouses in the Netherlands and in the colony usually remarried. Of the ninety-six marriages performed in the Reformed Church in New Amsterdam between 1661 and 1664, thirty involved a widow or a widower, and in ten more both parties had lost a spouse.[17] Some of New Netherland's youngsters, therefore, grew up in families that had a mixture of children and stepchildren.

With death occurring at relatively frequent intervals, the sight of a healthy baby was, by contrast, a great joy. Jeremias van Rensselaer is one of but a few parents who noted the pleasure he took in his children, although his remarks are brief and interspersed among the numerous pages of his correspondence (1651–1674). His eldest son, Kiliaen, born in August 1663, was, he wrote, "a beloved child to his mother and a welcome son to his father." The babe had survived a bout of jaundice and a rash within the first three weeks of life, but he was also "fond of suckling," all signs, remarked Van Rensselaer, that he would "abide with us." In October 1664 the fourteen-month-old toddler was running "around everywhere." At twenty months, he was talking "a little in broken language." Shortly after his second birthday, Kiliaen remembered the departure of his grandmother Anneke Loockermans and other family members, who had probably been present at the birth of his sister Anna in August 1665. Van Rensselaer noted that "Kiliaen kept calling for a long time" for them, so that after their departure, when asked about them, he answered with a sad voice, "Ah," and pointed to the yachts on the river. Kiliaen's sister Anna was "quite a big baby," her father observed, when he compared her to her brother's birth size. At twenty-two months, she had begun "to say everything." A second son, Hendrick, arrived in November 1667 and was "a strong little fellow" at eight months. In January 1670 tragedy struck when Van Rensselaer and his wife, Maria van Cortlandt, buried "the little body" of an unnamed son, "who [had] died in the agony of birth." However, another son, Johannes, arrived in December 1670. Van Rensselaer used the endearment *poppetie* (poppet) to describe the babe to his father-in-law, Oloff van Cortlandt. He was "a strong child, like his brother Hen[d]rick," he wrote. The births of Van Rensselaer's last children, Maria and Jeremias, are not mentioned in the extant correspondence, although by June 29, 1674, he commented that his "five" children were well. Jeremias was born sometime after Van Rensselaer's own death in October 1674.[18]

NURTURING INFANTS

As noted above, Van Rensselaer declared in 1663 that his son Kiliaen was "fond of suckling." Mother's milk was, of course, vital for an infant's survival. Whether Kiliaen was suckled by his mother was not mentioned in the correspondence. European women of rank often employed a wet nurse, but contemporaries encouraged healthy Dutch mothers, from all levels of society, to nurse their newborns. Adriaen van der Donck observed that Native American mothers, regardless of rank, also nursed their babies for about a year. They did not "have their children breast-fed or nursed by others," he wrote. He does not mention what occurred if mothers fell ill or died in childbed. Such events were not uncommon in the seventeenth century, and among Dutch residents, the custom of employing a wet nurse was followed in those situations.[19] This practice is corroborated in the accounts of the deacons of the Dutch Reformed Church of Beverwijck, who offered relief to the town's poor. In October 1665 two women were hired to nurse the newborn twins of Carsten de Noorman after his wife died in childbirth. The contracts written to sustain the infants were valid for one year, and each wet nurse received 35 guilders a month. The twins were probably weaned in December 1666, when the last nursing fees were paid, and new boarding contracts were recorded for the children at 32 guilders a month each.[20]

The deacons also provided the twins, and other poor and/or orphaned babies, with diapers made of blue or Osnabruck linen or of thick woolen fabrics, like baize or duffel. These were used for swaddling, the baby being rolled in the linen and then the woolen diaper. Caps of linen or durable serge covered their heads, and yarn was knit into shirts to keep their bodies warm. When Beverwijck's babies became toddlers, they wore outfits made of baize or of a woolen cloth called *dosijntiens*. These outfits, of which tops and bottoms were made out of one piece of cloth, were worn underneath a sleeping gown.[21]

CHILDHOOD ACTIVITIES: PUNISHMENT AND REWARDS

The accounts of Beverwijck's deacons and Van Rensselaer's correspondence make it possible to imagine New Netherland's babies wrapped in blue linen diapers and toddlers running around in their baize outfits before they graduated to breeches or petticoats and before their parents, or those entrusted with their care, anticipated the weighty concerns about their futures. Extant records, however, rarely mention the activities of childhood. Five-year-old Maria Ebbingh played with her silver doll accessories during the last days of her life. Somewhat older children may have participated in the games (trundling hoops, spinning tops, jumping rope, and playing leapfrog) depicted in the numerous paintings, prints, and tiles of the Dutch Republic's Golden Age. Surely many of the amusements prohibited in New Netherland on the Sabbath and on Days of Fasting and Prayer—including card and ball games, backgammon, ticktack, ninepins, and dancing—must have been learned in childhood, perhaps from grandparents, parents, or older siblings.[22]

Children were not caught breaking the Sabbath by indulging in one of the forbidden pastimes, but an occasional youngster was discovered behaving boisterously. Take, for instance, Gerrit Hendricksz, who was eleven years old when he stood before New Netherland's Council in 1644. There he acknowledged that he had accidentally hit Jacob Melyn in the eye with a potsherd, although he claimed that he had actually been aiming for Jacob's dog. Jacob's sister had struck Gerrit for his deed, and consequently during the fracas he had stepped on and torn her neckerchief when it fell from her shoulders.[23] Gerrit did not appear again regarding this case, and it is unclear why Jacob's father, Cornelis Melyn, had requested Gerrit's statement; perhaps he wanted to seek damages from the boy's father. The son of Frans Clasen, on the other hand, did not stand before the municipal court of New Amsterdam in 1656 when Jan Vinje accused him and his schoolmates of trampling his peas and corn. The clerk of the court did not bother to record the boy's name and age, but his father defended him and his friends, protesting that the children had "not taken or injured anything to the value of a pea's pod." Besides, "many other children, when they came out of school," had been among the peas. Vinje, who was Clasen's neighbor, acknowledged that he had struck the boy because he "could not catch any other but him." The boy's folly, therefore, was that he had not scampered out of Vinje's way as quickly as his mates, and thereby he had received such a beating from Vinje with a stick that he had arrived home black and blue, the other children having escaped unharmed. The court ruled that the boy had already received enough punishment for his deed, and Vinje, by his actions against the child, had "destroyed his rights" to sue for damages.[24]

Jan Vinje's use of a stick or rod was not an unusual form of punishment to correct a recalcitrant youngster, like Frans Clasen's son. A ferule and a cane, as well as the rod, were common disciplinary tools and were considered to be less severe than a whip. However, the pain produced by the rod may have depended on who wielded it or where it was applied (back or buttocks) and if that particular part of the body was covered, or not, with clothing.[25] Some Dutch moralists urged parents not to spare the rod and to avoid spoiling their children; others advocated fear of the rod rather than its use, for harsh punishment could harden children "into expectations of brutality and wickedness." Allowing "willfulness to go unchecked and unpunished," on the other hand, was considered foolish.[26]

Nevertheless, the Dutch generally frowned upon corporal punishment. The harsh notions of "breaking the will" that were advocated by some Puritan and evangelical cultures were absent in the Netherlands. Humanist thought prevailed there, including the idea of curbing a child's natural instincts, to some extent, and simultaneously coaxing him or her into learning.[27] Some parents in New Amsterdam were apparently influenced by the humanistic philosophies of their Dutch homeland, for they prohibited the schoolmaster of the Latin School in 1661 from punishing their sons, though the boys had fought among themselves and torn "the clothes from each others bodies."[28] The incident in the school did not mean, however, that New Netherland's parents failed to correct unruly children, but they did perhaps object to the punishment that was administered by someone other than themselves. Lambert Huybertsen Mol gave a bristling reply to the magistrates of New Amsterdam in 1663 when he and his son appeared before them for fighting and drawing a knife. He admitted giving his son a blow, "saying a father may well strike his child."[29]

Dutch parents were equally responsible for the moral, as well as the physical and mental, development of their children. They were required to provide the necessities of life—food, drink, clothing, and shelter—and to give children comfort, ease, and discipline.[30] Bringing them safely through infancy and childhood was not always in the parents' control, due to illness and accidents. Ensuring their futures, however, was achieved through several different means. Consider Leendert Aertsen and Joris Rapalje, two men who leased several cows from the West India Company in 1638. Their contracts stipulated that the first heifer calf produced by the leased herd would be kept for their daughters—that is, Aertsen's unnamed youngest daughter and Rapalje's daughter Judith. The cattle were valuable assets, and the arrangements made by their fathers offered two young girls an investment, not only in the colony, but also for their future well-being.[31] Juriaen Blanck and Tryntie Claesen, on the other hand, provided for their children's prospects by writing a joint will in 1662. They stipulated that the survivor of the two was "to bring up their children, clothe them, make them go to school, provide for all their needs, let them learn a trade or an art, by which they may earn their own living, educate them to be virtuous, teach them to know and fear God and to endow them, when they marry or arrive at some other approved condition, as the estate will allow in conscience and equity."[32] Many parents followed Blanck and Claesen's example, assured that the community of New Netherland would adhere to the Dutch civil law and customs of inheritance.[33]

Unlike the English customs of primogeniture and entail, the Dutch followed the rules of partible inheritance. Upon the death of a parent (whether mother or father), an estate was divided in half, one portion given to the surviving spouse and the other divided equally among sons and daughters alike. When the second parent died, the offspring received the remaining half, again in equal shares. A surviving parent with underage children often retained the entire estate and presented each child with his or her portion at majority (twenty-five years) or at marriage, whichever came first.[34] In cases of remarriage, some fathers or mothers made sure that the children from a previous marriage were cared for before the ceremony ensued. When the widow Geertruyt Jacobsen intended to marry Rouloff Jansen in 1643, a premarital contract was drawn up, whereby the bride promised to give her sons, Jan and Jacob van Vorst, 75 guilders each at the age of majority. The money was each boy's portion of their deceased father's estate and was apparently invested, for Jacobsen and her groom promised to rear the boys, "keeping their capital safe and not touching more than the interest." Furthermore, they would "send them to school and have them taught reading, writing and a good trade, as decent and God-fearing and honest parent[s] are bound to do, but all according to their means and not more."[35]

EDUCATION

The wills and marriage contracts preserved among New Netherland's manuscripts stressed the importance of educating one's children. It was, in fact, expected of parents "according to each one's condition and opportunity."[36] Contemporary philosophers in the Netherlands maintained that an education, when combined with parental guidance, allowed children to make responsible choices between goodness and evil, diligence and sloth, duty and disloyalty.[37] Learning was also a fundamental part of becoming a responsible and vital member of the community, and New Netherland's parents used various strategies in achieving that end. They sent their offspring to school, taught them at home, apprenticed them to skilled craftsmen, or used a combination of all three.

In matters of schooling, New Netherland followed the educational practices of the Netherlands, which differed from her European neighbors by her willingness to teach girls, as well as boys, to write and by the perception that it was beneficial to teach the poor. Therefore, boys and girls attended New Netherland's elementary schools, generally at their parents' expense, and the poor, who asked to be "taught for God's sake," were admitted for free.[38] In the 1660s through the early 1680s, the curriculum in the schools of New Amsterdam and the village of Midwoud (now Flushing) on Long Island included reading, writing, and ciphering (essentially arithmetic), as well as studying the fundamentals of the Reformed or "true" religion.[39] Attendance could begin as early as the age of three, as with Kiliaen van Rensselaer, whose parents sent him to school before his fourth birthday.[40] Beginners first learned the alphabet, then spelling, reading, and grammar, each in turn as their skills increased. Learning to read took about three years in the city of Utrecht and probably a similar length of time in the colony. A child of six or seven could, therefore, have a full understanding of the reading skills. Writing, which took dexterity with the quill and the watchful eye of a demanding teacher, was not considered until reading had been mastered. Most pupils probably also learned to count and recognize figures; however, ciphering, like writing, was a separate subject and was only taught to those whose parents agreed to pay the schoolmaster for such instruction.[41]

Religious instruction began by learning the answers to simple questions about the Bible, to which were added, over time, the catechism and the recitation of the "usual prayers," the Ten Commandments, the Psalms, and other Bible verses.[42] In 1661 the schoolmasters in New Amsterdam and Breuckelen were guided by the "very concise little catechism" entitled *A Brief Method of Instructing the Youth in the Principles of the Christian Religion*. Its author, Johannes Megapolensis, a minister of the Dutch Reformed Church in New Netherland, had it published in 1651. The book's endorsement by the consistory (minister, elders, and deacons) of Breuckelen's Reformed Church reads like the promotional material on the back covers of today's paperbacks. It comprised, they noted, "not only the means to attain godliness and salvation, but also the explanation of the Apostles' Creed and, moreover, of the Lord's Prayer, both of which are explained by the Rev. in a very learned and concise way and are presented in the form of questions and answers."[43]

Children in New Netherland began their school day at 8 a.m. In Midwoud the schoolmaster chose a pupil to read the "morning prayer" as it was found in the catechism. Latecomers were warned by three to four pulls on the bell that lessons were starting. The morning session closed at 11 a.m. "with the prayer before meals," and the afternoon session (1 to 4 p.m.) followed the same pattern, beginning and ending with "the prayer after dinner" and "the evening prayer," respectively. The evening school, for which no time was stated, opened "with the prayer of our Lord Jesus Christ and close[d] with a hymn from the Psalms of David." Catechism instruction commenced on Wednesday and Saturday, so the children could recite the questions and answers before the congregation on Sundays before the afternoon sermon. In the Reformed Church of New Amsterdam, the catechism was also taught every Sunday afternoon.[44] The forty-four boys and twenty-one girls, aged seven to fourteen, who had attended the catechism class of the Reverend Henricus Selyns in New York City in 1698 could recite "all the Psalms, hymns and prayers in rhyme." The "girls," noted Selyns, "although fewer in number, had learned and recited more in proportion than the boys."[45]

In the village of Midwoud pupils attended school for "nine months in succession" from September to June or May through November. During the summer months the schoolmaster was obliged to keep the school open for any number of children, as long as their parents would pay the tuition for a total of ten pupils. If just a few children appeared and agreed to pay the fee for ten, the schoolmaster's wife took on the responsibilities of instruction. In New Amsterdam the school may have been open all year, as were the schools in the Netherlands. The desire for knowledge was apparently strong among New Netherlanders. According to the Evert Pietersz, the schoolmaster in Nieuw Amstel (now Newcastle, Delaware), in 1657, young and old appeared at his school to learn reading, writing, and ciphering as "soon as winter begins and they can no longer work the soil."[46]

Schoolmasters like Evert Pietersz were allowed to charge a quarterly fee for imparting their knowledge to New Netherland's children, the cost for each subject clearly delineated in their contracts. For example, in 1661 New Amsterdam's parents paid 1½ guilders to have a child taught the ABCs, spelling, and reading; 2½ guilders for reading and writing; and 3 guilders for reading, writing, and ciphering. In 1670 Midwoud's villagers paid their schoolmaster 2 guilders for "ABC children and spellers" and 2½ guilders "for reading and writing together." Evening readers and writers in Midwoud paid 3 guilders for each subject.[47]

The contracts recorded in Midwoud also stipulated that a schoolmaster be tactful, sober, and industrious. He was to be patient with the children as the circumstances demanded and friendly in teaching them. He and his colleague in New Amsterdam were also required to keep strict discipline, while children were expected to behave and to follow instructions.[48] In the Netherlands, the school rules were hung on the wall, and the pupils who had read such rules but failed to heed them received two whacks with the ferule or a whipping. Among the offenses were failing to take off one's cap "before a man of honor"; running, screaming, swearing, gambling, lying, stealing, or playing with knives; racing "wildly or improperly through the streets"; chasing other people's animals; resisting the wishes of one's parents; "run[ning] into the fields, or jump[ing] into the hay with sticks"; "stay[ing] at home without the teacher's or parents' leave"; bathing in the nude and walking through peas and carrots; making "noise in church"; not saying one's prayers; tearing books and spoiling paper; "call[ing] one another names"; slinging snot, fleas, and lice at each other; not going nicely to church and home again; and lastly, smiting each other with baskets or jugs.[49]

While some of the seventeenth-century indiscretions above are dated, others are a telling reminder that the momentary blunders of youth change little with the passage of time. Whether or not schoolmasters in New Netherland hung the rules on the walls of their schools was not documented. Certainly, the boys who attended the Latin School in New Amsterdam went unpunished by their master, Alexander Carolus Curtius, when they fought and tore each other's clothes, as noted earlier. Curtius was criticized by the city's burgomasters for not keeping "strict discipline over the boys," while Curtius entreated them to "make a rule or law for the school."[50]

Curtius's appearance before the Burgomasters' Court confirms that some of New Netherland's boys graduated from the elementary school to the Latin School in New Amsterdam for more advanced learning. Girls would not have attended, for they were barred from higher education, both in Europe and the colonies. Some boys and girls ended their elementary schooling after they had learned to read and may have never acquired the ability to write. Sending a child to school was, in fact, a parental prerogative, and if a future occupation did not warrant reading, writing, or arithmetic, there was no social necessity to attend.[51]

Labor and Vocational Training

Schooled or not, all children were expected to contribute to the household economy, infants and invalids being the only exceptions.[52] Contemporary attitudes promoted the beneficial effects of labor that could begin at the age of seven or according to each child's strength. Working without the benefit of instruction, however, was disapproved of, for the primary goal of labor was to teach young New Netherlanders an occupation, so that as adults they could make a positive contribution to their community.[53]

Many of New Netherland's parents prepared their own children for a lifetime of labor. Studies of New York City's male residents have shown that more than a third of the sons born to men who were in the city in 1664 performed the same work as their fathers; forty-two percent did so in the following generation. Girls also learned various skills from their parents. Consider Maria van Cortlandt, who became a successful brewer in Rensselaerswijck after her marriage to Jeremias van Rensselaer, having learned her father's brewing and entrepreneurial acumen while still at home in New Amsterdam.[54] If parents opted to continue a child's training beyond the household environment or elementary schooling, they could make other arrangements by binding their youngsters to the colony's artisans, merchants, professionals, and farmers.

The system established in New Netherland for vocational training and indentures for service was based on Old World customs and regulated by Dutch civil law.[55] Parents and guardians had a right to bind out a child or ward by means of a formal contract, which was usually executed by a local notary or secretary.[56] Hans Jansen, for example, bound his daughter Marritjen, in 1644, to serve the tavern keeper Philip Gerritsen or his wife for three years. Gerritsen agreed to provide the girl with "board, lodging and the necessary clothing, and also have her taught sewing, in such a manner as a father should or might do with his child, all however according to his circumstances." Two days later, the secretary also recorded an indenture for Maria, "a young Negro girl belonging" to the West India Company and the daughter of Big Pieter. She was bound by director Willem Kieft and became the servant of Nicolaes Coorn, a resident of Rensselaerswijck. Maria received no prospects for special training. Her master was obliged to feed and clothe her for four years and then restore her to the director or his successor, "if she be living."[57]

The formal contracts of apprenticeship or service recorded in the secretarial registers were but one way to direct a child's future. Many parents and guardians also made oral or casual agreements with neighbors and friends, and consequently their arrangements were never recorded. Countless contracts have also been lost through the passage of time,[58] as is indicated by the fact that parents and masters presented copies of indentures as evidence on numerous occasions to court magistrates.

The contracts, whether oral and written, were binding, and contracting parties sued each other if the terms were neglected. Take the suit brought against

Aert Pietersen Tack by Gerrit Heergrins in the court of Wiltwijck (now Kingston, New York), in 1662. Heergrins demanded the wages his son had earned, namely four *schepels* of wheat and a pair of leather breeches. The boy, however, had left his master's service prematurely and had gone to Manhattan; therefore, Tack refused to pay. The court agreed and ordered Heergrins to return his son, because he had been hired out "under a written agreement," which Tack himself had prepared. Also, the boy had left without his master's consent.[59] Several other parents, who were also sued to return their runaway children, accused masters of abusing them. For example, Grietje Provoost's "little son" ran home without leave, but she charged his master, the shoemaker Adriaen van Laer, with beating and ill-treating the child. The boy still had a half-year to serve on a two-year contract, and his master demanded his return. Despite his mother's assertions, the magistrates decreed that the boy serve out his time. Concurrently, they admonished his master to treat his apprentice "properly and not show him a bad example."[60] Local magistrates enforced the laws but used their discretionary power when necessary to serve the needs of the colony's children.

Contracts and court cases concerning children and their work in New Netherland offer a window into the world of working children. They contain specific information, such as the names of the contracting parties and of the child involved. Some also record the intended vocation, the length of apprenticeship or service, the child's age, the recompense, and whether the master would impart some form of education besides vocational training. The four-year apprenticeship contract of Françoys Pietersz, the fifteen-year-old son of Pieter Winne, can be used here as an example. In 1674 his father apprenticed him to the shoemaker Rutger Arentsz, who promised to feed Françoys, provide the materials to make his clothes, grant him time all winter to go to school every evening, and allow him to "help his father three weeks every year in the harvest." At the end of four years, he would fit Françoys out "burgher wise with a workaday and a Sunday suit of clothes and linen to correspond." Françoys' father agreed to have his son's clothes made during the four-year period, both woolen and linen, and to have them mended and repaired. He would also arrange to have his linens washed. Françoys promised to serve his master with "all diligence faithfulness as well in the shoemaking business as in all other work in which the master may need him."[61]

Françoys Pietersz would spend four years with his master to learn the shoemaker's trade. The term of apprenticeship or service in the contracts made on behalf of other children ranged from one to eleven years, with an average length of about four—younger children serving longer apprenticeships than older children. The occupations and skills mentioned included glazier (glassmaker), shoemaker, smith, tailor, gun-stock maker, carpenter, millwright, tile maker, bookkeeper, sewer or needle worker, surgeon, and turner. Françoys Pietersz was also given the opportunity to attend the evening school in Albany during the winter in 1674. Not all contracts included this stipulation, but when masters agreed to provide learning other than vocational, they had various options. In 1662 the master of

Jochim Anthony Robberts had to "teach him, or cause him to be taught, reading and writing"; Laurens Haf's master had "to send him to school in the winter or teach him properly himself," while Laurens' half-sister Anna Tielemans could go to "school during the winter evenings." Gysbert Schuyler was also allowed to attend school in the evening in 1665 "without neglecting his master's service, but at his father's expense."[62]

Clothing

The details in Françoys Pietersz's contract concerning his clothes allude to the challenge of keeping ever-growing youngsters properly clothed. Masters were obliged to provide their trainees with the basic necessities, which included clothing,[63] and those who neglected to provide them were, at times, sued in the colony's courts, as was Jan Hendrick. Caspar Stynmets demanded the "breeches, two shirts, one pr. stockings, and 1 pair shoes" that were due to his brother-in-law, who had served Hendrick for nine months in 1656. The clothes, Stynmets stated, would allow the boy to "engage with other persons," meaning perhaps that he would make a good impression in his new outfit.[64] The end-of-service clothing that children had earned by working for their masters saved them and their parents the costs of purchasing others, for clothes were dear and valuable possessions. Garments outgrown by older children were given to younger family members or auctioned off to the highest bidder.[65] Garments of the deceased, like those of Teuntje Straetmans, were bequeathed to her eldest daughter, Margariet Meijring, who received her mother's black undershirt, a linen undershirt, a black apron, a smaller apron, and a round handkerchief in 1662.[66]

Clearly, children's clothes, like those of adults, were made of linen and woolen textiles that were imported to the colony from the Netherlands and elsewhere in Europe.[67] A child's wardrobe usually consisted of old and new clothes and garments for special occasions or for everyday use. There would be several pieces of underwear, including shirts, chemises, and drawers that were made of linen, a durable fabric that could be washed regularly. It was not unusual, therefore, for apprenticeship contracts to include arrangements for washing, either at the master's or a parent's expense. Linen underwear was worn next to the skin to protect it from the coarseness of the outerwear, which was made from a range of woolen fabrics like kersey, serge, and baize, as well as deerskin. These garments were rarely washed, and therefore underwear also protected the outerwear from body soils. Girls wore petticoats or skirts, coats, bodices with stays, and tight-fitting under-vests worn between an undershirt and the outerwear. Boys wore woolen coats, waistcoats, breeches, and mantles. The wardrobe would also have included sundries like head wear (hats and caps), neckwear, footwear, aprons, linen handkerchiefs, and removable sleeves made of durable baize and serge (these added warmth to the bodice or were worn as a protective covering). Ribbons,

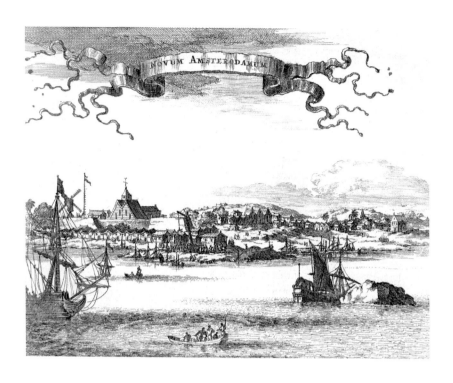

Augustine Herrman (attributed), Novum Amsterodamum *(The Montanus View), ca. 1650. Courtesy of the Museum of the City of New York, L231.2.*

L. F. Tantillo, The Half Moon at Newburgh Bay, 1609. *Henry Hudson pilots his famous ship northward, exploring the river which today bears his name. Reproduction courtesy of the artist.*

L. F. Tantillo, Curiosity of the Maguas, *ca. 1650. Arent van Curler's bark, carrying a pair of workhorses, is approached by Mohawk warriors six miles north of Fort Orange, on the site of present-day Albany. Reproduction courtesy of the artist.*

L. F. Tantillo, rendering from a digital study model of Asser Levy's house on the north side of Stone Street, New Amsterdam, ca. 1660. Reproduction courtesy of the artist.

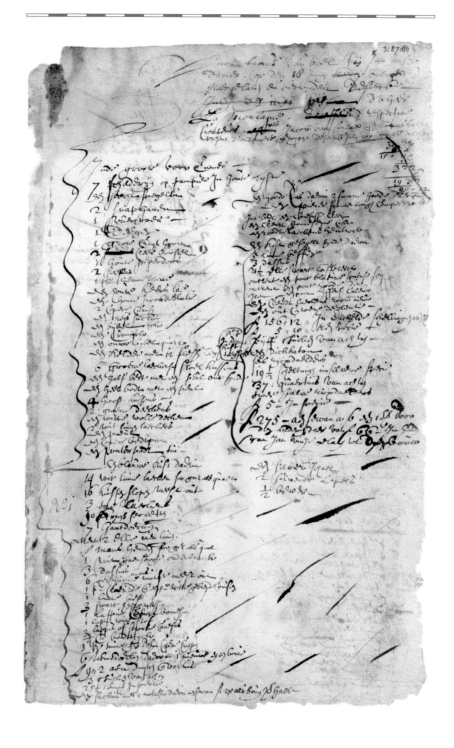

Inventory of the personal estate of Jan Jansz Damen, July 6–7, 1681. Dutch Colonial Manuscripts, Vol. 3, New York State Archives. Reproduction courtesy of the New York State Archives.

Pieter de Hooch, Woman with Children in an Interior, *ca. 1658–1660. Oil on canvas, 67.9 x 55.6 cm (26¾ x 21⅞ in). Fine Arts Museums of San Francisco, Gift of Samuel H. Kress Foundation, 61.44.37.*

Jan Havicksz Steen, Leiden Baker Arend Oostwaert and His Wife Catharina Keyzerswaert, *ca. 1658.*
Courtesy of the Rijksmuseum, Amsterdam, the Netherlands.

Jan Havicksz Steen, The Feast of St. Nicholas, *ca. 1663–1665. Courtesy of the Rijksmuseum, Amsterdam, the Netherlands.*

Willem Cornelisz Duyster, The Wedding of Adriaen Ploos van Amstel and Agnes van Bijler, *1616. Courtesy of the Rijksmuseum, Amsterdam, the Netherlands.*

lace, braid, buttons, and buckles decorated and added color to the outerwear or adorned shoes, hats, caps, and stockings.

The list of clothes belonging to the fourteen-year-old orphan Laurens Haf allows a rare glimpse of one boy's wardrobe. It was compiled in 1664 when Willem van Couwenhoven was given custody of Laurens by the deacons of the Dutch Reformed Church in Breuckelen. Laurens owned four new shirts, an *innocent* (a loose-fitting dressing gown), serge trousers, and a new red kersey dress coat. The coat may have matched a pair of red trousers made of barracan, a coarse woolen fabric that was durable and waterproof. Laurens also owned trousers made of white linen and another pair of leather. His sundries included stockings, Iceland stockings, new shoes, half-worn shoes, two black hats, a serge cap, gloves, two handkerchiefs, and two scarves. Whether or not Laurens Haf's wardrobe was typical for a boy his age is difficult to determine. No list was made of the clothing belonging to his half-sister Anna Tielemans. When their mother Teuntje Straetmans died in October 1662, the inventory of her estate noted that part of the linen cloth found at her house would be made into shirts for the children, while some blue linen would be made into aprons for the eight-year-old Anna.[68]

CONCLUSION

Dressed in their woolens and linens, children like Laurens Haf and Anna Tielemans played along Hudson's river, walked on New Netherland's streets, attended her schools, and worked in her fields, shops, and homes. They were New Netherland's future generations, and they occupy a unique niche in the colony's history. For a brief moment in time—that is, from infancy through adolescence—they were not concerned about the burdensome matters of politics and government that so often preoccupied their elders. Neither were they responsible for the affairs of trade and the growth margins of crops. Yet, children's lives were profoundly affected by the myriad of decisions made by their parents and those who governed them. How they reacted to the choices made on their behalf was seldom recorded. New Netherland's records, nevertheless, allow us to peer into their world. Most children were born at home, swaddled in diapers, and nursed by their mothers. The devastating effects of childhood diseases and epidemics greatly reduced their numbers. Those who survived prepared for their futures. The glimpses of childhood in New Netherland remind us that a child's journey toward adulthood in the seventeenth century was very different from that of a twenty-first-century child, yet, in certain respects, so similar.

I want to thank the editor Martha D. Shattuck for her comments on an earlier version of this paper.

NOTES

1. J. Franklin Jameson, ed., *Narratives of New Netherland, 1609–1664* (New York: Charles Scribner's Sons, 1909), 48; Arnold J. F. van Laer, trans. and ed., *Documents Relating to New Netherland, 1624–1626 in the Henry E. Huntington Library* (San Marino, Calif.: Henry E. Huntington Library and Art Gallery, 1924), 136, 139–140; Adriaen van der Donck, *A Description of the New Netherlands*, Jeremiah Johnson, trans., Thomas F. O'Donnell, ed. (Syracuse: Syracuse Univeristy Press, 1968), 11; A. J. F. van Laer, trans. and ed., *Correspondence of Jeremias van Rensselaer, 1651–1674* (Albany: University of the State of New York, 1932), 375–376 (hereafter cited as *CJVR*).

2. For extant manuscripts, see Charles T. Gehring, ed., *A Guide to Dutch Manuscripts Relating to New Netherland* (Albany: University of the State of New York, 1978).

3. Arnold J. F. van Laer, trans., "Letters of Nicasius de Sille, 1654," *Proceedings of the New York State Historical Association* 18 (1923): 101–102, 105.

4. Thomas G. Evans, ed., "Baptisms from 1639 to 1730 in the Reformed Dutch Church, New York," in *Collections of the New York Genealogical and Biographical Society*, vol. 2 (1901; repr., Upper Saddle River, N.J.: Gregg Press, 1968), 9–117 (hereafter cited as "Baptisms"); A. P. G. Jos van der Linde, trans. and ed., *Old First Dutch Reformed Church of Brooklyn, New York: First Book of Records, 1660–1752* (Baltimore: Genealogical Publishing Co., Inc., 1983), 109–116 (hereafter cited as *Reformed Church*).

5. *CJVR*, 432; Berthold Fernow, ed., *The Records of New Amsterdam from 1653 to 1674 Anno Domini*, 7 vols. (1897; repr., Baltimore: Genealogical Publishing, 1976), 3:193 (hereafter cited as *RNA*); Adriana E. van Zwieten, " '[O]n her woman's troth': Tolerance, Custom, and the Women of New Netherland," *de Halve Maen* 72, no. 1 (1999): 12. Some women returned to the Netherlands to give birth. See Jaap Jacobs, *New Netherland: A Dutch Colony in Seventeenth-Century America* (Leiden and Boston: Brill, 2005), 421–422.

6. G. D. J. Schotel, *Het Oud-Hollandsch Huisgezin der Zeventiende Eeuw.*, 2nd ed., improved and illustrated by H. C. Rogge (Arnhem, Netherlands: A. J. G. Strengholts's Uitgeversmaatschappij and Gijsbers & Van Loon, 1903), 31–32; Janny Venema, *Beverwijck: A Dutch Village on the American Frontier, 1652–1664* (Hilversum and Albany: Verloren and State University of New York Press, 2003), 230–231.

7. Dean R. Snow, Charles T. Gehring, and William A. Starna, eds., *In Mohawk Country: Early Narratives about a Native People* (Syracuse: Syracuse University Press, 1996), 43, 114–115.

8. See for example *CJVR*, 326–327, 380, 393, 432–433, where the children of Jeremias van Rensselaer are carried by godparents to the church for baptism.

9. Schotel, *Hollandsch Huisgezin*, 54–61; *CJVR*, 367.

10. Edward H. Tebbenhoff, "Tacit Rules and Hidden Family Structures: Naming Practices and Godparentage in Schenectady, New York, 1680–1800," *Journal of Social History* 18 (1985): 567–585; David Steven Cohen, *The Dutch-American Farm* (New York: New York University Press, 1992), 147; Willem Frijhof, *Wegen van Evert Willemsz. Een Hollands weeskind of zoek naar zichzelf 1607–1647* (Nijmegen, Netherlands: Uitgeverij SUN, 1995), 134–135.

11. "Baptisms," 2: 54, 62, 72, 85, 94, 102, 123; Joyce D. Goodfriend, "Recovering the Religious History of Dutch Reformed Women in Colonial New York," *de Halve Maen* 64, no. 4 (Winter 1991): 56.

12. For Maria's story see Jacobs, *New Netherland*, 439–440.

13. Van Laer in *CJVR*, 328, 332–333, translated the word *kinderpockjens* (literally "children's pox") as "chicken pox;" however, Venema, in *Beverwijck*, 405, n. 322, avers that the word refers to "smallpox." For "children's pocks" in New Amsterdam in February 1663, see Berthold Fernow, trans. and ed., *The Minutes of the Orphanmasters of New Amsterdam, 1655 to 1663*, 2 vols. (New York: Francis P. Harper, 1902–1907), 2:33, 34–38 (hereafter cited as *MONA*).

14. Janny Venema, trans. and ed., *Deacons' Accounts 1652–1674: First Dutch Reformed Church of Beverwyck/Albany, New York* (Rockport, Maine: Picton Press, 1998), 102–104, 106 (hereafter cited as *Deacons' Accounts*).

15. *RNA*, 5:189–190, 195, 197. The ages of the children were calculated from the baptismal register, "Baptisms," 2:54, 68.

16. Firth H. Fabend, *A Dutch Family in the Middle Colonies, 1660–1800* (New Brunswick, N.J.: Rutgers University Press, 1991), 39–40, 43–45. For infant-mortality rates in the Netherlands, see Dirk Damsma, *Het Hollandse Huisgezin (1560-heden)* (Utrecht, Netherlands: Kosmos – Z & K Uitgevers, 1993), 38–39. For Maryland, see Lois Green Carr and Lorena S. Walsh, "The Planter's Wife: The Experience of White Women in Seventeenth-Century Maryland," *William and Mary Quarterly*, 3rd ser., 34 (October 1977): 552.

17. Rudolf Dekker, *Uit de schaduw in 't grote licht. Kinderen in egodocumenten van de Gouden Eeuw tot de Romantiek* (Amsterdam: Wereldbibliotheek, 1995), 18; David E. Narrett, *Inheritance and Family Life in Colonial New York City* (Ithaca: Cornell University Press, 1992), 63.

18. *CJVR*, 6, 326-327, 329, 364, 377, 380, 382, 392–393, 402, 417, 432–433, 462; A. J. F. van Laer, trans. and ed., *Correspondence of Maria van Rensselaer, 1669–1689* (Albany: University of the State of New York, 1935), 3, 14, 14–15 n. 19, 57; Jacobs, *New Netherland*, 423–424.

19. Damsma, *Hollandse Huisgezin*, 64–65; Simon Schama, *The Embarrassment of Riches* (Berkeley: University of California Press, 1988), 538–540; Snow et al., ed., *Mohawk Country*, 115.

20. *Deacons' Accounts*, 126–127, 146, 154–157, 161–171; Venema, *Beverwijck*, 341. For examples of wet nursing in New Amsterdam, see *RNA*, 1:298, 2:222.

21. *Deacons' Accounts*, xv, 40, 53–55, 161, 163, 166, 169, 173–174, 180, 262; Schotel, *Hollandsch Huisgezin*, 39.

22. Jacobs, *New Netherland*, 440; A. T. van Deursen, *Plain Lives in a Golden Age. Popular Culture, Religion and Society in Seventeenth-century Holland*, trans. Maarten Ultee (Cambridge, UK: Cambridge University Press, 1991), 131–132; Schama, *Embarrassment of Riches*, 497; *RNA*, 1:24–27, 2:40–42; E. B. O'Callaghan, *Laws and Ordinances of New Netherland, 1638–1674* (Albany: Weed, Parsons, 1868), 258–263.

23. Arnold J. F. van Laer, trans., *New York Historical Manuscripts, Dutch*, vol. 4, *Council Minutes, 1638–1649*, ed. Kenneth Scott and Kenn Stryker-Rodda (Baltimore: Genealogical Publishing Co., Inc., 1974), 249 (hereafter cited as *Council Minutes*).

24. *RNA*, 2:122, 134, 137.

25. S. Groenveld, J. J. H. Dekker and Th. R. M. Willemse, *Wezen en boefjes. Zes eeuwen zorg in wees- en kinderhuizen* (Hilversum, Netherlands: Verloren, 1997), 222–223. A ferule (*plak* in Dutch) was a flat, round, wooden disk attached to a short stick.

26. Schama, *Embarrassment of Riches*, 555–556; Van Deursen, *Plain Lives*, 130.

27. Schama, *Embarrassment of Riches*, 556.

28. *MONA*, 2:76.

29. *RNA*, 4:205.

30. Van Deursen, *Plain Lives*, 115.

31. Arnold J. F. van Laer, trans., *New York Historical Manuscripts, Dutch*, vol. 1, *Register of the Provincial Secretary, 1638–1660*, ed. Kenneth Scott and Kenn Stryker-Rodda (Baltimore: Genealogical Publishing Co., Inc., 1974), 1: 17–18, 20–21 (hereafter cited as *Provincial Secretary*).

32. *MONA*, 2:19–23.

33. The community of New Amsterdam also established a special municipal institution to transfer property to successive generations. See Adriana E. van Zwieten, "The Orphan Chamber of New Amsterdam," *William and Mary Quarterly*, 3rd ser., 53 (April 1996): 319–340.

34. Narrett, *Inheritance and Family Life*, 54, 56; Hugo Grotius, *The Jurisprudence of Holland*, 2nd ed., 2 vols., trans. Robert W. Lee (1953; repr. Aalen, Germany: Scientia Verlag, 1977), 1: 40–49.

35. *Provincial Secretary*, 2:115–116.

36. Van Deursen, *Plain Lives*, 115.

37. Schama, *Embarrassment of Riches*, 555; Van Deursen, *Plain Lives*, 130.

38. Margaret Spufford, "Literacy, Trade and Religion in the Commercial Centres of Europe," in *A Miracle Mirrored. The Dutch Republic in European Perspective*, ed. Karel Davids and Jan Lucassen (Cambridge, UK: Cambridge University Press, 1995), 259–260; William Heard Kilpatrick, *The Dutch Schools of New Netherland and Colonial New York* (Washington, D.C.: Government Printing Office, 1912), 30–31, 228; Van Deursen, *Plain Lives*, 116; *MONA*, 2: 116; Venema, *Beverwijck,* 150.

39. *MONA*, 2: 116; David William Voorhees, trans and ed., *Records of the Reformed Protestant Dutch Church of Flatbush, Kings County, New York*, vol. 1 (1677–1720) (New York: Holland Society of New York, 1998), 101, 103 (hereafter cited as *Records of Flatbush*).

40. Venema, *Beverwijck*, 150; *CJVR*, 392.

41. Venema, *Beverwijck*, 150; Van Deursen, *Plain Lives*, 122; Groenveld, et al., *Wezen en boefjes*, 194; Kilpatrick, *Dutch Schools*, 227.

42. *MONA*, 2:116; *Records of Flatbush*, 1:85, 101, 103, 107; Venema, *Beverwijck*, 150. The series of questions and answers in the catechism were used to test the religious knowledge of one preparing for Christian confirmation.

43. *Reformed Church*, 23, 31; Venema, *Beverwijck,* 151.

44. *Records of Flatbush*, 1:85, 101, 107, 109; *MONA*, 2:116. In 1661 the school schedule in New Amsterdam was similar to that of Midwoud. Lessons began at 8 a.m. and 1 p.m., with an evening session commencing at an unspecified time; ibid.

45. Edward T. Corwin, trans. and ed., *Ecclesiastical Records. State of New York*, 7 vols. (Albany: James B. Lyon, 1901–1916), 2:1235 (hereafter cited as *ER*); Goodfriend, "Recovering Religious History," 54–55.

46. *Records of Flatbush*, 1:87, 107; Kilpatrick, *Dutch Schools*, 216; *ER*, 1:402; Venema, *Beverwijck*, 148–149.

47. *MONA*, 2:115–116; *Records of Flatbush*, 1:85, 87, 103, 109.

48. Ibid.

49. Kilpatrick, *Dutch Schools*, 31–32; Schotel, *Oud-Hollandsche Huisgezin*, 82–83.

50. *MONA*, 2:76.

51. Kilpatrick, *Dutch Schools*, 30; Venema, *Beverwijck,*150; Van Deursen, *Plain Lives*, 116.

52. This section on children and labor in New Netherland is based on Adriana E. van Zwieten, "Preparing Children for Adulthood in New Netherland" in *Children Bound to Labor*, ed. Ruth W. Herndon and John E. Murray (Ithaca: Cornell University Press, forthcoming).

53. Stefan Bielinski, "How a City Worked: Occupations in Colonial Albany," in *A Beautiful and Fruitful Place. Selected Rensselaerswijck Seminar Papers*, ed. Nancy A. McClure Zeller (Albany: New Netherland Publishing, 1984), 121; Dekker, *Uit de schaduw*, 18; Van Deursen, *Plain Lives*, 115.

54. Joyce D. Goodfriend, *Before the Melting Pot: Society and Culture in Colonial New York City, 1664–1730* (Princeton: Princeton University Press, 1992), 173–176, 231 n. 17; *CJVR*, 377–378.

55. The guild system, although still prevalent in the Netherlands during the seventeenth century, was not transferred to the colony. Its establishment, however, was attempted. See Charles T. Gehring, trans. and ed., *Fort Orange Court Minutes, 1652–1660*, New Netherland Documents Series (Syracuse: Syracuse University Press, 1990), 190; *RNA*, 2: 410.

56. Grotius, *Jurisprudence*, 1: 43, 299, 301; Robert W. Lee, *An Introduction to Roman-Dutch Law*, 5th ed. (Oxford: Clarendon Press, 1953), 243 n. 3.

57. *Provincial Secretary*, 2: 222–224.

58. Charles T. Gehring, "Documentary Sources Relating to New Netherland," in *Colonial Dutch Studies: An Interdisciplinary Approach*, ed. Eric Nooter and Patricia U. Bonomi (New York: New York University Press, 1988), 33–51.

59. Dingman Versteeg, trans., *New York Historical Manuscripts, Dutch*, vol. 6, *Kingston Papers*, ed. Peter R. Christoph, Kenneth Scott and Kenn Stryker-Rodda (Baltimore: Genalogical Publishing Co., Inc., 1976), 1:45. One *schepel* of wheat was equal to 0.764 bushels. For seventeenth-century Dutch weights and measures, see Charles T. Gehring, trans. and ed., *New York Historical Manuscripts, Dutch*, vol. 9, *Council Minutes, 1652–1654* (Baltimore: Genalogical Publishing Co., Inc., 1983), 238.

60. *RNA*, 5: 243.

61. Jonathan Pearson, trans., *Early Records of the City and County of Albany and Colony of Rensselaerswyck*, 4 vols., rev. and ed. Arnold J. F. van Laer (Albany: University of the State of New York, 1869–1918), 3: 422–423.

62. Edmund B. O'Callaghan, trans., *New York Historical Manuscripts, Dutch*, vol. 6, *The Register of Salomon LaChaire*, ed. Kenneth Scott and Kenn Stryker-Rodda (Baltimore: Genalogical Publishing Co., Inc., 1978), 9; *Reformed Church*, 194–199; A. J. F. van Laer, "Albany Wills and Other Documents, 1665–1695," in *The Dutch Settlers Society of Albany Yearbook*, vol. 6 (Albany: Dutch Settlers Society of Albany, 1930–1931), 14.

63. Van Deursen, *Plain Lives*, 127.

64. *RNA*, 2: 247.

65. *Clothing the Colonists. Fashions in New Netherland* (Rensselaer, N.Y.: Friends of the Crailo State Historic Site, 1995).

66. *Reformed Church*, 50–53.

67. The information for this paragraph can be found in *Clothing the Colonists*. For various materials and items of children's clothing, see *Deacons' Accounts*, xv, 13, 44, 51, 53–54, 89, 98, 119, 155, 157, 161–162, 164, 166, 177–178, 189, 191, 193, 220, 246, 253, 255, 258.

68. *Reformed Church*, 50–53, 194–195, 200–201, 254 n. 4–7.

Bread: Staff of Dutch Life

IN THE OLD AND THE NEW WORLD

PETER G. ROSE

Bread was the mainstay of the Dutch diet in the seventeenth century. It was consumed with butter or cheese for breakfast, paired with meat or *hutspot* (a one-pot dish of meats and vegetables) for the midday main meal, and served with, or as part of, the porridge at night. Baked goods accompanied the human life cycle, from the rusks with comfits served for celebrations of a birth to funeral biscuits served at the time of a death. Bread and *koek* (gingerbread-style cake or flat hard cake)—then and now, prominent items in Dutch food consumption—were brought to the New World, where they assumed a similar position in the diet of Dutch settlers and their descendants.

The detailed record books of the Amsterdam Municipal Orphanage provide an insight into bread consumption of the poor (the orphans) and of the lower middle class (the staff). Ann McGants, in her analysis of the diet of the burgher orphans in Amsterdam, finds that the bread ration in the years 1639 to 1699 fluctuates between ten and eleven ounces per day per orphan and averages about ten and a half ounces of bread daily. Indeed, "bread occupied a prominent place in the daily diet of the Burgerweeshuis" and accompanied nearly every meal, as excerpts from the orphan menu for 1640 in the same publication show:

> *Sunday noon:* beans with a piece of bread; salted or smoked meat with a piece of bread
> *Sunday evening*: whole milk with rice made into a porridge
> *Tuesday noon*: white beans with butter and with a piece of bread; smoked or salted bacon with carrots, turnip, or cabbage and bread
> *Tuesday evening*: buttermilk with rye bread
> *Thursday noon:* beans with a piece of bread; salted or smoked meat and bread
> *Thursday evening*: buttermilk with wheat bread cooked together[1]

In a contemporary painting that still hangs in the building where the orphanage was housed, now the Amsterdam Historical Museum, we see the orphans at an evening meal for which such a porridge is served, along with dark, whole-grain bread. Bread not only had a major place in the orphans' meals; it was also the mainstay in poor children's fare elsewhere in Holland. A. Th. van Deursen asserts that a poor family with two young children in the rural part of Holland, where they would eat little else but bread, would eat about five pounds of rye bread a day. If we assume that the children would eat less than a pound each, the adults would have about a pound and a half or a little more per person.[2]

Janny Venema has investigated the care of the poor in Beverwijck, now Albany, circa 1650–1700 by the deacons of the First Reformed Church. The deacons decided each case individually. Sometimes the poor received monthly cash allotments; sometimes they were helped by providing them with a piece of land for growing their food or with a cow; and at other times they received food outright. Between 1652 and 1700 more than 850 bushels of wheat, 265 bushels of corn, and 60 bushels of peas were given to the poor. And bakers, such as Jochem Wessels, Wouter Albertsen, and several others, baked bread specifically for the poor. According to the deacons' records, the poor were always given wheat bread, which cost 14 stuivers between 1656 and 1658 for an eight-pound loaf,[3] because wheat was the main grain of the Beverwijck area. We may conclude that care for the poor and orphans took place in the New World in the same painstaking manner as is evident from the records of the Municipal Orphanage in Amsterdam.

The orphanage records also give us a good idea of the bread consumption of the working class. Coarse and fine wheat bread was reserved for the staff. McGants found that the staff ate a diet remarkably similar to that of the orphans, except for quality and quantity: at least ten pounds of wheat and four and a half pounds of rye bread per week, in addition to goodly quantities of other foods. This generosity leads her to speculate that some of the bread was meant to be shared with family members or was sold by the staff on the side. However, since the Dutch have always been known as big eaters, the staff may have eaten most of the food due to them.[4]

Another source of information on bread consumption of the working class is an ordinance of 1647 in New Amsterdam. This document sets the weekly ration for the West India Company ships as follows: "stew according to circumstances; 3½ pounds of hard tack [twice-baked sea biscuits, which keep for months, even years]; 1½ gills of vinegar; 1 pound of dried fish; and 2½ pounds of pork or beef." These rations conform more or less to those of the East India Company.[5]

While in the Netherlands, the working class ate rye or coarse wheat bread; daily consumption of white bread was seen as a symbol of affluence. The well-to-do burgher class continued the same plain-but-plenty meal pattern of the orphanage staff but showed off its wealth in the different kinds of white breads on their tables, which accompanied fruit, perhaps from their gardens, as well as fowl or meat for a frugal but ample dinner. These rich burghers often built themselves country homes, where they had beautiful gardens full of not only fruit bushes and trees and vegetables but also the newest exotic plants brought in from faraway lands. They grew all sorts of produce for their immediate use. Recipes for these vegetables were provided by *De Verstandige Kock (The Sensible Cook)*, acknowledged as the definitive Dutch cookbook of the seventeenth century and meant for owners of such houses. Portrayed on its frontispiece is a kitchen in such a wealthy home. On the right is a large bake oven, being heated for the baking of raised pies, which are readied in the foreground. We may assume that various kinds of white bread were baked in that oven, as well.[6]

Native Americans in New Netherland liked the wheat bread of the Dutch. Wheat had been unknown to them, and the bread made from it had a very different texture and taste from the boiled corn bread that was a staple in their diet. Harmen Meyndertsz van den Bogaert relates in his diary of 1634–1635 that when he was more than a day's walk away from Fort Orange, an Indian who had just come from the fort offered him a piece of wheat bread.[7] An ordinance for Fort Orange and the village of Beverwijck gives a clear picture of the impact of the Indians' fondness for Dutch bread on life in the Dutch communities in New Netherland. The baking for trade purposes made flour scarce, because the bakers preferred to prepare baked goods for the Indians, which was more profitable, to baking regularly (twice a week) for the settlers' community. The ordinance reads:

> Having heard the manifold complaints of the scarcity of coarse bread
> which the bakers, contrary to the ordinance…of 6th of October Anno
> 1659, do not bake twice a week, …consuming, to the serious prejudice
> of the community, their flour in baking Koeckjens [cookies] and white
> bread for the Indians, without [standard] weight…every one who
> follows the trade of baking shall from this time forth twice a week
> bake coarse bread for the accommodation of the community…[8]

The four basic ingredients of bread are grain, leavening, salt, and water. While bread subtly differs from day to day depending on outside temperature and circumstance—even the mood of the baker—its main ingredients of grain or flour, liquid, and leavening remain constant. Rye and wheat were the two main grains used for bread in the seventeenth-century in the Netherlands. Rye bread in the north was darker and sweeter, while that in the south—below the great rivers of Rhine, Meuse, and Waal—was lighter in color and consistency. Wheat produces a lighter bread with a softer crumb than rye. When properly bolted (finely sifted), a fine-textured white bread is obtained.

The western provinces of Holland with their wet clay grounds were not particularly suitable for the growing of grain and instead were used for grazing and horticulture. By the seventeenth century, bread grain imported from the Baltic states and Amsterdam had become an important transit market. In the first half of the seventeenth century, 50,000 last (roughly 120,000 tons) of grain were brought to Amsterdam, where they were traded. The prices set in Amsterdam influenced those in other, less-important regional markets. Most of the grain was used to feed the local population, and the rest was traded to France, northern Spain, and Portugal. Some wheat was grown locally; the province of Zeeland had been known since the Middle Ages for the quality of its wheat. The drier eastern provinces of Drente, Overijssel, Gelderland, and the southern provinces of Brabant and Limburg grew mostly rye, which requires less moisture and ripens earlier than wheat.[9] A study of the agricultural productivity of Rensselaerswijck by Jan Folkerts shows that from 1642 through 1646 the main crops were oats and wheat: "The prices of wheat and oats generally were in the ratio of 5 to 2, so in fact wheat was the leading crop in the patroonship." He points out that while the Netherlands had become dependent upon the Baltic region for its grain, "in the American colony a one-sided directedness towards the cultivation of grain" is seen.[10]

In the Dutch cities the baker purchased his grain from the grain trader and stored it in his attic. The rural baker would buy directly from the grower, a practice that was followed in New Netherland. There, as in the Netherlands, grain was ground at a mill as needed for a milling fee set by the local government. An early privilege granted to the city of Haarlem in 1274 by Floris V mentions the standard grain mill, which can be turned as needed in the changeable winds of Holland.[11] In Cryn Fredericksz's city plan of New Amsterdam, dating from around 1626 and the earliest known, a mill is already present, and a mill is also shown in the same location on the 1655 Visscher map.[12]

What we now know as the sourdough method was the early way of leavening bread. A portion of a previous dough was set aside to ferment and used to leaven the next batch. A natural by-product of beer brewing is yeast, and brewer's yeast was used for bread baking in the seventeenth century in the Netherlands. The same method was probably followed in New Netherland. According to an Amsterdam ordinance of 1652, the yeast for bread baking had to be unadulterated, just the way it came from the brewery, and measured with a verified and approved measure.[13] In Leiden in the middle of the seventeenth century, yeast was sold in a *gist-huis*, or "yeast-storage house," but numerous petitions made clear that the bakers preferred to obtain their yeast directly from the brewery.[14]

Salt is found in some places on earth close to the surface and can simply be dug up. Salt can also be obtained through natural evaporation of sea water. The Netherlands do not have salt deposits readily available, and the climate is not conducive to the evaporation method; therefore, another way of obtaining salt—so important to food preservation and preparation—was devised. In the medieval province of Zeeland, the salty peat bogs were dug, dried, and then burned. The resulting *zel-as*, or salty ash, was mixed with sea water, and the salt was extracted by boiling down the mixture. By the sixteenth century rough salt was imported from France and Spain and refined in Zeeland.[15] During the Eighty Years' War, Spain tried to curtail the salt trade, and the Dutch needed to go farther afield to obtain the precious commodity. By 1622 the West India Company had a salt monopoly in the Caribbean at Punta de Araya.[16] Its loss to the Spaniards caused the Dutch to mount an expedition to seize Bonaire, St. Eustacius, and Curaçao; both the Netherlands and New Netherland were then supplied with the salt from these islands.

The water used in bread must be wholesome. However, water in the canals of Amsterdam was so polluted that beer brewers employed ice-breaking boats during the winter so water boats could get through to the river Vecht in order to obtain clean water.[17] Recipes in *The Sensible Cook* sometimes specify the kind of water to be used, such as "cold rain water." Undoubtedly, bakers made similar efforts to ensure pure water for their doughs.[18] In New Netherland the situation was different, as no tanners, dyers, fullers, paper makers, or glue makers had yet polluted the waters. Adriaen van der Donck sings the praises of streams from which the water may be drunk without danger even in the hottest weather.[19]

Not quite as simple as his four basic ingredients are the baker's tools. Most important among them is the cavernous wall oven, stoked by *takkenbossen,* fagots or reeds used to create the lively fire necessary to heat the bricks. A petition of the Leiden bakers' guild of 1685 asks to be allowed to burn reeds, peat, or sawdust and buckwheat shells. Attached to this petition is a resolution that allows the burning of reeds on certain conditions.[20] In New Netherland fuel was not this scarce. Van der Donck reports how the new country's giant oak trees, sixty to seventy feet high, were not only used for all sorts of farming purposes but also made "excellent firewood, surpassing every other kind."[21] The baker's implements included an ash rake to rake out the fire prior to baking, a mop to clean out the ashes, an ash pot to keep the hot coals, a grain shovel, sieves, a trough for mixing and kneading, a table for shaping, a scale for weighing the dough pieces, boards and cloths for rising, baking sheets for small breads and rolls, and a peel to "shoot" the dough pieces into the oven.

The bakery shops were but a simple extension of the workroom, sometimes no more than a window to the street. In his workroom the baker mixed the flour, salt, yeast, and water into a dough, which was then kneaded to the right consistency. Wheat doughs were kneaded by hand; the heavier rye doughs were kneaded in a trough with the feet while the person doing the kneading would hang onto a rail affixed above the trough. Hands or feet were not allowed to be washed with soap but were cleaned with hot water and then rubbed with flour.

Seventeenth-century Dutch art provides pictorial proof of the large assortment of breads, which varied in shape, size, weight, filling, and ornamentation and often differed from town to town or region to region not only in shape but also in name. The common shape of the utilitarian bread was the round-balled floor bread; baked on the floor of the oven, it could be either coarse or white bread. These breads were also made in rectangles or squares, depending on the region. White breads were also shaped in a variety of forms and sizes, as illustrated in Jan Steen's painting *Leiden Baker Arend Oostwaert and His Wife Catharina Keyzerswaert.* As shown in Baker Oostwaert's assortment we find displayed on the left and held by the baker's wife *zotinnenkoeken,* a baked good akin to rusks. Leaning against the wall is a *duivekater,* a fine white bread, baked for the holidays of St. Nicholas Day on December 6 through Epiphany on January 6 but apparently also for Easter. Hanging above it on their typical rack are pretzels and below them *schootjes,* portioned dough strips baked together, often shaped in a form that looks somewhat like an ice-cube tray. Behind the baker is a display of *halsjes,* small round breads baked together, like little heads held together by their *hals,* or neck, hence the name. In other works of art we often encounter baskets with rolls of various sizes and shapes, some plain, others filled with currants or raisins, and as in the *Baker Oostwaert* painting, pretzels displayed on their typical rack are featured dominantly. In a 1753 booklet for *koekbakkers* (bakers) and their apprentices, an early guide for the profession, a recipe for pretzels calls for a pound each of wheat flour and sugar, fourteen grams of cinnamon, fifty-two grams of butter, and a bit of potash. Together with eggs, the ingredients are made into a dough, which is divided into pieces of forty-two grams each. These are baked on a buttered baking sheet.[22] They are similar in shape but not in taste to the salty pretzels now sold on the streets of New York City. Pretzels were baked in New Netherland, as well: bakers petitioned the court of Fort Orange on March 4, 1653, requesting mitigation of the ordinance against baking white bread, pretzels, and cookies for the Indians.[23]

Some breads, particularly *duivekaters* (holiday breads), were decorated with *patacons,* earthenware disks, generally painted with either biblical or worldly images, pre-baked, and baked again onto the bread as decorations. Small and larger *patacons* were used between the sixteenth and eighteenth century in the Netherlands (mostly in the south) and far longer in Flanders. Recently some were found in a garden of a house in Deventer in the eastern Netherlands.[24] One might think of them as little gifts, similar to the way a ring or toy is placed in a Cracker Jack box or a paper parasol garnishes a drink in a restaurant: they remain after the treat is consumed. *Duivekaters* were baked in the New World, as well, and given to the poor at holiday time. We do not know whether they were decorated with *patacons.*

Breads were often flavored with the spices brought by the East India Company to Dutch shores, such as nutmeg, cloves, and especially cinnamon, and they were filled with "sweetmeats," such as currants or raisins. New Netherland ordinances forbidding the baking for the Indians in time of grain scarcity often specifically mention breads with sweetmeats.[25] An Amsterdam ordinance from as early as 1601 forbids excessive ornamentation with, for example, gold, which was probably gold leaf. The ordinance explains that such ornamental breads displayed in the baker's window offend pious people and cause sad feelings of longing for such adorned breads among the poor.[26]

In addition to shape or ornamentation, each baker placed his own identifying mark—perhaps a circle with a cross or what now looks like an asterisk—on the bottom of each bread. Housewives, who preferred to prepare their bread dough at home, both in the Netherlands and New Netherland, gave their breads a mark as well before they sent it out to be baked. For this service the baker received an amount set by the local authorities in both locales. While there is no evidence that bread marks were registered in New Netherland, we know that they were in Holland. The Municipal Archives in Leiden still have a list of bread marks from the late eighteenth century.[27]

After the bread had been weighed, shaped, risen, and finally baked, a baker would blow on an animal horn—a common means of communication—to let his clientele know it was ready for sale. The *Fort Orange Court Minutes* provide evidence that the practice of bakers blowing their horn was brought to the New World. Jochem Becker Backer, for example, was summoned to an extraordinary session of the court called on April 12, 1653, because "in violation of the ordinance he had in the absence of the commissary publicly blown the horn to sell white bread."[28]

It was not the bakers who set the price for their bread but the local government. Part of a government's task was to ensure sufficient food to protect its people against famine. Consequently, the municipal governments in the seventeenth century regulated the size, weight, and price of the different kinds of bread. Bread prices were established in relation to grain prices. Rye bread loaves had a stable weight of six and twelve pounds, but their price would vary; this was called *zetting*, or fixing of the price. For example, in Leiden between 1596 and 1620, the price for a twelve-pound loaf fluctuated between 5 and 9.4 stuivers.[29] For white bread the price would be stable, but the weight would vary; this is called called *rijding*, a term hard to translate but indicates that the price moves or varies. Price and weights were announced in bulletins affixed to prominent structures in town, such as church doors. The same was true in New Netherland, where, for example, an ordinance of October 6, 1659, reads: each coarse loaf of eight pounds shall cost "18 stivers, counting eight white and four black wampum beads to one stiver…"[30]

In order to ensure that the bread was of the right size, weight, and quality, the Dutch government appointed *brood-weger*s, or bread-weighers, and inspectors. The same custom was practiced in New Amsterdam. On October 13, 1661, two men were elected and confirmed as "overseers of the bread" and charged with the responsibility of ensuring that "the bread is made of good material, proper weight and well baked." Immediately after their appointment, they were put to work and asked to give their opinion on a loaf seized by the *schout* (equivalent to a sheriff), "which is not as it ought to be." They concluded that the bread "was made of honest material" but badly baked, possibly by someone who was in a hurry. The baker, brought to the council, explained that he was out and had put "his boys" to work. He was excused, but in a later discussion he was admonished for blaming his apprentices, something that "would not be done in Holland."[31] Through time, both in the Netherlands and New Netherland, bakers were fined for selling bread with short weight or for adulterating bread with extra bran or other materials, even sawdust. Their practices served to keep the overseers on the alert to spot infringements of government rules. Simon Middleton, of the University of East Anglia, points out that the customers themselves were quite alert, as well. "The cases of customers suing when loaves were a fraction under weight, sold wet, or with impurities suggests that the buyers of bread were no less precise in their calculations than the sellers."[32]

In the Netherlands the bakers were organized in guilds, which not only petitioned the government on behalf of their members but had as their main purpose the regulation and curtailment of the bakers' trade. These restrictions were necessary to ensure an adequate market share for each bakery. To be a full member of the baker's guild, one had to be a citizen of the town, to have completed a certain amount of training in a bakery, and to have passed the baker's exam. Apprentices paid an entry fee to register with the guild and worked for several years in a bakery. Once this training time was completed, they were given a certificate of competence and could start work as journeymen. After completion of the master-baker exam, they could start their own bakery. One of the five requirements of the *bakkersproef,* or guild's bakers exam, of 1652 in Amsterdam was preparing and placing twenty *schooten,* literally "shots," of common bread (in other words, the amount of bread (of varying weight) that could be placed [shot] into the oven at one time with a wooden peel, a method not unlike the way pizza is placed in a modern-day wood-burning pizza oven). [33] From personal experience, I can add that it takes a certain amount of skill and precision to place loaves of bread in an oven with a peel in precisely the right way—some close together, others separate with the right amount of room between each dough piece to allow for air circulation. These exams varied from city to city, as the kinds of bread varied from place to place.

The guilds were close-knit societies. Members were obliged to attend their colleagues' funerals. Some guilds owned a special bier to carry the guild brother to his grave and in addition provided a silver shield to decorate the coffin on its last journey. In an exhibit in the early 1990s, the Westfries Museum in Hoorn showed the funeral shield of the Hoorn bakers' guild. It portrays a baker at his work, forming his dough into balls of equal size, standing at his worktable displaying a scale and the necessary weights. Another obligation for the members was the attendance at a yearly guild meal. Such meals were accompanied by tobacco and pipes, music, food, and ample drink, as remaining bills show. One of these documents also indicates that such feasts were rowdy affairs, as it includes payment for broken glasses and trampled beer pitchers.[34]

I have found no documentary evidence of a bakers' guild in New Netherland, except for a petition of the bakers to be able to form a guild that was turned down by the Court of Fort Orange on May 9, 1655.[35] However, at various times the New Netherland bakers did band together when petitioning their governments. For example, bakers in Beverwijck requested that it should be left up to them whether or not to use sweetmeats in their baking for the Indians. Numerous other instances exist of requests for mitigation of government rulings.[36]

Bread had such an important place in everyday life that it became part of the language. In order to eat, you do what you have to do: "for the lack of bread, you eat the crust of raised pies." Or when times are hard, "you hang the bread basket high." When times improve, "there is bread on the [cutting] board." A spoiled child might be called "a white-bread child." White bread is referred to as *heren-brood*, or "gentlemen's bread," while the first weeks of marriage, presumed to be the best times, are called "the white-bread weeks." Finally, the man who bakes the staff of life assures you that "it is better to spend [your money] at the baker's than at the pharmacist."[37]

Bread was a symbol of seventeenth-century social services, as evidenced in the painstaking care for the provisions of the orphans and other poor in both the Netherlands and New Netherland. The supply and trade of its ingredients have great economic and historical consequences, such as the success of the Amsterdam grain market or the seizure of Curaçao and Bonaire for their salt supplies. Government regulations for bread provide insight into social customs and circumstances. Period art gives visual documentation and adds to the knowledge of this richly diverse part of Dutch culinary history. But when we bite into a freshly baked piece of crusty bread, savor its chewy texture, and are enveloped in its fragrant smell, we forget the connection between this nourishing food and a set of complex issues with far-reaching impact.

NOTES

1. Anne McGants, "Monotonous but not Meager: The Diet of Burgher Orphans in Early Modern Amsterdam," *Research in Economic History* 14 (1992): 69–116. *Burgerweeshuis*: orphanage for children of burghers (citizens), in this case of the City of Amsterdam.

2. A. Th. Van Deursen, *Het Kopergeld van de Gouden Eeuw: het dagelijks brood.* (Assen: Van Gorcum, 1981), 15.

3. Janny Venema, *Kinderen van Weelde en Armoede: Armoede en liefdadigheid in Beverwijck/Albany* (Hilversum: Verloren, 1993), 52–54. Jan Folkerts, "Kiliaen van Rensselaer and the Agricultural Productivity in his Domain: A New Look at the First Patroon and Rensselaerswijck before 1664" (paper presented at the Rensselaerswijck Seminar, Albany, New York, 1995).

4. McGants.

5. A. J. F. van Laer, trans. and ed., *New York Historical Manuscripts, Dutch*, vol. 4, *Council Minutes 1638–1649.* (Baltimore: Genealogical Publishing Co., Inc.,1974), 4: 53.

6. Peter G. Rose, trans. and ed., *The Sensible Cook: Dutch Foodways in the Old and the New World* (Syracuse: Syracuse University Press, 1989), frontispiece.

7. Charles T. Gehring and William A. Starna, trans. and eds., *A Journey into Mohawk and Oneida Country 1634–1635: The Journal of Harmen Meyndertsz van den Bogaert* (Syracuse: Syracuse University Press, 1988), 21.

8. A. J. F. van Laer, trans. and ed., *Minutes of the Court of Fort Orange and Beverwijck 1651–1660,* 2 vols. (Albany: The University of the State of New York, 1923), 2: 166–167.

9. Jan Bieleman, *Geschiedenis van de Landbouw in Nederland 1500–1950.* (Meppel: Boom, 1992), 35–100.

10. Folkerts, 10–12.

11. *Brood: De Geschiedenis van het Brood en het Broodgebruik in Nederland,* catalog for an exhibit by the same name (Rotterdam: Museum Boijmans-van Beuningen, 1983), 17.

12. The 1655 Vischer map, reissued by Schenk, Junior, imprinted ca. 1690, # 12280, Manuscripts and Special Collections, New York State Library.

13. Renee Kistemaker, "Brood, Bakers en de Stedelijke Overheid: De Zorg voor het Amsterdamse Brood tot Omstreeks 1750," *Ons Amsterdam* 35, no. 8 (1983): 222.

14. R. C. J. Van Maanen, *Inventaris van het Stadsarchief van Leiden (1253) 1574–1816 (1897)* (Leiden: Gemeentearchief, 1986), 127.

15. *Zout op Tafel: De Geschiedenis van het Zoutvat,* catalog for an exhibit by the same name (Rotterdam: Museum Boijmans-van Beuningen, 1976), 4.

16. Ruud Spruit, *Zout en Slaven: De Geschiedenis van de Westindische Companie* (Houten: de Haan, 1988), 24.

17. R. E. Kistemaker and V. T. Van Vlisteren, eds. *Geschiedenis van een Volksdrank.* (Amsterdam: De Bataafsche Leeuw, 1994), 67.

18. Rose, 55.

19. Adriaen van der Donck, *A Description of the New Netherlands,* ed. Thomas F. O'Donnell (Syracuse: Syracuse University Press, 1968), 16.

20. Van Maanen, 127.

21. Van der Donck, 19.

22. B.G., *Volmaakte Onderrichtinge ten Dienst der Koek-bakkers, of hunne Leerlingen* (1753), n.p. 7.

23. Van Laer, 1:58. Charles T. Gehring, *Fort Orange Court Minutes, 1652–1660* (Syracuse: Syracuse University Press, 1990), 45. (Hereafter cited as *FOCM.*)

24. This information was obtained through the Department of Archeology of the City of Deventer.

25. *FOCM,* 242.

26. Kistemaker, 221.

27. Gemeentearchief Leiden, Archief, 2536-2539, 1596–1845. I gratefully acknowledge the help of Dr. J. A. Jacobs in obtaining this information from the Municipal Archives.

28. *FOCM,* 49.

29. *Brood: de Geschiedenis van het Brood,* 33.

30. Van Laer, 1:167. *FOCM,* 415.

31. Berthold Fernow, *Minutes of the Orphanmasters Court of New Amsterdam, 1655–1663* (New York: Francis P. Harpers, 1907), 113–115.

32. Simon Middleton, "Baking, Carting and the Transition to English Rule in Seventeenth Century New York" (paper presented at the Conference on New York State History, 1996).

33. *Handvesten*, Vol. 5, 1183.

34. D. Barneveld, *De Oude Banketbakkerij* (Bussum: C. A. J. van Dishoeck, 1968), 33.

35. *FOCM*, 190.

36. Ibid., 276.

37. J. H. Nannings, *Brood en Gebaksvormen en Hunne Betekenis in de Folklore,* n.p., n.d. 183–186.

From Amsterdam to New Amsterdam:

WASHINGTON IRVING, THE DUTCH ST. NICHOLAS, AND THE AMERICAN SANTA CLAUS

ELISABETH PALING FUNK

Throughout the Netherlands the celebration of St. Nicholas's feast day on December 6 is a joyful public and domestic occasion. Dressed as a Catholic bishop, with miter and staff, and accompanied by at least one Moorish servant, called *Zwarte Piet* (Black Peter), in colorful, sixteenth-century Spanish attire, *Sinterklaas* arrives either on horseback—in conformance with early tradition—by motorized ship, or by even more modern conveyance, for his triumphant entry into towns large and small. In homes with young children, *Sinterklaas* himself may put in a surprise appearance, and shoes are set near the hearth on St. Nicholas Eve in the hope that all wishes will be fulfilled by morning. Adults and older children celebrate St. Nicholas Eve with anonymous gifts that either are found at the door, their arrival heralded by loud knocks, or are hidden throughout the house. Poems created for the occasion, often gently ridiculing the gift, the giver, or the recipient, accompany the inventively wrapped, often homemade presents and are part of the evening's merriment.[1]

Within the past thirty years a growing number of Dutch families have begun to exchange gifts at Christmas as well. Along with this custom, Santa Claus, called *de kerstman*, or "the Christmas man," arrived from America. This second occasion for gift giving in December has created concern for the survival of the earlier celebration to the point that associations have been formed to promote the St. Nicholas traditions in the Low Countries. Comparisons between the two figures are invariably to the disadvantage of the newcomer. Mirjam van Leer speaks of the foreign Santa Claus with a sled full of packages devoid of poetry and surprises. Rien van den Heuvel calls him a meaningless figure who lacks St. Nicholas's long tradition and is pure fabrication by the author Washington Irving, who simply appropriated Nicholas's name.[2] Irving receives too much credit here: his talent was not for invention.[3] Rather, his imagination drew upon a superior ability to absorb what he read, heard, and observed and to re-create his subject in a graceful, gently satirical manner.

Washington Irving (1783–1859) was America's first internationally known author. A first-generation American of Scottish-English descent, he was born in New York City, as were his seven surviving older siblings. With about 23,000 inhabitants at that time, the town retained a recognizably Dutch character in structures, speech, and customs. Surrounded from birth by Dutch-American friends and in-laws, Irving's remarkable skill at bilingual punning and his ability to coin Dutch phrases prove that he had successfully absorbed Dutch as he had heard it spoken daily until he was twenty. Much of his reading was eighteenth-century neoclassical English literature, marked by realism and satire. Yet Gothic romances, notably Ann Radcliffe's, and later Sir Walter Scott's poetry appealed to his antiquarian bent and romantic spirit, which had been nourished by his youthful explorations of rural Manhattan Island and the Hudson region and by travel in Europe. These interests are reflected in the prominence of history and popular culture in his works. They dominate his first major work, *A History of New York, by Diedrich Knickerbocker* (1809), a burlesque history of the seventeenth-century Dutch colony of New Netherland. Here and in the extensively revised second edition of 1812, the Dutch St. Nicholas appears, not as a pale invention but as an imaginative re-creation endowed with all the attributes of the legendary and traditional figure.

The *Knickerbocker History* is a treasure trove of Hudson River Valley Dutch popular culture. Although its Dutch customs and folk beliefs and those of the later Knickerbocker folk tales were reworked by the literary artist, their variety and vividly observed rendering have earned Irving the right to be called America's first folklorist. All major elements of Dutch folk belief occur in the *History*: religious and historical legends; *spotsagen*, derisive or tall tales; and the supernatural, which includes demonism, witchcraft, omens, and visions. The religious legend is represented by the Dutch St. Nicholas.

Any attempt to reconstruct the historical Nicholas leads almost instantly into legend. Biographical data, such as they are, are limited and, together with the records of his miracles, were accumulated over later centuries. He is believed to have been born in the fourth century in Patara, now in Turkey, near Myra, where he became bishop. Legends associated with St. Nicholas of Myra reached Greece in the sixth century, where his feast day, the day of his death, was established as December 6. During the seventh and eighth centuries his cult spread to Russia and westward to southern Italy, from where it progressed north through western Europe. In the eleventh century his presumed remains were brought to the Italian seaport of Bari and subsequently buried in the basilica that bears his name. By this time he had become the most popular saint, venerated nearly as much as Mary, mother of Christ.[4]

As his cult spread north, the inhabitants of the European coastal regions turned to him for protection against the dangers of the sea. St. Nicholas churches arose along the entire North Sea coast. In the Netherlands, where the cult arrived via France and Flanders, these mostly thirteenth-century churches also encircled the former *Zuiderzee* and bordered the rivers. At the same time the Dutch guilds chose him as their patron. Nicholas's legendary sea voyages provided the foundation for his patronage of seafarers, who were largely responsible for spreading his cult. Other such specific events made him the patron, for example, of children, marriage, and fertility and associated him with anonymous gift giving. His attributes early included the ability to overcome a demon or the devil, bind or chain him, and ban him. Other feats, such as the reanimation of murdered students, made Nicholas the subject of medieval miracle plays, which turned him "into a folk hero of the market place."[5]

The distinction is crucial. From this point on, two figures are embodied in one person: a legendary saint and a popular hero. Further elements of the St. Nicholas cult contributed to this development. St. Nicholas's patronage of school children was expressed in yearly medieval processions, led by a boy dressed as bishop. His followers were frightening figures, often bearing chains. Moreover, the earliest legends show that the benevolent saint could also be a stern and sometimes angry disciplinarian. He functioned as the latter in the medieval monastic schools, where a monk disguised as St. Nicholas would question and admonish the students, reward the good with sweets, and apply the traditional birch twigs to the sluggards. It is mainly this practice, which began in northern France as early as the fourteenth century, that is the origin of the secular Dutch St. Nicholas celebration, which begins on the eve of his feast day and could, in the Middle Ages, last until December 28.[6]

In the Netherlands St. Nicholas, or *Sint Nicolaas*, is familiarly called *Sinterklaas*, a contraction of *Sint Heer Claes* or Saint[ly] Lord *Klaas*, the modern Dutch abbreviation of *Nicolaas*. In old prints he is depicted with or without a beard, but he is always dressed as a western European bishop, with a bishop's staff and a rod of birch twigs. The rod, symbol of the saint's punitive function, is still present in an 1840 series of Flemish woodcuts, where he is also portrayed riding his white horse, a common attribute of saints, on roofs as well as on *terra firma*. Charity was one of the legendary St. Nicholas's earliest attributes. In the Netherlands anonymous gift giving was associated with shoes as early as 1360, when they were filled in church with money for the poor. By the sixteenth century children had begun to place a shoe, or wooden shoe, at home. Gifts, sweets, and nuts for good children came down the chimney and into their shoes, replacing the hay or oats they had left there for the saint's horse. Misbehavior was rewarded with a bunch of twigs. Although the shoe remained the receptacle of choice in the Netherlands, stockings evidently were also used. The main scene in a drawing entitled *Het Sint Nicolaasfeest* (*The St. Nicholas Celebration*) by Cornelis Dusart (1660–1704) depicts a three-generational family scene set in the interior of a simple farm house. Although a shoe filled with toys is present, the picture's background shows a mantel hung with a stocking. Another has been thrown to the floor, still holding a bunch of birch twigs.[7]

Nowhere is the St. Nicholas celebration as expressive of the character of its people as in the Netherlands, says Karl Meisen. And here most of all, occasional songs devoted to St. Nicholas are found.[8] These songs were part of the St. Nicholas celebration since the Middle Ages. First, existing folk songs were transformed to suit the occasion, to become a major, lasting element. Original composition followed, but between 1750 and 1840 almost no new children's songs devoted to St. Nicholas were composed.[9]

With the Protestant Reformation of the sixteenth century, public aspects of the St. Nicholas celebration, such as the boy-bishop procession, disappeared. Although laws against the practice of Catholicism were generally evaded without consequences, especially after the Eighty Years' War with Spain ended in 1648, the secular St. Nicholas celebration, in origin and appearance a Catholic observance, was outlawed along with those of the other saints. Seventeenth-century ordinances even forbade the filling of children's shoes and the manufacture and sale of the traditional bakery products bearing St. Nicholas's portrait. These ordinances were disregarded with impunity, however. Families continued to purchase such products at the St. Nicholas market of Amsterdam, for example, which continued without interruption.[10] Nevertheless, extant, but rare, wooden cookie molds from areas of the Netherlands that became Protestant upon the Reformation show St. Nicholas dressed not in his expected attire but as a horseman with, for example, a feathered hat, skirted coat, and knee-high boots with wide flaps below puffed breeches. In some, a miter or miter-like hat, a staff, and a beard remain of his traditional appearance. Filled baskets, or other reminders of his legend, also allude to his identity. J. J. Schilstra suggests that these alterations functioned as camouflage to meet the continued popular demand for the traditional St. Nicholas bakery products while avoiding possible fines.[11]

The Reformation eradicated St. Nicholas as an object of veneration, along with all other saints; but as the folk hero he had become in the Middle Ages, he proved indestructible. J. L. de Jager posits that the secular aspect of the St. Nicholas celebration had become too entwined with the relatively early domestic life of the Netherlands to be suppressed. Instead, its importance grew, while it waned elsewhere, and became increasingly domestic.[12] A well-known painting by Jan Steen (1626–1679), entitled *Het Sint Nicolaasfeest* (*The Feast of St. Nicholas*), attests, like Dusart's drawing, to this domestic celebration. Its scene, replete with traditional bakery products, is that of the morning of December 6, when children discover toys and treats in shoes placed under the chimney the night before, while one boy is weeping because he received the birch twigs instead. Fast-forward one hundred years for a picture of another St. Nicholas celebration: a print, showing the morning of St. Nicholas in an affluent setting, is by P. Fouquet, Jr., dated 1761 and entitled *Het St. Nicolaasfeest* and *La Fête de St. Nicolas*. It is dedicated to Dionis Muilman, an Amsterdam city councilman, whose family, and a maid, may be the subject of the picture.[13] Again, there are the traditional baked goods, two girls and a little boy delighted with their presents, a shoe holding the birch twigs, and its presumed owner, the oldest son, crying and in a temper. Common among these seventeenth- and eighteenth-century pictures by Dusart, Steen, and Fouquet is the central position of the nuclear family, the absence of St. Nicholas, and the tenacity of traditions surrounding his celebration.

It is not until the first half of the nineteenth century that Nicholas's actual, solitary appearance on the eve of his feast day is mentioned on rare occasions. Heralded by loud noise and chain rattling, the figure is decked out in fear-inspiring attire, gruffly asking to be informed about the children's behavior.[14] Until the early twentieth century, however, the most common signs of his presence were rattling chains and loud knocks on doors and windows.[15] It is, therefore, the invisible, secular, post-Reformation folk hero, his appearance evident only through his disguised portrait imprinted on some of the traditional baked goods, who accompanied the Dutch settlers to seventeenth-century New Netherland. Given his solid entrenchment by that time in Dutch domestic life and the general tenacity of Dutch customs in the area of the former colony, the secular Nicholas undoubtedly continued being celebrated on the feast day of the legendary bishop to whom he owed his existence.

The nature of domestic celebrations anywhere generally precludes their being recorded; discovery of such written evidence is exceedingly rare. The first evidence of public, rather than private, interest in St. Nicholas appears in accounts of Nicholas celebrations among New Yorkers of Dutch descent in the 1770s. One of these refers to "St. a Claus," showing the progress toward "Santa Claus" under the influence of English upon *Sinterklaas*. In 1773 a New York newspaper reports that a group calling itself "The Sons of St. Nicholas" celebrated St. Nicholas Day. At a banquet of the New-York Historical Society in January 1809, where Washington Irving was nominated for membership, the memory of St. Nicholas and Dutch-American traditions in general were toasted. John Pintard, one of its founders, who was of Huguenot descent and a scion of New Netherland settlers, commissioned a broadside concerning the saint, which the Society published in 1810. In the broadside's woodcut Nicholas's miter is replaced by a halo, but as of old he is dressed in bishop's garb, holding a twig in his right hand. This punitive aspect is reinforced by the presence of a crying boy, also with a twig in his hand. A smiling girl at his side shows off her apron filled with toys or treats. Both children seem to be standing on top of the mantel, which is hung with filled stockings, one with toys and treats, the other with a birch rod. Under the double-paneled picture is a Dutch St. Nicholas rhyme, flanked by its English translation.

Its likely source, according to Charles W. Jones, was Mrs. John Hardenbrook, a member of the Dutch-American community of Manhattan, who was born in 1730.[16] The song's "Sancte Claus" is asked to travel to Amsterdam, then from Amsterdam to Spain, where oranges and pomegranates are rolling through the streets. The allusions to Spain and to fruits that, centuries ago, were exotic to the inhabitants of the Low Countries, indicate that the lyrics were written prior to 1750, the beginning of a fallow period of nearly a century in the creation of new St. Nicholas songs. In fact, they point to its oral existence in as early as the sixteenth century, when, with the advent of Dutch trade with Spain, Netherlandic folk belief began to associate St. Nicholas with that country and Spain became a motif in St. Nicholas songs.[17] The song's earliest written version in the Netherlands, a quatrain consisting only of a near-verbatim version of the Hardenbrook song's first and final two lines, is of 1645–55.[18] Significantly, this version is the only one recorded in the Netherlands that shares its conclusion with the Hardenbrook song, one that suggests composition in a period predating the Reformation. The lines in the latter version read: "SANCTE CLAUS, my good Friend/ I have always been devoted to you,/ [If] you will give me something now,/I shall devote myself to you all my Life."[19] This appeal demonstrates an interesting mixture of familiarity with Nicholas the folk hero in "Friend" and in the lines' implied *quid pro quo,* with a dominant element of servitude consistent with the veneration of Nicholas in his function of legendary Catholic saint. It can be posited, therefore, that the song existed prior to Hudson's discovery in 1609 and arrived in New Netherland with the generation of Mrs. Hardenbrook's grandparents. It has survived in the Netherlands, albeit with significant alteration: the above concluding lines have disappeared in favor of a variety of endings, all of them secular in nature. This substitution leaves no doubt that, like all St. Nicholas songs in those provinces of the Netherlands where Protestantism became dominant, the song celebrates a secular hero.

As tenacious in the former colony as it was in the Netherlands, the song is quoted again in a mangled but recognizable form in Katherine Schuyler Baxter's recollections in 1897 of her paternal grandmother, Catherine Van Rensselaer Schuyler, born in 1781, the daughter of Philip Schuyler and Catherine Van Rensselaer. As in the modern Dutch version, the St. Nicholas song here is wholly secular. The devotional final lines of the song recorded in the Hardenbrook and seventeenth-century versions are missing; instead, "Santa Klaus" is asked to bring some fun things for the children. Baxter further relates that in her grandmother's household, the children sang their St. Nicholas songs at the fireplace on New Year's Eve. [20]

Presence of the traditional bakery products further attests to the fact that St. Nicholas continued to be celebrated in the New World. The unpublished Van Rensselaer Manor Papers record that, in 1675, "Maria Van Rensselaer paid f2-10 to baker Wouter Albertsz vanden Uythoff for some *Sinterklaasgoet*" (St. Nicholas baked goods).[21] From seventeenth-century Rensselaerswijck, located near present-day Albany, to nineteenth-century New York, descendants of the original New Netherland families remained faithful to their secular St. Nicholas traditions. John Pintard, in a letter to his daughter Mary in 1819, writes: "In old times…St. Class [sic] used to cross the Atlantic and brought immense supplies of cookies etc. from Amsterdam." And into the 1820s and 1830s Pintard continued to refer to and describe his family's essentially Dutch St. Nicholas celebrations.[22] Finally, it is Washington Irving's thorough familiarity with the Dutch St. Nicholas that confirms his presence as folk hero in the author's day. Informed by his Dutch-American in-laws, friends, and surroundings, and perhaps inspired by the bishop's public revival as a quasi-patron saint, Irving put all of St. Nicholas's attributes to extensive use in the *Knickerbocker History*.

Although St. Nicholas makes a few fleeting appearances in *Salmagundi* of 1807–1808, written with James K. Paulding and Washington Irving's brother William, it is with the publication of Irving's burlesque history, published deliberately on December 6, Nicholas's feast day, that the secular Dutch folk hero begins his journey toward center stage as a truly national figure. Throughout the *History* Irving interweaves the Dutch St. Nicholas tradition and his own fictive lore. This fiction begins with St. Nicholas as a figurehead on the *Goede Vrouw*, the ship that carries the first Dutch settlers across the Atlantic. In this portrait he is "equipped with a low, broad brimmed hat, a huge pair of Flemish trunk hose, and a pipe that reached to the end of the bowsprit."[23] Here, Nicholas's appearance has lost all kinship with the legendary bishop and instead assumes that of a seventeenth-century New Netherland settler. The pipe's description is that of the Dutch *Gouwenaar*, a long clay pipe for whose manufacture the city of Gouda, among others, was known.

In the following passage, added to his 1812 edition of the *History*, Irving provides further descriptive detail. Having landed on Manhattan Island, Oloffe Van Kortlandt dreams:

> the good St. Nicholas came riding over the tops of trees in that selfsame wagon wherein he brings his yearly presents to children; …And the shrewd Van Kortlandt knew him by his broad hat, his long pipe, and the resemblance he bore to the figure on the bow of the Goede Vrouw. And he lit his pipe by the fire and he sat himself down and he smoked; …And when St. Nicholas had smoked his pipe, he twisted it in his hatband, and laying his finger beside his nose gave the astonished Van Kortlandt a very significant look; then mounting his wagon he returned over the treetops and disappeared.[24]

St. Nicholas's appearance in Oloffe's dream and on the *Goede Vrouw*'s bowsprit incorporates some elements of the Dutch St. Nicholas in disguise, except for the pipe, as he was portrayed in the earlier-mentioned cookie molds. No such molds are known to have come to America; be that as it may, Irving was not the first to divest the bishop of his accoutrements. In addition, St. Nicholas's demeanor has lost all the austerity and dignity of the Dutch folk hero. Instead, he companionably joins Oloffe by the fire to smoke his pipe, and he gestures in a folksy manner. Like the Dutch folk hero, he is seen "riding over the tops of the trees," but his steed now pulls a wagon, an addition that further confirms his transformation into a seventeenth-century Dutch-American farmer.

St. Nicholas customs are deftly woven into Irving's narrative of New Netherland. The centuries-old Dutch tradition of occasional St. Nicholas songs is transformed into one appropriate for battle: in the relation of the historical altercations with the Swedes at Forts Casimir and Christina in the Delaware, "the valiant men of Sing-Sing…assisted marvelously in the fight by chaunting forth the great song of St. Nicholas."[25] The transformation, ludicrous as it may seem, is not inconsistent with the public, pre-Reformation tradition, when people liked to refer to themselves as men of St. Nicholas,[26] a habit that resembles the earlier described, wholly secular, public revival in late-eighteenth-century New York. The inclusion of the "festival" of St. Nicholas as one of the few occasions when the front door is opened[27] is consistent with the Dutch custom to leave gifts there on St. Nicholas Eve. Irving takes advantage in this context, however, to gently ridicule the exceptional status of the front door in some of the Dutch provinces, while he elevates the importance of the Dutch St. Nicholas customs.

Gift giving on the occasion of St. Nicholas is further explored in the *History*'s second edition:

> in the sylvan days of New Amsterdam, the good St. Nicholas would often make his appearance in his beloved city of a holiday afternoon, riding jollily among the tree tops or over the roofs of the houses, now and then drawing forth magnificent presents from his breeches pockets and dropping them down the chimneys of his favorites. Whereas in these degenerate days of iron and brass he never shows us the light of his countenance nor ever visits us, save one night in the year; when he rattles down the chimneys of the descendants of the patriarchs, confining his presents merely to the children in token of the degeneracy of the parents.[28]

The passage demonstrates that the austere, disciplinarian traits of the Dutch St. Nicholas, legendary saint and folk hero, have largely disappeared. Irving's Nicholas is kind; punishment is directed exclusively at adults and takes the form of withholding his presence. Moreover, the "days of iron and brass" refer to Irving's contemporary scene. In a time marked by devotion to progress, Irving indicates, all myths are lost except to those who retain their innocence.

In retirement, former director-general Stuyvesant, or, as Irving calls him, governor, continues to observe Dutch holidays, "nor was the day of St. Nicholas suffered to pass by, without making presents, hanging the stocking in the chimney and complying with all its other ceremonies."[29] The chimney is the right location for presents, whether homemade or store bought, but Irving departs from the uninterrupted, centuries-old prevailing European tradition of the shoe as receptacle. Instead, he adopts what perhaps, judging by the above-mentioned Dusart print, was a simple, rural tradition of a stocking that may have prevailed among New Netherlanders and their descendants, who may have inaugurated the stocking as part of the American tradition.

Irving not only perpetuates the traditions associated with the secular folk hero, but also resurrects the legendary saint. Raised a Presbyterian and fully realizing the preposterousness of his undertaking, he revives the legendary St. Nicholas in his capacity of protector and performer of miracles. In keeping with the saint's function as the patron of seafarers, his image adorns the ship that brings him and the settlers to the New World; under the guidance of the "blessed Nicholas," they establish a "settlement, which they called by the Indian name *Communipaw*."[30] In imitation of the mother city, says Knickerbocker, "they dedicated [the church in the fort] to the great and good ST. NICHOLAS, who immediately took the infant town of New Amsterdam under his peculiar patronage, and has ever since been . . . the tutelary saint of this excellent city." St. Nicholas's statue that adorned the *Goede Vrouw* is, according to "a little legendary book . . . written in low dutch," placed "in front of this chapel." Irving reinforced the connection with St. Nicholas in a seventeenth-century view of New Amsterdam, copied and somewhat altered, that is folded into the first edition of the *History*. Although all other explanatory legends of the original are correctly translated, he changed "de Kerck" (the Church) to read "Church of St. Nicholas."[31] The actual building was constructed in 1642 during director Kieft's tenure and was located within the confines of the fort.

In this instance, what Irving undoubtedly intended as easily recognizable, humorous fiction came to be accepted as fact. St. Nicholas's patronage of New York is proclaimed on guided tours of the city; and the unknown author of "The Church of St. Nicholas" writes that the building "was known as 'The Church in the Fort,' although it was dedicated to its patron St. Nicholas."[32] The history of St. Nicholas in his functions as Catholic bishop and patron saint in the Netherlands following the Reformation makes abundantly clear that such a formal dedication to St. Nicholas or any other saint is out of the question. As in the Netherlands, New Netherland's official church was the Dutch Reformed Church, although other rites were permitted to be practiced in seclusion. Nevertheless, Irving's name for this structure and St. Nicholas's fictional patronage of the city have tended, over the years, to be repeated as accepted facts.

Firmly established in Knickerbocker's *History* as New Amsterdam's protector, St. Nicholas is also New Netherland's and Stuyvesant's patron saint. Like his legendary counterpart, the *History*'s Nicholas performs miracles, but these can best be described as mixed blessings. In Knickerbocker's New World, St. Nicholas is paradoxically credited with causing an outbreak of witchcraft in New England so that the Yankees' attention will be diverted from their Dutch neighbors. During the battle of Fort Christina, Nicholas protects Stuyvesant from harm. As befits his metamorphosis into a New Netherland farmer, he provides a cushion of manure to soften the governor's fall. Finally, to put an end to the wrangling of the New Amsterdam city council, he miraculously produces a messenger to announce the arrival of the hostile British fleet.

Upon the surrender in 1664, says Knickerbocker, the English allow Nicholas to remain the only saint "in the calendar" and "thenceforward, as before, be considered the tutelary saint of the city."[33] Not only has he remained, but he has enlarged his realm. Arrived in the New World as a secular Dutch folk hero, Nicholas is reinvested with his legendary powers in Irving's *History*. His bishop's attire is permanently exchanged for that of a seventeenth-century New Netherland farmer and his stern, austere demeanor for that of a jolly companion. Like the Dutch Nicholas in the early nineteenth century, the Santa in an 1821 American juvenile still gives equal emphasis to reward and punishment, the latter by means of the traditional birch twigs. But, except for his turban and slender posture, the figure depicted here resembles the modern Santa Claus. The booklet's pictures demonstrate that St. Nicholas's physical metamorphosis begun by Irving had become fixed.[34]

The later Knickerbocker tales contain a few references to St. Nicholas, but solely as patron saint. The pre-Reformation religious legend Irving used and expanded upon in the *History* is treated as fact; apart from its perpetuation, these references serve only as part of the backdrop for Dutch-American folk life as it is portrayed in these tales. Others would build upon Irving's portrait of Nicholas, the secular folk hero, whose lean figure had begun to assume the stout proportions of some of the *History*'s New Netherlanders, a trait that later illustrators would accentuate. Notably Thomas Nast turned Irving's Nicholas into the rotund, jolly elf he is today. In 1836 Irving's friend and one-time co-author James K. Paulding, who himself was of Dutch descent and whose sister Julia was married to Irving's brother William, wrote his *Book of St. Nicholas*, in which he endows the saint with a wife and children. This fantasy was not as original as it may seem: an old children's rhyme from the province of Friesland relates that St. Nicholas's wife, called *Sintele Zij*, and his son and daughter, would stay around for three nights after December 6 to monitor children's behavior for backsliding.[35] It hardly requires a side-by-side comparison to recognize Clement Clarke Moore's indebtedness to Oloffe Van Kortlandt's dream of St. Nicholas for his 1822 poem, *A Visit from St. Nicholas*.[36] It is Irving's *History of New York*, however, that presents the transformations in appearance and character of the Dutch St. Nicholas; these are the genesis of what would become the American Santa Claus.

Not Irving, but Pintard and others are responsible for the shift of Nicholas's celebration to Christmas Day in the later 1800s. The attention subsequently bestowed on Santa Claus notwithstanding, this American folk hero over time became less colorful and exciting than the Dutch original and his portrayal in Irving's *History*, whose many, centuries-old traditions appeal to young and old alike and foster cohesion within the circle of family and friends. Recent fears in the Netherlands that *Sinterklaas* may bite the dust are evidently unfounded: an inquiry conducted by the *Nederlands Centrum voor Volkscultuur* (Netherlandic Center for Popular Culture) in 2007 demonstrated that *Sinterklaas* is considered by far the most important tradition among the Dutch, even among those without children.[37] More than the comparatively static American Santa, *Sinterklaas* demonstrates his viability as a true folk hero by adapting to and changing with the times. But both heroes will continue to exist on their respective sides of the Atlantic as long as they help to satisfy the need for cheer and good fellowship in the darkest days of the year.

NOTES

1. The above description relates dominant practices; in parts of the Netherlands sharply divergent Nicholas traditions prevail, notably on the islands north of the provinces of Friesland and North-Holland. The origins of *Zwarte Piet* are unclear, but it is certain that Nicholas arrived alone in New Netherland. The servant was not part of the St. Nicholas tradition in the seventeenth and eighteenth centuries, and even later he seems to have appeared only sporadically. Nicholas is portrayed without a servant until 1800, when a centsprent, a penny picture with verse, portrays him on horseback with a white servant on foot. Not earlier than in a text of 1832 is Nicholas accompanied by a dark-complexioned young man dressed as he is in the modern celebration. For the servant's attire and his depiction in the nineteenth century, see Eugenie Boer-Dirks, "Nieuw Licht op Zwarte Piet" ["New Light on Black Peter"], *Volkskundig Bulletin* 19.1 (April 1993), 8–9. Dutch and German authors cited here are scholars of popular culture. The author's translation of titles follows in brackets.

2. Mirjam van Leer, "Wie gelooft er nog in Sinterklaas" ["Who Still Believes in St. Nicholas?"], *Volkskundig Bulletin* 22.3 (Dec. 1996), 258–259; Rien van den Heuvel, "Het verhaal van St. Nicolaas" ["The Story of St. Nicholas"], *Traditie* 4.4 (1998), 22–23. Among the consulted Dutch texts, Van den Heuvel's is the only one to mention Irving in this regard.

3. See Henry A. Pochmann, introduction, *Washington Irving: Representative Sections* (New York: American Book, 1934), xl.

4. The Catholic Church removed Nicholas from the saints' calendar in the 1970s. See S. J. van der Molen and Paul Vogt, *Onze Folklore* [Our Folklore] (Amsterdam: Elsevier, 1980), 166; and A. P. van Gilst, *Sinterklaas en het Sinterklaasfeest: Geschiedenis en Folklore* [*Saint Nicholas and the St. Nicholas Celebraetion: History and Folklore*](Veenendaal: Midgaard, 1969), 40. Van Gilst notes that Paul VI's apostolic letter of May 9, 1969, announces this event.

5. Martin Ebon, *Saint Nicholas: Life and Legend* (New York: Harper & Row, 1975), 57–58.

6. For the history of the St. Nicholas cult, see J. L. de Jager, *Volksgebruiken in Nederland* [*Folk Customs in the Netherlands*] (Utrecht: Spectrum, 1981), 143–144, 146; Ebon, 3, 32; Karl Meisen, *Niklauskult und Niklausbrauch im Abendlande* [*Nicholas Cult and Nicholas Customs in the Western Half of the Old World*] (1931; repr., Dusseldorf: Schwann, 1981), 172, 273, 307, 326, 331; Sigrid Metken, *Sankt-Niklaus in Kunst und Volksbrauch* [*Saint Nicholas in Art and Folk Customs*] (Duisburg: n.p., 1966), 4–12, 63; C. Catharina van de Graft, *Nederlandse Volksgebruiken bij Hoogtijdagen* [*Netherlandic Customs on Feast Days*], rev. ed. Tj. W. R. de Haan (Utrecht: Spectrum, 1979), 119–121; Boer-Dirks, 4.

7. For the saint's name, appearance, and secular celebration, see Jan de Schuyter, *Sint Niklaas in de Legende en in de Volksgebruiken* [*Saint Nicholas in Legend and in Folk Customs*] (Antwerpen: Dirix, 1944), 33, and for the woodcuts see De Schuyter, n.p.; De Jager, 147–148; and Metken, 66. Dusart's drawing is part of the collection *Stichting* [*Foundation*] *Atlas Van Stolk* of the historical museum *Het Schielandshuis* in Rotterdam.

8. Meisen, 9, 76.

9. Bert van Gelder, "Makkers staakt uw wild geraas: veranderde opvattingen over Sint Nicolaas en Zwarte Piet" ["Companions, stop your wild noise: changed opinions concerning Saint Nicholas and Black Peter"], *Traditie* 4.4 (1998), 31. The first part of this title is a quotation of a line in a St. Nicholas song, anticipating the St. Nicholas Eve celebration.

10. For St. Nicholas upon the Reformation, see J. L. Price, *Culture and Society in the Dutch Republic during the 17th Century* (New York: Scribner, 1974), 33, and Van de Graft, 127–129.

11. J. J. Schilstra, *Prenten in Hout: Speculaas-, Taai- en Dragantvormen in Nederland* [*Pictures in Wood in the Netherlands: Forms of brittle Gingerbread, Gingerbread of stiff dough, and Sweets consisting of a mixture of powdered sugar and gelatin*] (Lochem: De Tijdstroom, 1985), 47, 133–134. According to tradition, *taai* or *taaitaai*, "tough" or "toughtough," is the oldest known Netherlandic bakery recipe. J. J. Schilstra is the author of several books on Dutch material culture.

12. De Jager, 148–149.

13. The Steen is at the *Rijksmuseum* at Amsterdam. The Fouquet is part of the collection *Stichting Atlas Van Stolk* at the historical museum *Het Schielandshuis*, Rotterdam.

14. Boer-Dirks, 8.

15. Van de Graft, 127–129.

16. For Pintard's woodcut, see Ebon, 86. For the 1770s celebrations, see Peter R. Christoph, "St. Nicholas," *The Encyclopedia of New York State*, ed. Peter Eisenstadt et al. (Syracuse: Syracuse University Press, 2005), 1489. For the 1773 newspaper account, and the rhyme and its provenance, see Charles W. Jones, *Saint Nicholas of Myra, Bari, and Manhattan: Biography of a Legend* (1978; repr., Chicago: University of Chicago Press, 1988), 333, 341–342. Ignorant of St. Nicholas's dual role as venerated saint and secular hero and the fact that as popular hero Nicholas survived the Reformation in Dutch family circles, Jones, professor emeritus at the University of California, Berkeley, and later Stephen Nissenbaum, professor of history at the University of Massachusetts, Amherst, deny Nicholas's seventeenth-century arrival in New Netherland and wholly credit his emergence in late-eighteenth- and early-nineteenth-century New York to the need for a patriotic rallying point. See Jones, 333–335; and Nissenbaum, *The Battle for Christmas* (New York: Vintage Books, 1997), x. Citing Jones, Nissenbaum calls "the ritual . . . an invented tradition," 63–64. Neither author offers an explanation of, or speculates upon, the means whereby Mrs. Hardenbrook would have learned the Dutch song and have remembered it at the age of eighty if she had not thoroughly absorbed it in childhood.

17. See Van Gelder, 31, for hiatus in composition, and Van Gilst, 40, 62, for the association between St. Nicholas and Spain. The Hardenbrook song, in two stanzas and in orthography that is reminiscent of the seventeenth century, reads "*Sancte Claus goed heylig Man!/ Trek uwe beste Tabaert aen,/ Reiz daer me'e na Amsterdam,/ Van Amsterdam na 'Spanje,/ Waer Appelen van Oranje,/ Waer Appelen van granaten, Wie rollen door de Straaten./ SANCTE CLAUS, myn goede Vriend!/ Ik heb U allen tyd gedient,/ Wille U my nu wat geven,/ Ik zal U dienen alle myn Leven.*" Author's translation: St. Nicholas good holy Man!/ Put on your best tabard,/ Travel with it to Amsterdam,/ From Amsterdam to Spain,/ Where [there are] Apples of Orange,/ Where [there are] (Apples of) Pomegranate[s],/ That roll through the Streets./ ST. NICHOLAS, my good Friend!/ I have always served [been devoted to] you,/ [If] you will give me something now,/ I shall serve [devote myself to] you all my Life.

The English translation of Pintard's broadside is rhymed and less precise. See Jones, 341–342.

18. The full text of the 1645–1655 Netherlandic quatrain is as follows, with author's translation: "*Sinter Klaas, ô Heil'ge Man,/ Trek je beste Tabbaart an;/ En wilje me dan wat geven,/ Zo dien ik je al men* [sic] *leven.*" (St. Nicholas, O Holy Man,/ Put on your best tabard;/ And will you then give me something,/ Then I shall serve [be devoted to] you all my life.) For this text, see Henk van Benthem's collection of original texts and melodies of all known, traditional St. Nicholas songs, entitled *Sint-Nicolaasliederen* [*Saint Nicholas Songs*] (Amersfoort/Leuven: Acco, 1991), 61. Van Benthem's collection contains eight more versions of this song, varying in length from quatrain to ten lines, in from one to three stanzas (61–64). Apart from the first and the two latest (1960s), their transcriptions from the oral tradition date from 1863 to 1907. Where St. Nicholas is in motion, he rides instead of travels; the pomegranates have permanently disappeared and been

replaced by "little pears" or "little plums," or candy, gingerbread, nuts, or rusk, depending on the version. Only one version, recorded in 1903, reiterates the incident of fruit and other treats rolling through the streets. Piet de Boer's important contribution, in the form of his expertise and copies of Van Benthem's pertinent pages, in response to my request for information directed to the *Nederlands Centrum voor Volkscultuur* (Netherlandic Center for Popular Culture), is gratefully acknowledged (March 2, 2008). Thanks are due as well to Sonja Blom, Monique van Grunsven, Joekie Gurski, Josina van der Maas, Anneke Oranje, Ria Perne, Adriana Phillips, Riet Rose, Renée Schaaf, Marion Strauss, and Cocky Vogels, who generously responded with their recollections of the song's lyrics and melodies.

19. The general meaning of the verb *dienen* in the Dutch text is "to serve," with the same wide application as it has in English. Specifically, it means "to devote oneself" to a higher cause, such as God, the Church, or the king.

20. Katharine Schuyler Baxter, *A Godchild of Washington: A Picture of the Past* (New York: F. Tennyson Neely, 1897), 650–651.

21. For the quotation from the unpublished Van Rensselaer Manor Papers, see Janny Venema, *Beverwijck: A Dutch Village on the American Frontier, 1652–1664* (Hilversum: Verloren/State University of New York, 2003), 112. The "f" preceding the amount paid is the abbreviation of "florin" or guilder.

22. Jones, 338, 339; Nissenbaum, 61–62.

23. Washington Irving, "A History of New York, by Diedrich Knickerbocker," *History, Tales, and Sketches*, 1809 edition, ed. James W. Tuttleton (New York: Library of America, 1983), 435. Irving's anomalies of spelling and punctuation are copied without comment. Further references to this volume appear as *K*1809.

24. Washington Irving, *A History of New York*, 1812 edition, ed. Edwin T. Bowden (New Haven: New College and University Press, 1964), 109. Further references to this text appear as *K*1812.

25. *K*1809, 651.

26. Van de Graft, 120.

27. *K*1809, 498. In rural areas of the Netherlands, the back door is most commonly used. In some Dutch provinces, use of the front door is strictly limited to weddings and funerals. See, for example, Petra Clarijs, "De Wooncultuur" ["Habitation Culture"] in *Volkskunst der Lage Landen* [*Folk Art of the Low Countries*], ed. Tjaard W. R. de Haan (Amsterdam: Elsevier, 1965), 3:48, 66.

28. *K*1812, 132–133.

29. *K*1809, 725.

30. *K*1809, 436. Communipaw was an early Dutch settlement across the Hudson from Manhattan, in the area of present-day Jersey City, N.J.

31. *K*1809, 454. This view is credited to "Justus Danckers, at Amsterdam," and to "Justus Danker" in a textual note (*K*1809, 527n). Justus Danckerts was a seventeenth-century art dealer, publisher, and engraver, who copied and may have slightly retouched a map of New Netherland and surroundings published in the early 1650s by Nicolaes J. Visscher. Danckerts copied the view of New Amsterdam in all pertinent details, including the legends, as it appears on the Visscher or prototype map as an inset in the lower right corner. For Danckerts, see Abraham van der Aa, *Biografisch Woordenboek der Nederlanden* [*Biographical Dictionary of the Netherlands*] (Amsterdam: Israel, 1969); G. M. Asher, *A Bibliographical and Historical Essay on the Dutch Books and Pamphlets Relating to New Netherland* (Amsterdam: Israel, 1960), 11; and I. N. Phelps Stokes, *The Iconography of Manhattan Island, 1498–1909* (New York: Dodd, 1915), 1: plate 7a.

32. "The Church of St. Nicholas," *The Saint Nicholas Society of the City of New York. Genealogical and Record Book* (1968), 6.

33. *K*1809, 714.

34. Duncan Emrich, "A Certain Nicholas of Patara," *American Heritage* 12 (1960), 22–27. Called *The Children's Friend*, this booklet, consisting of eight pages and reproduced in Emrich's article, pertains to "Santeclaus." Each page has a picture and a quatrain with secular content. Gifts are distributed on Christmas Eve. The conveyance, a first, according to Emrich, is a sled and one reindeer. Only two copies of the booklet are known to exist.

35. Waling Dijkstra, *Uit Friesland's Volksleven* [*From Friesland's Folk Life*], 2 vols. in 1 (1895–1896; repr., Leeuwarden: Hugo Suringar, 1970), 1: 337.

36. Andrew Burstein accepts Donald Foster's claim that Henry Livingston, a Hudson Valley New Yorker of Dutch-Scottish descent, was the actual author of this famous poem and that he recited it "at a gathering as early as 1807–1808." *The Original Knickerbocker: The Life of Washington Irving* (New York: Basic Books, 2007), 142.

37. "Recente enquéte wijst Sinterklaas als belangrijkste traditie aan" ["Recent inquiry points to St. Nicholas as the most important tradition"], *The Windmill Herald*, December 7, 2007, U.S.A. edition.

Searching for True Love:

LETTERS FROM KILIAEN VAN RENSSELAER

JANNY VENEMA

The New Netherland Project transcribes, translates, and publishes the archival records of the seventeenth-century colony of New Netherland. In addition to its translation work the New Netherland Project tries to locate documents relating to New Netherland. The best-known repositories have been searched pretty well, and a "good find" has become rare. One of the most valuable contributions was made some hundred years ago and came from a private family, a collection of papers concerning the patroonship of Rensselaerswijck, which has become known under the name of Van Rensselaer Bowier Manuscripts. The original manuscripts are now in the Scheepvaart Museum of Amsterdam. My curiosity was aroused when, at the Centraal Bureau voor Genealogie at The Hague, I saw a typewritten page quoting part of a letter written in 1615 by Kiliaen van Rensselaer, who, as a director of the Amsterdam chamber of the Dutch West India Company and patroon of the area of the present-day Albany and Rensselaer counties at the upper Hudson, would play an important role in populating New Netherland. I had not seen this letter at the Amsterdam Scheepvaart Museum or at the Amsterdam municipal archives, which also holds many documents relating to Van Rensselaer and Rensselaerswijck.

A search eventually brought me to Mrs. Reins Mangert-Doeksen, who appeared to be in the possession of copies of twenty-one documents unknown to me, among which were two letters written by Kiliaen van Rensselaer in 1615, one of them a copy of the entire letter that I was looking for.[1] Unfortunately, however, Mrs. Mangert-Doeksen did not know the location of the original documents, as around 1948 her grandmother had donated them to an unknown place for safekeeping. Although I have not yet been able to locate the original letters, I could not think of anything more appropriate for this liber amicorum than to offer a translation of the copies. The letters shine a light on the point in Van Rensselaer's life when he is on the threshold to success—a period in which the seeds for New Netherland's history were planted. He wrote the two letters in 1615 to Hillegond van Bijler, who would become his wife within the next year and with whom he would have three children. Shortly after the birth of their daughter

Maria in 1626, Hillegond died, leaving Kiliaen with their two sons, Hendrick and Johannes. The baby girl also died.

In the following pages I will first summarize the history of the Van Rensselaer Bowier Manuscripts, since it may provide an indication as to where the original documents could be located. In order provide a context for the two letters and their relevance, I will then briefly sketch Van Rensselaer's surroundings in 1615: part of his circle of friends, a glimpse of Amsterdam at that time, and, since they are love letters, some contemporary views on marriage.

The Van Rensselaer Bowier Manuscripts: A Short History

In the spring of 1888 Nicolaes de Roever, archivist of the city of Amsterdam, met with *Jonkheer* (esquire) M. W. van Rensselaer-Bowier, who showed him a small chest with documents of the Van Rensselaer family archives that had been handed down in the Van Rensselaer family in the Netherlands. De Roever published two articles based on these manuscripts, but his death in 1893 prevented subsequent publications. The documents were returned to the widow of the deceased Jonkheer van Rensselaer-Bowier and his two surviving sons, H. J. J. and M. W. M. M. van Rensselaer-Bowier. Around 1896, people in America learned about the article and the collection of documents, but a search in 1902 brought to light that the documents had been loaned to "a friend" of the Van Rensselaer-Bowier family, J. F. Pieters, alias Pieters van Wely, who had taken them to America in 1895 in order to sell them at private sales. Pieters van Wely did not succeed and returned to the Netherlands, where he died soon after. Part of the collection he had left with a certain George Waddington. This collection eventually reached Arnold J. F. van Laer, then archivist at the New York State Library, who inspected, transcribed, and translated the documents into English. The result was the publication of the Van Rensselaer Bowier Manuscripts (VRBM) in 1908—just in time for the tricentennial celebrations of Henry Hudson's voyage on the Hudson.[2]

Another part of the collection, containing some eighty-three documents, was left by Pieters van Wely with Stephen van Rensselaer Townsend, of New York. After his death they came into the possession of his brother Howard Townsend, who had them examined by Van Laer. It was not surprising that they assumed these papers, which dated from 1476 to 1795, to be the documents described by De Roever as "papers of a personal nature, which would indeed be valuable for an accurate genealogy, but which are unimportant for our purpose."[3] Van Laer made transcripts of forty-nine of the eighty-three documents and provided the New York State Library with a list noting dates and topics of all eighty-three documents, which he named the "Van Rensselaer Bowier Manuscripts, series 2—Papers relating to various members of the Van Wely, Van Rensselaer and Van Bijlaer families."[4]

Both collections were restored to the Van Rensselaer-Bowier family. In 1922 Jonkheer Van Rensselaer-Bowier loaned the Van Rensselaer-Bowier Papers to the Scheepvaart Museum at Amsterdam, and in 1961 the heirs of Jonkheer

M. W. M. M. van Rensselaer-Bowier and Mrs. J. M. van Rensselaer-Bowier-van Zanten Jut donated the documents to the same museum.[5]

With the same generosity as the Van Rensselaer-Bowiers once had showed to De Roever and Van Laer, Mrs. Mangert-Doeksen offered the papers to me so that I might copy them and do with them as I desired. About their authenticity I have no doubt, as Mrs. Mangert-Doeksen is a direct descendant in the female line of Richard van Rensselaer, Kiliaen's fourth son of his marriage to Anna van Wely.[6] Furthermore, not only does the regular, neat handwriting of the two letters resemble that of the letters written by Van Rensselaer in his later life, but we can also recognize the person of the later patroon: just as he later provided such detailed instructions for the government and organization of his patroonship in North America, so did he explain in these early letters to his future wife the reasons for success of their possible marriage. The originals of these documents could have been all or part of the personal papers to which De Roever and later Van Laer referred and of which it was assumed that they had remained in possession of the family. The possibility that they did not belong to that collection, however, is greater, since Mrs. Mangert-Doeksen descends not from Jonkheer M. W. van Rensselaer-Bowier but from one of his sisters.[7]

Through Van Laer's translation of the VRBM in 1908 we have met Kiliaen van Rensselaer as one of the directors of chamber of Amsterdam of the West India Company and as the patroon of his colony of Rensselaerswijck. By reading through his letters we can imagine this man in his early forties: a man of importance with important friends and acquaintances; a precise, orderly, enthusiastic, energetic, and enterprising man with political ideals, as well as with ideas about colonization, agriculture, and religion. We can follow him through the manuscripts and, in later years, picture him trying to hold on to his ideas and expressing his frustration when he seems to lose control of his colony in New Netherland.[8] The two letters of 1615 create an image of Van Rensselaer as a younger man with religious principles, who participated in the literary culture of his day. Above all, however, we see a glimpse of a man in love, with ideas about marriage as a social, religious, and economic partnership for which he considered love, reason, discretion, and fairness important ingredients. The letters show Van Rensselaer making an important step on his way to success, some ten years *before* he became a West India Company director, when he could not even envision what was to come in the near future.

1602–1615: KILIAEN'S SURROUNDINGS

FRIENDS AND FAMILY

The letters show the twenty-nine-year-old Kiliaen in September 1615 in Frankfurt am Main for the Frankfurt fair—one of Europe's greatest auction places for jewelry and precious stones at that time. Three months before, his former master, Wolfert van Bijler, a trader in jewelry, had died childless. In his will Van Bijler had appointed his associate and nephew Jan van Wely and Kiliaen administrators of his entire estate. Being further removed from him as a relative than Wolfert's brothers, sisters, and their children, the position of administrator must have been a great sign of confidence and trust to Van Rensselaer.

This course of events was not yet known in 1602, when Kiliaen had come from his birthplace, the small town of Hasselt (Overijssel), to Wolfert's house in Amsterdam as a merchant apprentice. It had been the wish of his father, Hendrick van Rensselaer, who as a captain in Maurits's army had died in the battle of Ostend in 1602, that his son would end up in the economic and social circles of his relative Wolfert van Bijler. Hendrick van Rensselaer had seen Hasselt's poor economic situation and the rapidly growing prosperity of North-Holland, especially Amsterdam. His family ties with Van Bijler stemmed from the area of Nijkerk, where they both came from. During the 1580s Van Bijler had lived and worked as a jewelry trader in London, after which he had settled in Amsterdam.[9] Here he kept in touch with Van Rensselaer, while he continued the jewelry business together with his nephews Jan and Willem van Wely.[10] Wolfert had been widowed twice, and by the time of Kiliaen's arrival he seems to have been living at the Nieuwezijds Kerkhof near the Nieuwe Kerk and old city hall with his third wife, Anna Willekens, and Jonas, his fourteen-year-old son from his first marriage.[11] Perhaps Fabiaen de Vliet, his twenty-year-old stepson from his first marriage, who studied law at Leiden, came back to live with them again for a while, while Jonas would leave in 1606 to study philosophy in Leiden.[12] Wolfert's older brother Jan lived nearby in the Eggertstraat with his wife and daughter. Leonora Haukens, Anna's thirty-three-year-old daughter from her first marriage, lived with her husband (Wolfert's associate) Jan van Wely and their growing number of children in the then-stately, upper-class Warmoesstraat.[13]

WORK AND THE CITY

In this family setting Kiliaen learned about gold, silver, precious stones, jewelry designs, perhaps something about diamond cutting, and other details of the jewelry trade. Generally, work of jewelry traders included, among other tasks, dealing with gold- and silversmiths, diamond cutters, artists, designers, jewelers, and traders in gold, silver, and precious stones such as diamonds and pearls. Most likely Van Bijler sent his apprentice on business trips as well, and Kiliaen probably learned the languages and customs of other countries, which would have been required for the international trade.[14] As a merchant apprentice he was part of Amsterdam's great development as a staple market. Especially since the fall of Antwerp in 1585, many merchants from the Southern Netherlands had come to Amsterdam, taking along their capital, experience, and trading networks. They were active in many trading expeditions and played an important role in the newly established Dutch East India Company (VOC). In 1609, when a twelve-year truce in the war with Spain was officially proclaimed and when Kiliaen witnessed the opening of the new exchange, there may have been about 450 merchants from the Southern

Netherlands in Amsterdam. Other institutions were established to promote trade, such as the brand-new building of the bourse, which was opened in 1611. Amidst these great developments Kiliaen learned about trade in general: for example, the trade in VOC shares and dealing with price lists, different coins, and bills of exchange.[15]

The almost endless stream of immigrants (especially after the Alteration in 1578, when Amsterdam accepted the Protestant religion) had created economic growth, and architects, painters, musicians, and other artists found a ready market in the growing wealth of Amsterdam's inhabitants. Many of the growing number of wealthy merchants and well-to-do entrepreneurs and businesspeople made showpieces of their private houses by having them decorated with skillful reliefs and gable stones, such as those of Hendrick de Keijser, whose decorations adorned government buildings and gates in the city. He designed many of the later famous buildings that Kiliaen saw arise, such as the Southern and the Western churches and the bourse. Other arts developed, as well: Kiliaen lived amidst an explosive development of luxury products and art dealing that accompanied the growing wealth. I imagine that he frequently attended the daily organ concerts by Jan Pietersz Sweelinck in the Oude Kerk. But I wonder whether he enjoyed Nicolas Vallet's little orchestra that played at weddings and parties or the private music and dance lessons that this Frenchman taught after he settled in Amsterdam in 1613 or whether he appreciated Gérard Thibault's fencing school, the *Académie de l'Espée*. He may have visited the music houses, statue gardens and labyrinths that inns began to offer. I am curious to know how he would have felt about the exuberant ways of life of the southern immigrants, who brought along their extravagant Brabandish fashion with its bright colors, which, in spite of continuous protests of Calvinist preachers, filled the taverns, colored the streets, and found their way to Rembrandt's or Jan Steen's canvasses. Perhaps Kiliaen met for business with artists, such as Hendrick Golzius, an engraver who may have made jewelry designs for Van Wely.[16]

The jewelry business profited of the city's prosperity, as well. During the last fifteen years of the sixteenth century the number of goldsmiths had quadrupled, and between 1576 and 1625 some 156 gold- and silversmiths operated in Amsterdam, of which eighty-two came from the Southern Netherlands.[17] But if Van Bijler, like other successful merchants, had hopes of keeping the business within his own family, they ended abruptly in 1609, when his only son, Jonas, died. By 1610 Kiliaen may have been keeping the business running. In February 1614 he entered into a company to trade in jewelry with the Van Wely family. Although the Van Welys carried the largest share, the ƒ24.000 (one-eighth share) brought in by Kiliaen, the youngest partner, seemed to mark a promising start of his own career.[18]

MARRIAGE

By 1614 Kiliaen was twenty-eight, and other young men of his age were usually married around that age. A random-sample survey undertaken by Amsterdam's city archivist, Simon Hart, in 1976 indicates that from around 1626 and 1627 the average age for a man to marry was twenty-five years and eight months.[19] For a woman it was twenty-four years and six months. The general thought was that too great an age difference would be contrary to one of the purposes of marriage, as instead of increasing the human race, it would decrease the hope of many children. Besides, the age difference might promote discord and sexual abuse.[20] Kiliaen, nevertheless, approached the seventeen-year-old Hillegond, the only child of Wolfert's eldest brother, Jan van Bijler.[21] After Jan's death Wolfert had become her guardian, and the fact that parental consent was required for marriage may have been a reason for Kiliaen to mention that Wolfert would have wanted them to marry and that her mother had already approved of Kiliaen's guardianship.[22]

Kiliaen was probably right when he wrote that Wolfert would have wanted their marriage. His former master had been a great merchant master, but since business and marriage were closely linked, he also may have given good advice when it came to marriage. Wolfert's own marriages—he had married three wealthy Flemish widows—had greatly expanded his network, and most likely he and Anna had arranged Jan van Wely's marriage to Leonora in 1597. I would not be surprised if they also influenced or arranged other marriages, such as those of Willem van Wely and Fabiaen de Vliet to daughters of the wealthy Antwerp trader Jan van Valckenburgh.[23] Like other successful merchants, Wolfert and the Van Welys intended to expand the business and keep it within the family. It was therefore important, and generally accepted, that sons and daughters would marry within their own social class. Authors such as the poet-grand pensionary (*raadpensionaris*) Jacob Cats—who, like Willem van Wely and Fabiaen de Vliet, married a Van Valckenburgh girl—were adverse toward social mobility and strongly advised people to look for a partner within their own social circles. In their opinion, marriage between classes would only affect the relations of authority within the family, especially if the man was of a lower social status than the woman. This social status was determined by one's family, unless one had broken away from it and had established oneself independently.[24] Kiliaen had lost his parents a long time previously, but he certainly felt that he belonged and wanted to be in Van Bijler's circles. Not only were they related, but by 1614 he had gathered enough capital to put f24,000 into a company for jewelry trade with the Van Welys.[25] A combination with Hillegond's capital (on certain conditions she would inherit f12,000 from her uncle Wolfert) would greatly improve Van Rensselaer's opportunities and definitely keep the jewelry business within the family.[26] The attention Kiliaen paid to the fact that she could be assured of his financial situation, that they were an only son and daughter, and that they both had honorable friends, who were much alike in their social behavior, suggests that social status was important to him.[27]

In addition to age and social status, religion was important for a successful marriage. Throughout the seventeenth century the church would advocate that marriage partners be of the same religion. Minister Wittewrongel wrote as late as

1661 that marriages between people of a different religion were "a horror in the eyes of God."[28] It is therefore not surprising that Kiliaen emphasized that both he and Hillegond, and their parents as well, had the same religion and belief, which was the reformed belief of the Oude Kerk, where Hillegond's father at various times had been a consistory member.[29] Having been brought up with the principles of Calvinism, Kiliaen considered it important that their personalities would agree well and that they would treat each other with reason, discretion, and fairness. Calvin himself had described marriage as a natural social institution that created the necessary order in human life. Its goal was especially companionable, or in Calvin's words: "La femme a été jointé á l'homme pour compagne, pour l'aider á vivre plus commodément."[30]

The boundaries within which one should look for a partner were thus more or less established, but that did not mean that love was not considered important. Calvin himself had written that once a marriage was made according to God's plan, love would exist between the partners. This love would be expressed by sexual intercourse, which, if not dishonored by immoderacy, was not sinful, but pure and dignified. Reproduction then would be a result of, and not a reason for, the marriage. Man and woman were equal, according to Calvin, and there was only a functional difference, an "égalité differanciée," which would create order and discretion.[31] Throughout the two letters it is clear that Kiliaen hoped that his love and longing for her would be mutual, and before summing up their so-important similarities, he mentioned his pleasure and joy in Hillegond's person. Although he apologized for not being expert in expressing his feelings, he probably was well aware of the recent publications of love literature. Love poetry and the erotic *Emblemata Amatoria* by P. C. Hooft, the leader of the Amsterdam chamber of rhetoric named *d'Eglentier*, for example, had been published in 1605 and 1611 respectively and were very popular.[32] Kiliaen's rhymes at the end of his letters (if he produced the text himself) suggest that he may have taken the *rederijkers*, or rhetoricians, as an example and that he was part of the literary part of the population, among whom playing with sayings, thinking them up, and making variations on existing ones were very popular. Texts and sayings were common knowledge and circulated verbally, were sung, and appeared in many example texts. Kiliaen's saying *Niemandt Sonder* + (including the rebus-like character of the cross sign) is typical for *rederijker* productions, as well as for *alba amicorum*, and could very well have been his personal saying.[33]

In 1615 Kiliaen was very ready to find a bride and saw in Hillegond van Bijler the right combination of love, social status, and religious conviction. Hillegond said yes, and their marriage took place the following year.[34] Perhaps they lived for a while in Jan van Bijler's house in the Eggertstraat, but within not too long they moved to the Keizersgracht. The marriage not only confirmed Kiliaen's social and economic situation; it also greatly strengthened and improved it, as it connected him more closely to the Van Welys and Van Bijlers and added enough capital to buy several lots at the newly dug Keizersgracht, to start renting land in Het Gooi for reclamation, and in future years to invest enough in the West India Company, founded in 1621, to become one of its largest shareholders.

Translation:

Kiliaen van Rensselaer to Hillegonda van Bijllaer, 10/20 September 1615

The honorable virtuous *joffr*
Hillegonda van Bijllaer
My gracious cousin
Dwelling at Vuijtrecht
Amij qui Dieu garde
Laus Deo Adij 10/20 September 1615 in Francfordt an de Maijn

Honorable, gracious, and very dearest cousin *juffrouw* Hillegonda van Bijllaer,

After my very willing obliging recommendation and compliments to you, I would be truly pleased and delighted if I personally could be the messenger or carrier hereof, or if I could verbally present to your honor what now has to take place in writing. Then, considering the inconvenience of the time and the distance of the places, I hope that your honor will understand the intention of this little letter, and remember me while reading this over, just as I, while writing this, and always, think of your honor. First, I hope to hear, when it is possible, about your honor's good health, as well, as I myself am thanking God Almighty now that he has brought me and the entire company here in good health without any danger, hoping that he will let me come back, as well, and find your honor in a virtuous condition. The cause of my writing is, moreover, to give you, my most dearest cousin, not any suspicion or thought of carelessness, forgetfulness, or thoughtlessness, as if I, following up on my promise and bounden duty, would not observe the same; and, moreover, [I] immediately annul and undo the common saying "far out of sight, far out of the heart," which should not be like that. And as far as I am concerned, this does not apply to me, and on your end, I trust that your honor does not completely forget me either, and that your honor, at least in your honor's prayers for the traveling people will think of me too. And then I wished that your honor were longing as much for my arrival as I am longing for my homecoming, and that your honor accept this letter with as much fondness as I dedicated to it, and wrote the same to your honor out of sincere affection. And if I don't use the charming style and cannot think of the pleasing words that I wish and feel in my heart, your honor's discretion won't hold that against me, and excuse me for it, also considering that the necessary work (especially here at the Frankfurt fair) makes the same impossible, as well, all the more since I am inexperienced and unpracticed in such matters, and that one first has to be a disciple before one becomes a master. Likewise, do I not want to busy you with detailed reasons, but herewith end this. Praying (my most dearest cousin) with all my heart to the God of peace that by the powerful effect of his holy spirit he will give to your honor and me that we always be unanimously disposed, and that he, who has the hearts of all people in his hands, will bless the work I began, and, if it is his godly will and our bliss, also move our mutual friends thereto. I commend your honor and your honor's beloved mother in his grace, along with my hearty greetings and a little three-double kiss when I will come visit your honor. Meanwhile, always remaining

> your honor's obliging servant, and hoping to remain your honor's most dearest cousin, and to become all yours until death,
> Kiliaen Van Rensselaer

God shall unite it
[It] will please me
Whatever God unites pleases me

Kiliaen van Rensselaer to Hillegonda van Bijllaer, 17 September 1615

The honorable virtuous *joffr.*
Hillegonda van Bijllaer
My gracious cousin
Dwelling at Vuijtrecht
[M?] Amij qui Dieu garde
[Received on the first of October old style]
Laus Deo Adij 17 September 1615, Francfordt ande Maijn, *stilo veterij*

Honorable, gracious, well beloved cousin, my very dearest and only lady friend, *joffrouw* Hillegonda van Bijllaer,

After my whole-hearted greetings this serves to follow up on the promise I made, and the obligation I owe you from a small letter that I wrote to you a few days ago, in which I informed your honor of service, hoping that the same will have reached your honor in good order. Meanwhile, longing with a steady longing, I hope to learn, when the occasion arises, that your honor will have accepted the same note with pleasure, read it with discretion, and after consideration, re-read it, not paying attention to the imperfection and flaws of the same, but to its simple purpose and sincere intention, which is, to sufficiently assure you of my honest and sincere intention, as I, in my humble opinion, have sufficiently expressed the same verbally to you and your honor's beloved mother, not doubting that the almighty God will bless such intention, give me good patience in everything, and cause your honor's heart and affection to incline thereto, so that I, as the country-man does when work is over, may receive the blessed fruits at harvest time.

Because something has begun in vain if the Lord does not complete it; therefore, my most dearest, let us leave this matter to him—he certainly will make it as it will be best. Further, my most dearest (who after the characteristic of wisdom elaborates and takes caution in resolving things), be not hasty believing it, if in my absence or otherwise it would happen that on account of either jealousy or selfishness some malicious people slander or speak badly about me on anything, because generally in such matters it is customary with many people that they don't speak of the best of a young man, but of the worst, and not only of the worst, but also of things that are not true at all. Sometimes one does not know where it comes from. But I think the best of everyone, and apologize for not being able to refrain from communicating this to you, and at the same time send your honor reason and word of what moved me (after I had prayed to God many a time for a honest partner) to address your honor's person. [It is], you see, because of many agreeing similarities, along with the pleasure and joy in your person, as [is] first, that your honor and I, as well as your honor's parents and mine are, and have been, of one religion and faith. Second, that we are not of strange, foreign families, but from one country and moreover, of one descent and relationship, being related to each other last removed and in the first member to marry [*bestaende malcanderen inden lesten graet ende eerste lit omme te trouwen*]. Also, that on both sides we have honest friends, and that your honor is an only daughter and I am an only son, although I have one only sister, who is peaceful and virtuous. Further, that after your honor's late father's death your honor's uncle Wolfaert van Bijllaer, deceased, has been like a father and caretaker for your honor, whom by my father, deceased, in his lifetime was also entrusted to supervise me, and therefore, after my father's death, I have considered him as a father too, whose wish and desire certainly has also been that your honor and I unite, as I can prove sufficiently; all the more because I had served him not for only seven, but for almost fourteen years—since my childhood—and in my time [I] have helped him gain most of his resources, with which I certainly should have deserved his daughter, if he had had one, and now, by the lack thereof, your honor, his eldest brother's daughter, and therefore, the closest daughter. Concerning our nature, I have no doubt that we will agree well, and that we will always treat each other with reason, discretion and fairness. Also, that your honor's friends and mine are of a same character and nature, and not unlike each other in contact and communication. Also, that God the Lord has blessed your honor in resources and goods, and I thank him, that he has not forgotten me either, as I will show sufficiently, if it is necessary. And whereas I was given the good opportunity and chance when your uncle, deceased, (upon whom, next to God, I relied most, and whereas, because of his death I considered myself half abandoned) died, that through his will he also had appointed me administrator of his estate, for which I was invited by the general heirs as well, and besides, as far as it concerns you, I am also authorized by your honor's mother to administer your affairs. From all of which I conclude, that because your honor's uncle Bijllaer, being your guardian, has died, and your honor's uncle Mauwerits refuses to accept the guardianship, that your honor will accept me as such, because Bijllaer, deceased, has entrusted me together with cousin van Weelij, to administer his entire estate. From which your honor and your honor's mother and the friends may deduce sufficiently and should be well assured of my person; and on account of the aforesaid reasons I am assured sufficiently of your honor's person, so that I further pray the Almighty God that he will give his blessing thereto, in honor of his holy name to the edification of his community and our fellow human beings [*even naesten*] and to the salvation of our souls. Amen. And ending herewith, my very dearest cousin, I pray your honor, not to blame me for this long story, but to consider it carefully. And your honor may think that one word brought along the next, and that people who are in love only possess half of their senses. Meanwhile, I commend your honor and your honor's beloved mother in the merciful protection of the very highest God, who will grant your honor and me, and all of us whatever is blissful. *Vale* and I remain

> your honor's faithful servant and very dearest cousin
> as much as is in me, Kiliaen van Rensselaer

J'adore Dieu et suis serviteur de Madame
L'Un pour le corps et l'aultre pour l 'ame
Nobody without + [*Niemandt Sonder.* +]

NOTES

1. With thanks to Zwanette Plomp at the Centraal Bureau voor Genealogie for her assistance.

2. A. J. F. van Laer, trans. and ed., *Van Rensselaer Bowier Manuscripts, being the letters of Kiliaen van Rensselaer, 1630–1643, and other documents relating to the colony of Rensselaerswyck* (Albany: University of the State of New York Press, 1908). (Hereafter cited as *VRBM.*)

3. *VRBM*, 42.

4. A. J. F. van Laer, "Van Rensselaer Bowier Manuscripts, series 2—Papers relating to various members of the Van Wely, Van Rensselaer and Van Bijlaer families," in Report of the Director 1909, in *State of New York. No. 58 Assembly; 92d Annual Report on the New York State Library* (1910) 18–30.

5. With thanks to Anton van Oortwijn and Diederick Wildeman of the Nederlands Scheepvaart Museum, Amsterdam. For a more detailed history of the Van Rensselaer-Bowier collection, see the introduction to the *VRBM*, 19–20, 37–42, and Van Laer, *92d Annual Report*, 17–30, Report of the Director 1911 in *State of New York, in Assembly*, and Van Laer, *94th Annual Report of the New York State Library* (1912), 30.

6. *VRBM*, 38–39.

7. *VRBM*, 42.

8. Several people have written about Van Rensselaer using the publication of the *VRBM*. In 1917 J. S. C. Jessurun wrote a 213-page dissertation about Van Rensselaer, "*Kiliaen van Rensselaer, van 1623 tot 1636*" (PhD diss., Den Haag, 1917); S. G. Nissenson, *The Patroon's Domain* (New York: Columbia University Press, 1937); L. Van Nierop, "Rensselaerswijck 1629–1704" in *Tijdschrift voor Geschiedenis* 60 (1947): 1–39, 187–219; Jan Folkerts, "*De pachters van Rensselaerswijck, 1630–1664. Nederlandse boeren in de wildernis van Noord-Amerika. Een onderzoek naar landbouw en pacht in Nieuw Nederland*" (Rijksuniversiteit of Groningen, 1984); Jan Folkerts, "Kiliaen van Rensselaer and Agricultural Activity in His Domain: A New Look at the First Patroon and Rensselaerswijck

Before 1664," in *A Beautiful and Fruitful Place: Selected Rensselaerswijck Seminar Papers*, ed. N. A. McClure Zeller (Albany: New Netherland Publishing, 1991), 295–308. One recent publication paid attention to his Hasselt roots: D. Westerhof and Js. Mooijweer, *Tussen Hasselt en Amerika. De Hasselter wortels van drie Amerikaanse pioniersfamilies: Van Rensselaer, Lansing en Cuyler/ Between Hasselt and America. The Hasselt roots of three American pioneer families: Van Rensselaer, Lansing and Cuyler.* (Hasselt: Historische VerenigingHasselt, 1996).

9. Van Bijler was originally from Barnevelt, not far from Nijkerk. For genealogical information on Hendrick van Rensselaer, see W. De Vries, "De Van Rensselaer's in Nederland," *De Nederlandsche Leeuw* 66 (1949): 150–172, 194–211. For Van Bijler, see W. A. van Bijlaer, *Enkele genealogische byzonderheden betreffende een in de zeventiende eeuw te Amsterdam en Dordrecht woonachtige familie van Bijlaer (later van Bijlert)* (Rhenen, 1942).

10. Gemeente Archief Amsterdam, Notarieel Archief, 53/510 (8 October 1599) (hereafter cited as GAA, NA).

11. GAA, Doop, Trouw en Begraafboeken, 407/77 (10 September 1594) (hereafter cited as GAA, DTB).

12. GAA, DTB, 414/381 (29 September 1610); *Album Studiosorum Academiae Ludugno Bataviae Hague Comitum* (Leiden: Sijthoff, 1875), 85: 31 augustus 1606.

13. GAA, Kwijtscheldingen, 5062-12-89 (1599–1601); GAA, DTB, 408/112 (2 January 1597).

14. In 1608 he sent a report to Van Bijler from the court of Rudolph II in Prague, 1 March 1608, Amsterdam Scheepvaart museum, box BIII, 828 III, folder 16. See also *VRBM*, 44–45.

15. During Kiliaen's lifetime Amsterdam would become the third largest city of Europe; from 30,000 in 1586 it grew to 120,000 in 1632. For the expansion, economics, immigration, politics, culture, and religion in Amsterdam at that time, see Willem Frijhoff and Maarten Prak, eds., *Geschiedenis van Amsterdam, Centrum van de wereld, 1578–1650* (Amsterdam: SUN, 2004). For South-Netherlandish immigration, see Oscar Gelderblom, *Zuid-Nederlandse kooplieden en de opkomst van de Amsterdamse stapelmarkt (1578–1630)* (Hilversum: Verloren, 2000), 116–117, 264–265, 294–320. For the city's commerce at that time see also Cle Lesger, *Handel in Amsterdam ten tijde van de opstand. Kooplieden, commerciële expansie en verandering in de ruimtelijke economie van de Nederlanden ca. 1550–1630* (Hilversum: Verloren, 2001).

16. For the development of the arts in Amsterdam, see Boudewijn Bakker, "De zichtbare stad, 1578–1813," in *Geschiedenis van Amsterdam*, 17–101, especially 48–60, and Marijke Spies, "Kunsten op de troon. Culturele hoofdstad 1578–1713," in *Geschiedenis van Amsterdam*, 299–383, especially 311, 324; N. De Roever, "Een drietal brieven van Hendrick Goltzius," in *Oud Holland* (Amsterdam, 1888), 6, 140–153.

17. By 1600 some 62 master goldsmiths worked in the city, while 15 years before there were just 15. J. Briels, "Zuidnederlandse goud- en zilversmeden in Noord-Nederland omstreeks 1576–1625. Bijdrage tot de kennis van de Zuidnederlandse immigratie," in *Bijdragen tot de Geschiedenis* 54 (1971): 87–142.

18. According to De Roever, Kiliaen was doing business a few years later under the name Kiliaen van Rensselaer & Co, for which I have not been able to find the source. See *VRBM*, 45. In 1610 he kept a *schultboecxken* (small merchant's book, providing an overview of all debts and claims). GAA, NA, 747/281 (16 June 1622); Scheepvaartmuseum Amsterdam, Rensselaer handschriften, box BIII 828 III, folder 17 (28 February 1614).

19. Donald Haks, *Huwelijk en gezin in Holland in de 17de en 18de eeuw. Processtukken en moralisten over aspecten van het laat 17de- en 18de eeuwse gezinsleven* (Utrecht: Hes intgevers, 1985), 128–29; Simon Hart, "Onderzoek naar de samenstelling van de bevolking van Amsterdam in de 17de een 18de eeuw, op grond van gegevens over migratie, huwelijk, beroep en alfabetisme," in *Geschrift en getal. Een keuze uit de demografisch-, economisch- en sociaal-historische studiën opgrond van Amsterdamse en Zaanse archivalia, 1600–1800*, ed. Simon Hart (Dordrecht: Historische Vereninging, 1976).

20. Haks, *Huwelijk en gezin,* 106.

21. Ibid., 117.

22. Gertruit van Roen (Geertruyd de Roy/Rode), Jan van Bijler's second wife, was Hillegond's mother, and not his first wife, Hillegonda van Bijler, as is stated by Van Bijlert, W. A. van Bijlert, *Enkele genealogische bijzonderheden betreffende een in de zeventiende eeuw te Amsterdam en Dordrecht woonachtige familie Van Bijlaer (Later van Bijler en Van Bijlert)* (Rhenen: C. Waiboer, 1942), 6; GAA, DTB NK 38/661 (2 August 1598). NK is Nieuwe Kerk.

23. GAA, DTB 408/112 (2 January 1597); GAA, DTB, 413/344 (13 December 1608); ibid, 414/381 (29 September 1610).

24. The little research that has been done regarding this matter reveals that in 1750 two thirds of wealthy inhabitants of the town of Leiden appeared to have married within their own social position. Haks, *Huwelijk en gezin,* 106, 130.

25. By mentioning in the letter that he had worked for almost fourteen years instead of seven for Van Bijler, however, Kiliaen left open a possibility that Van Bijler may have contributed some money, while the share of the company to trade in jewelry was put in Kiliaen's name. In 1604 uncle Richard Pafraet had bought out the inheritance of Kiliaen and his sister at Hasselt for 534 Philips guilders, Westerhof and Mooijweer, *Tussen Hasselt en Amerika,* 50. A Philips guilder was worth about 2 guilders and 7 stuivers in 1603. With thanks to Arent Pol of the Koninklijk Penningkabinet/Geldmuseum, and after the death of his uncle, Captain Johannes van Rensselaer (his father's twin brother) in 1601, Kiliaen received a lifelong annual allowance of 100 pounds Flemish for his uncle's service between 1580 and 1595 (.B&MG IV, 7, aantek.2.).

26. In 1598 Jan van Bijler had been able to pay *f* 5,500 to the heirs of his first wife. Around 1600 he had bought a house in the Eggertstraat, Nieuwezijds Kerkhof, which Hillegond seems to have inherited. W. A. van Bijlert, *Enkele genealogische bijzonderheden,* 6; GAA, Kwijtscheldingen, 1599–1601; the house, east of the Nieuwe Kerk, where *de Roos* sign was hanging, was in 1643 noted for a value of *f* 7,000. Scheepvaart Museum Amsterdam, Rensselaer handschriften box BIII 828 III, doc. 48, *Beschrijving huysen en erven bij het sterffhuys Kiliaen van Rensselaer.*

27. Honor being one of the most important things in seventeenth-century society, both for an individual as for his or her family, it is not surprising that Kiliaen calls his sister, his closest relative, in that respect virtuous and peaceful and makes sure not to mention that in September 1605 she had given birth to her son Wouter van Twiller only a few months after her wedding with Rijckelt van Twiller, for which they registered 14 July 1605. Westerhof, *Tussen Hasselt en Amerika,* 45–48.

28. Haks, *Huwelijk en gezin,* 108, 132.

29. GAA, Oude Kerk 376/2, p. 155 (9 February, 1595); Oude Kerk 376/3 (3 February 1600).

30. Quoted in Haks, *Huwelijk en gezin,* 11.

31. Ibid.

32. In July 1615 the chamber of rhetoric *D'Eglentier* had performed *Moortje,* a play by Gerbrandt Adriaensz Brederode that ridiculed the amorous extravaganzas of wealthy young people. Around 1602 P. C. Hooft had become the leader of Amsterdam's chamber of rhetoric, *D'Eglentier;* his love tragedy *Theseus and Ariadne* was performed that year, and his play *Granida* about a platonic love story was very popular. Hooft's *Amoureus Liedtboeck* appeared in 1605 and his *Emblemata Amatoria, Afbeeldinghen van Minne, Emblemes d'Amour* in 1611. In 1612 Jan Pietersz Sweelinck, the organ player of the Oude Kerk, had added a collection of French love lyrics to his earlier published French songs and psalms.

33. Personal communication with Willem Frijhoff, 6 February 2008, and with Arjan van Dixhoorn, 12 and 18 February 2008. See also Willem Frijhoff, *Fulfilling God's mission. The Two Worlds of Dominie Everardus Bogardus, 1607–1647* (Leiden and Boston: Brill, 2007), 103, 103 n. 69, 168–69, and Arjan van Dixhoorn, *Lustige Geesten. Rederijkers en hun kamers in het publieke leven van deNederlanden in de vijftiende, zestiende en zeventiende eeuw* (PhD diss., Vrije Universiteit Amsterdam, 2004).

34. GAA, DTB, 763/48 (23 July 1616).

Family and Faction:
THE DUTCH ROOTS OF COLONIAL NEW YORK'S
FACTIONAL POLITICS

DAVID WILLIAM VOORHEES

On July 3, 1729, Elizabeth Rynders, the twenty-seven-year-old daughter of deceased New York City alderman, recorder, and justice of the peace Barent Rynders and his wife Hester Leisler, married wealthy merchant Nicholas Bayard, a son of Samuel Bayard and Margaretta Van Cortlandt, in the New York Reformed Protestant Dutch Church.[1] The union not only joined two young people with large fortunes, but it brought to a culmination a bitter family feud that had rent New York for three generations—its apogee being the infamous 1689 event commonly known as Leisler's Rebellion. Elizabeth was a granddaughter of Capt. Jacob Leisler, who had assumed the provincial administration of New York after a militia coup in the wake of England's 1688 Glorious Revolution.[2] The thirty-year-old Bayard was none other than grandson and heir to Leisler's chief adversary, Nicholas Bayard, and, on his maternal side, a grandson of Leisler's equally bitter enemy, Stephanus van Cortlandt.[3]

Considering that Bayard's grandfathers, Nicholas Bayard and Stephanus van Cortlandt, were the primary agents behind the 1691 beheading for treason of Elizabeth's grandfather, Jacob Leisler, and the subsequent persecution of her family, the marriage appears somewhat baffling. That Elizabeth's family had, after their restoration to political power in the late 1690s, similarly persecuted Bayard's family for another decade makes the marriage seem incomprehensible.[4] Conventional interpretations of New York's political factionalism during the pre-Revolutionary period have stressed class, ethnic, and religious tensions.[5] In a 1971 seminal revisionist work on colonial New York politics, *A Factious People*, Patricia Bonomi wrote, the "sharpest polarity was that between the landed and commercial interests" and that "this contest was at the heart of New York political rivalries in the early eighteenth century."[6] Sixty years earlier historian Carl Becker postulated that New York society consisted of a pyramid of three tiers, at the top of which was an aristocracy composed of great landlords and merchants, followed by independent freeholders and tradesmen, and, finally, disenfranchised tenants and mechanics. Becker argued that the aristocrats worked to maintain their self interest but were "so various [in] their backgrounds that they did not move together as one interest; families faced each other as Capulets and Montagues."[7] What all these theories fail to take into account, as the marriage of Elizabeth Rynders and Nicholas Bayard reveals to us, is the Dutch political culture within which New York's factions developed.

In the early Dutch Republic urban elites gained control of the governing councils of the towns, the *vroedschappen*, and, as a result, of the provincial states, such as the States of Holland and Zeeland, and, eventually, of the States General. Increasingly men gained access to public offices through family connections and cooption rather than through meritocracy and election.[8] In a study of the republic's oligarchic structure, Julia Adams notes that, as in "all patrimonial states, state officials had two concerns: securing the state that provided their offices, and maintaining the status and wealth of their families and lineages."[9] It has been shown, however, that the Dutch patriciate was not a closed group. Political control by one family was curtailed by limiting the *vroedschap* to one family member per term. To avoid this restriction, newly rich men were introduced through careful marital alliances. Through this tactic, elite families ensured and enhanced their wealth and power.[10] In the republic, however, the "private and public spheres were not rigidly separated," and faction often arose out of intrafamilial disputes and rivalries.[11] The West India Company directors transplanted intact into New Netherland not only the Old World Dutch legal forms and social structures but its political culture as well.[12] That the Dutch political legacy should long outlast actual Dutch rule in New Netherland becomes apparent when seen through the prism of the 1729 marriage of Elizabeth Rynders and Nicholas Bayard.

The legal and social forms that lay behind the development of New York's political culture were introduced into New Netherland at the very beginning of Dutch colonization. But family and faction would not appear until the population had increased to a point where a domestic oligarchy could develop and until conflicts within it superseded conflicts between colonists and the company's directors in the republic.[13] Elizabeth's and Nicholas's ancestors were part of this process. An example of the dawning of this change to the developing New Netherland oligarchy is found in an event that occurred during the administration of company director Willem Kieft. In the republic the public church and civic culture intertwined closely, and by 1642 New Amsterdam desperately needed a respectable church edifice.[14] The barn-like structure in which the Reformed congregation worshiped—the only doctrine allowed public expression—was rotting. Yet, the company directors refused to provide the funds necessary for a new building. At the June 1642 wedding of company surgeon Hans Kierstede and Sara Roelofse, stepdaughter of the congregation's pastor, Everardus Bogardus, who were also great-great uncle and aunt to both Elizabeth Rynders and Nicholas Bayard,[15] Kieft came up with a novel plan. He shrewdly told the wedding guests, "after the fourth or fifth round of drinking," how much he would contribute for the construction of a new church. "All then with light heads subscribed largely, competing with one another; and although some well repented when they recovered their senses, they were nonetheless compelled to pay—nothing could avail to prevent it."[16]

The subscription for the new building marked a turning point in New Amsterdam's civic consciousness. Kieft recognized that an appropriate church edifice heralded the civic maturity necessary to maintain Dutch corporate discipline. He thus tapped into the competitive vanity of New Amsterdam's newly emerging local social order. At the top of this community stood a small group of men whose familial and professional ties with European mercantile syndicates and West India Company officials gave them an edge in New Netherland's expanding commerce. What rooted them in North America, as we shall see, was a family of local women. Marital kinship through matrilineal alliances launched these men forward, as it did for the regent class in the Dutch Republic, and created the factional divisions that spurred New Netherland's, and later New York's, economic, political, and cultural development.

If New York has an Eve, she is Elizabeth Rynder's great-great grandmother, Tryn Jonas van Maesterland. From Tryn's womb came two daughters around whose offspring coalesced the core of New Netherland's nascent oligarchy. By the time of the American Revolution, virtually every member of New York's Anglo-Dutch elite claimed her as an ancestress. Although myth later maintained that she had wed an illegitimate son of William the Silent, liberator of Holland and Father of the Dutch Republic, in actuality Tryn was born in obscurity on the island of Marstrand (in Dutch, *Maesterland*), presently in Sweden but until 1658 part of Norway.[17] By 1633 she was living widowed in New Netherland with her daughter, Anneke, and son-in-law, Roelof Jansz, on *de Laets Burg* farm in the patroonship of Rensselaerswijck. The following year the family departed Rensselaerswijck to farm on Manhattan. Here, West India Company director Wouter van Twiller employed Tryn as New Amsterdam's midwife.[18] In the rudimentary medical conditions of New Netherland, with childbirth hazardous, Tryn attained as midwife a respectable status in the community.[19] Although she did not leave a substantial estate when she died in 1645, she left a legacy more valuable in a community scarce in females—two attractive, healthy, and fertile daughters.

Rome has its Romulus and Remus. New York City has its Anneke Jans and Marritje Jans. Like powerful magnets, Tryn's daughters and their offspring attracted into the family increasingly richer filings from all parts of the Atlantic world in a manner similar to the republic's regent class, which drew upon well-heeled marital connections throughout Europe.[20] After the death of her first husband, Anneke married New Amsterdam Domine Everardus Bogardus, originally from Woerden, Holland, but more recently minister at Elmina, Guinea (Ghana), West Africa. Marritje married successively company ship's carpenter Thymen Jansen from Monnickendam, Holland; land speculator Cornelis Dircksz from Wensveen, Holland; and, finally, merchant Govert Loockermans from Turnhout, Antwerp Province (Belgium), whose 52,702-guilder estate at the time of his death in 1671 made him New York's wealthiest merchant.[21] Corporate growth in the preindustrial world resulted from the merger of families whose capital and credit potential enhanced their members' economic prospects and extended their trade contacts into new regions. Family was the crux for individual economic advancement throughout early modern Europe. The career of Maritje's third husband, Govert Loockermans, reveals how marital ties aided this one particular family to rise to dominate the economic and political life of colonial New York.

Loockermans arrived in New Amsterdam in 1633 as a twenty-one-year-old cook's mate aboard the *St. Martyn*, which also brought West India Company director Van Twiller. Impressed by Loockermans, Van Twiller employed him as a company clerk. Loockermans remained in this capacity until 1639, when the company opened trade up to private individuals. In 1641 he became New Netherland agent for the Amsterdam firm of Gillis Verbrugge and married Verbrugge's widowed niece, Adriantje. Adriantje's previous husband, Jan van de Water, had been active with his brothers Isaack and Jacob in the Arctic trade. More important for American developments, the Van de Waters and Gillis Verbrugge were among the financial backers to a Swedish colony on the Delaware River promoted by disillusioned Dutch West India Company director Samuel Bloomart and led by former New Netherland director Peter Minuit. Jan van de Water, who subsequently disappeared at sea during a hurricane, captained the *Kalmar Nyckel*, lead ship of the two vessels the Swedish South Sea Company sent to the Delaware in 1637. In addition, Adriantje's sister, Hester, married Jacob van Couwenhoven, another prominent New Netherland merchant, while Govert's sister, Anna, married rapidly rising New Amsterdam merchant Oloff van Cortlandt.[22]

Loockermans's kinship ties provided him an edge in New Netherland's trade. Along with his brothers-in-law, he became a vocal proponent for the establishment of a municipal government in New Amsterdam.[23] The Company's 1653 grant of municipal privileges to the community opened up additional trade opportunities. In the dozen years thereafter, New Amsterdam's population tripled from a little more than 500 inhabitants to 1,500 residents, the size of a prosperous provincial European market town. Population increase and the city government's increasing administrative autonomy enhanced Loockermans' and his brothers-in-law's status, and they became part of the magisterial elite.[24]

Through marriage the network of siblings, cousins, and in-laws of Tryn Jonas's grandchildren—the generation of Elizabeth Rynders's and Nicholas Bayard's grandparents—developed an increasingly patrician oligarchy. In Dutch fashion carefully planned marriages brought good connections into the family while expanding the family's hold on offices.[25] The spouses of Anneke Jans's daughters, for example, included West India Company surgeon Hans Kierstede; wealthy merchant and New Netherland *fiscaal* Willem de Key; West India Company Curaçao director Lucas Rodenburg; Pieter Hartgers, brother of noted Amsterdam bookseller and printer Joost Hartgers; and Johannes Pietersz Verbrugge, or Van Brugh, a member of the elite Amsterdam mercantile house of Verbrugge. The spouses of Anneke Jans's sons included daughters of New Netherland councilor Nicasius de Sille and Beverwijck merchant Willem Teller. Marritje Jans's daughter, Elsie, married first senior company ship's carpenter Pieter Cornelisz van der Veen, then well-connected German-born merchant Jacob Leisler, while Marritje's son, Cornelis, married a daughter of New Amsterdam bread inspector Hendrick Willemsz. Her stepdaughters, Marritje Loockermans, married Balthazar Bayard, nephew of company director-general Petrus Stuyvesant, and Jannetje Loockermans married her cousin Hans Kierstede, son of Hans Kierstede and Sara Roelofse.[26]

By the late 1680s thirteen of the twenty-two New York City militia officers, nearly all of the city's Dutch Reformed Church officers, and many of the city's officials were related by blood, or through marriage of a relative, to a descendant of Anneke or Marritje Jans.[27] Studies of town councils in the Dutch Republic, such as of Leiden and Alkmaar, reveal that marital unions allowed members of the same elite families to sit simultaneously on the councils of, and hold offices in, various communities.[28] As in the Netherlands, where the arranged marriages of females were frequently used to consolidate political control, New York City's elite formed marital alliances with the emerging elite of other provincial communities as their social structures matured, most notably with Albany. Through such alliances, the extended de facto matrilineal familial network of the descendants of Anneke and Marritje Jans included by the late 1680s such prominent Albanian families as Cuyler, Schuyler, Staats, Van Rensselaer, Van Schaick, and Wendell.[29] Moreover, in Dutch fashion, in which the matricentric network played a greater role than in other western European cultures, New York's elite used the marriages of daughters to enhance their family's position in the emerging English mercantile world. This trend is evidenced by the marriages of Jacob Leisler's daughters: in 1685 Leisler's daughter Catharina wed Robert Walter of Plymouth, England, whose brothers were prominent merchants on the island of Jamaica; two years later daughter Susannah married Michael Vaughton of Staffordshire, England, whose half-brother, John Spragg, was English secretary of the province of New York; and in 1691 Mary Leisler married the widower Jacob Milborne, a London-born merchant, whose brothers were eminent in Bermuda.[30]

Under English rule, the familial unity that had propelled New Netherland's leading merchants forward began to fracture. At root was the competitive spirit that Kieft had so craftily manipulated in 1642. As the first generation passed, the division of their estates now became a bone of contention. The conflict between Dutch inheritance law, which favored equal division among male and female children, and English inheritance law, which applied primogeniture or descent to the eldest son or, in the absence of sons, in order of seniority in the collateral line aggravated dissension. Disputes over the Van Rensselaer, Loockermans, Delavall, and Steenwijck estates are the better known of these suits.[31] By the late 1680s the contesting male and female heirs in the various estate suits and their supporters were coalescing into two distinct camps. A foretaste of an emerging political struggle may be seen in the battle over the estate of former New Amsterdam burgomaster Cornelis Steenwijck. Steenwijck's children had predeceased him by the time of his death in 1684, and his widow, Margareta De Riemer, subsequently married New York City domine Henricus Selijns in 1686. Steenwijck's half-brother and half-sister, Jacob and Anna Mauritz, contested Margareta's and Selijns's claim to Steenwijck's estate. Drawn into the fray on Selijns's side were Bayards, Van Cortlandts, and De Keys, while Gouverneurs, Staatses, and Provoosts sided with the Mauritzes. The dispute eventually escalated into riots by supporters of the parties.[32]

Estates were not merely a possession, Julia Adams notes of the early modern Netherlands, but "functioned as lineage property as well as a kind of property in politics." And issues over what was passed down could result in "explosive" conflicts within families.[33] Contestants in New York's disputes, as in the Netherlands, courted official favor and public opinion to support competing claims. Faction arose as a method to promote particular interests. "In the political world of the Republic in the seventeenth century," historian J. L. Price writes, "access to power was through family and faction rather than party." But, he cautions, "faction was not the rival of party but part of its structure, and family and faction could and often did embody ideological values and aims."[34] To legitimate faction, theological doctrine was used to bolster ideological claims.[35] "Regent families tended to be the carriers of political traditions, factions were made up of alliances of families, and ideological sympathies were an important element in bringing families together. In this way factions could take on a political colour and begin, alone or with allied factions, to act as parties."[36] Politics and doctrine intertwined in New York as its elite, as elites in the Netherlands did, turned to theology as an ideological glue.

In the seventeenth century the Dutch body politic split into factions between the supporters of the fiscal office of *raadpensionaris*, loosely identified as the *Staatspartij*, and Orangists, supporters of the office of stadholder, or provincial military commander in chief, traditionally held by a prince of Orange.[37] At the beginning of the century *Staatspartij* and Orangists took opposing sides in the Arminian controversy over whether or not one could affect his or her own salvation.[38] Doctrinal conflict revived in midcentury between the followers of Utrecht University professor Gisbertus Voetius (1589–1676), a strict Calvinist who stressed moral precision and the need for a personal conversion to Christ, and the followers of the more liberal covenant theology of Leiden University professor Johannes Cocceius (1603–1669). In this dispute, Orangists allied with the Voetians, while the *Staatspartij* allied with the Cocceians. The factionalism came to a violent head when a devastating French invasion in 1672 resulted in a backlash against the *Staatspartij*'s policies of appeasing Louis XIV and Cocceian liberalism. Mobs forced numerous towns to replace their magistrates with Orangists; murdered the chief architects of *Staatspartij* policy, the De Witts; and forced the provinces of Holland and Zeeland to restore the stadholdership, which had been revoked in 1650, to William III, Prince of Orange.[39] These events had a direct bearing on New York's affairs.

The West India Company had established Reformed doctrine as formulated at the 1618-1619 Synod of Dordrecht as New Netherland's public church.[40] In New Netherland, as in the republic, "membership to the Dutch Reformed church was an important criterium for regents."[41] New Netherland, however, only palely echoed the conflicts within the republic's churches due to the sparse population and the scarcity of clergy. Not until the final quarter of the seventeenth century, when there was an explosive growth of congregations needing an ordained ministry, did doctrinal disputes begin to color New York's politics.[42] After 1677, in the wake of changes within the Amsterdam Classis, which oversaw the Reformed churches in New York and New Jersey, the Classis took a more pragmatic approach to the appointment of its North American domines. Seeking to preserve the Church's privileged position in provinces under English rule, the Classis began to send ministers whose progressive views would be more acceptable to their non-Calvinist English administrators.[43] This policy eventually brought these domines into direct conflict with the bulk of New York and New Jersey's more conservative Reformed communicants.

When royal authority collapsed in New York in the wake of England's 1688 Glorious Revolution, which saw Dutch stadholder William III replace the Roman Catholic James II on England's throne, the quarreling family factions openly vied for provincial control. In June 1689 Jacob Leisler, who had been battling his Bayard, Kierstede, and Van Cortlandt in-laws over the Loockermans's estate for nearly two decades, emerged as the Orangist leader. The political alignments between Leisler's supporters and their opponents in 1689 followed the alignments already evident in the above-mentioned estate suits. In 1690 Nicholas Bayard named the "principal authors of our principal miseries" as being Leisler, Jacob Milborne, Samuel Edsall, George Beekman, Peter Delanoy, Samuel Staats, Thomas Williams, Jonathan Couwenhoven, Benjamin Blagge, Hendrick Jansen, and Hendrick Cuyler.[44] Each of these men either was a litigant in or was related by marriage to a party involved in the estate feuds.[45]

Hendrick Cuyler serves as an example. Cuyler is credited with touching off the May 1689 militia uprising against King James II's government when, after a confrontation with New York's royal lieutenant governor, Francis Nicholson, he reported that Nicholson had declared he "would set the town on fire."[46] Cuyler was related to the Loockermans and Verbrugge families.[47] In 1688 his daughter, Sarah, married Peter van Brugh, son of Johannes van Brugh and Catrijntje Roelofse, daughter of Anneke Jans and first cousin of Elsie Leisler. In March 1689 Van Brugh's sister, Catharine, married Henrick van Rensselaer, son of Jeremias van Rensselaer and Maria van Cortlandt, daughter of Oloff van Cortlandt and niece of Elsie Leisler's stepfather. Maria was at this time in dispute with Robert Livingston and the Schuyler family over the Van Rensselaer estate. Moreover, Cuyler's wife, Annetje Schepmoes, had been raised after her father's 1656 death under the guardianship of Pieter Cornelisz van der Veen, Elsie Leisler's first husband.[48]

Following the lead of Orangists in the republic's 1672 uprisings, Leisler's faction increasingly acquired a confessional cast. Nicholas Bayard complained, "they have exercised their Jurisdiction not only in the Civill and Military, but alsoo in the Ecclesiastical affairs[,] prescribing to the severall churches rules and ordinances and enjoyned them by threatenings to be obedient thereunto."[49] Through charges of "papism," Leisler's faction sought to destroy their opponent's lineage claims, as they broadened their activities to secure the "true Protestants religion" against, as they noted, "false Protestants" and "false Priests of Baal."[50] "This arbitrary proud person Leysler, exalted himself above his brethren [and] disdains to own his very kindred unless they will entitle him Lieutenant Governor," Bayard wrote of his in-law in 1690, "nor will he free them from his Bullet-hole on any other terms."[51] Both factions manipulated public opinion to support their actions while accusing their familial opponents of doing the same. Faction in New York, as it did in the republic, became a manner to define and promote lineage interests within the elite, which now coalesced around two branches of a single kinship network: the relations of the deceased Anneke and Marritje Jans and the relations of Marritje's deceased third husband, Govert Loockermans. Faction energized society on their behalf, and ideology became faction's subsequent legitimation.[52]

The intrafamilial violence reached an operatic crescendo in spring 1691. When King William III's royal governor Henry Sloughter arrived, Leisler's in-laws rushed to greet the new governor with their version of events. Sloughter threw the Leislerian leadership into jail and attainted their estates on charges of treason. On May 16, 1691, Leisler and Jacob Milborne, who had become Leisler's son-in-law three months earlier, were executed by beheading. For a decade Milborne had been in litigation with Robert Livingston over the Thomas Delavall estate. Spying Livingston in the crowd from the scaffold, Milborne cried out, "you have caused the King [that] I must now die, but before gods tribunal I will implead you for the same."[53]

With Leisler's and Milborne's executions, Leisler's in-laws and their faction now seized control over the disputed estates. Modern historians have tended to see the political struggle between the two factions on the basis of wealth—greater merchants versus lesser merchants—using as an indicator of the disparities the wealth of the anti-Leislerians compared to the attainted Leislerians during the post-1691 period.[54] But they have failed to note the pre-1689 competing intrafamilial estate claims. Lobbying efforts by Leisler's son, Jacob Jr., and Abraham Gouverneur, Jacob Mauritz, Benjamin Blagge, and Kiliaen van Rensselaer before the English crown resulted in Parliament's nullifying the treason sentence against Leisler's party in 1695. With their properties restored, the Leislerians sought revenge against their relations. In the republic, patricians viewed themselves as heirs to the traditions of the republics of Florence and Venice, and, ultimately, of ancient Rome. New York's elite undoubtedly saw themselves within this Dutch context. In a self-conscious nod to similar disputes that rent the Florentine republic of the Medicis, New York's political factions, eighteenth-century commentator Pierre Du Simitiere noted, styled themselves "whites" [Bayard's faction] and "blacks" [Leisler's faction].[55]

Although the factionalism spawned by the elite's intrafamilial feud continued to rend New York's politics, the same centrifugal forces that created New York's oligarchy caused the combative family branches to close ranks. This trend also followed the pattern of elites in the Netherlands, where the patriciate "devised broad interelite pacts, deals, or settlements" to maintain their patrimonial control.[56] To resolve the estate suits and ensure lineages, the easiest method, of course, was for the contesting heirs to intermarry. As early as the 1690s cousins from the feuding family factions began to wed. The 1729 marriage of Elizabeth Rynders with Nicholas Bayard the Younger is, perhaps, the most dramatic of these unions. Elizabeth, however, was not the first of Leisler's granddaughters to intermarry with the opposition. On May 17, 1724, Jakoba, daughter of Francina Leisler, married her third cousin, Jesse Kierstede, son of the fanatically anti-Leislerian Lucas Kierstede.[57]

By the early eighteenth century, and despite a half century of English rule, New York's elite continued to reflect the patrician trends of the Dutch Republic. In the republic, in a period known as the Age of Periwigs (*Pruikentijd*), urban elites developed into "a closed patrician oligarchy, with a characteristic life-style of their own."[58] In contrast to elite formation in other European states, Dutch regents and New Yorkers "began to emphasize inherited genealogies of privilege rather than either mercantile prowess or strict aristocracy of blood."[59] In similar fashion Elizabeth's and Nicholas's network of siblings, cousins, and aunts and uncles formed an increasingly closed group that dominated provincial offices. Elizabeth's uncle Robert Walter was a member of the councils of governors Bellomont, Hunter, and Burnet, a Supreme Court justice, and mayor of New York City from 1720 to 1723, and her uncle Abraham Gouverneur was New York City recorder in 1700–1701, speaker of the Provincial Assembly in 1701–1702, and a political intellectual.[60] Her sister Johanna married David Provoost, son of David Provoost, mayor of New York in 1699 and New York councilor in 1708–1711.[61] Her sister Gertruyt married first her cousin Nicholas Gouverneur and, after his death, New Jersey justice David William Provoost.[62] Nicholas Bayard's sister, Judith, married Rip Van Dam, member of the governors' councils from 1702 to 1735 and acting governor of the Province of New York in 1731–1732. His brother, Stephanus, married Alida Vetch, daughter of Samuel Vetch, governor of Nova Scotia, and Margaret Livingston, a daughter of Robert Livingston and Alida Schuyler.[63]

The marriages of Elizabeth's aunt Francina demonstrate how the Leisler branch of the family maintained its status after 1691 through advantageous marital alliances within their kinship network. In 1694 Francina, daughter of Jacob Leisler and Elsie Tymens, married Thomas Lewis Jr., son of Thomas Lewis and Geesje Barents.[64] The elder Lewis, born in Belfast, Ireland, had emerged as one of New York's wealthiest merchants in partnership with Frederick Philipse.[65] After the untimely 1694 death of Thomas, Francina married in 1711 Jochem Staats, brother of Samuel Staats, a member of her father's council from 1689 to 1691. Samuel's daughter, Trintje, would in 1723 marry Lewis Morris Jr., leader of the opposition to Gov. William Cosby. Staats's sister Sarah, who died in 1683, had wed Johannes Provoost, also a member of Leisler's Council in 1690–1691, at which time he was married to his third wife, Anna Mauritz, half-sister of Cornelis Steenwijck and widow of Domine Wilhelmus van Nieuwenhuysen.[66] Jochem Staats, meanwhile, had previously been married to Antje Reyndertse, sister of Francina's brother-in-law Barent Rynders. Hence, Francina and Jochem were sister- and brother-in-law at the time of their marriage. Francina Leisler Staats died in New York City on September 13, 1728, leaving a considerable estate in New York City properties and eight household slaves.[67]

The marriages of Elizabeth's cousin Maria, daughter of Robert Walter and Catharina Leisler, provides another example of the family's marital pattern. In 1724 Maria married Arent Schuyler, son of Philip Pietersz Schuyler and Margaretta van Slechtenhorst of Albany. Schuyler had previously married in 1684 Anneke Teller, daughter of Willem Teller, who was one of Albany's wealthiest merchants and brother-in-law of Jacob Leisler, and Maria Dochesen (according to tradition an aunt of Robert Livingston), and second, in 1702, Swantje van Dyckhuysen.[68] The Schuylers formed in 1689 the leadership core of the anti-Leislerian branch of the family—Arent's sister Gertrude having married Elsie Leisler's cousin Stephanus van Cortlandt and sister Alida having married Robert Livingston. Initially, Arent opposed Leisler, but for unknown reasons he switched allegiances in 1690, for which change Leisler awarded him with several militia commissions. Schuyler owned extensive properties in New York and New Jersey, including land at Belleville, New Barbadoes Neck, New Jersey, where, in partnership with Maria's brother, John, he successfully operated a lucrative copper mine.[69]

After the death of Arent Schuyler in 1730, Maria Walter, following the Dutch practice of female unions outside the kinship network when it enhanced the family's status, married in 1736 Archibald Kennedy, receiver general of New York.[70] Kennedy, who was born in Kilhenzie, Scotland, served as receiver general of the province of New York from 1722 to 1754 and as collector of the Port of New York from 1758 to 1762. Upon Gov. William Burnet's recommendation, Kennedy was appointed to the New York Council in 1727, on which body he served until 1761. Kennedy's son by a previous marriage, Archibald Jr., later the earl of Casselis, married in 1764 Catharine Schuyler, daughter of Maria's niece and nephew, Hester Walter and Peter Schuyler. Through this marriage, according to Cadwallader Colden, the younger Kennedy "possessed more houses in New York than any other man."[71]

The Dutch oligarchic pattern becomes clearer through some lesser-known New York kinship alliances. Susannah, daughter of Jacob Leisler, for example, married for her second husband wealthy landowner Leendert Huygens de Kleyn, widower of Magdalena Wolsum, widow of Susannah's half-brother, Cornelis.[72] Jacob Walter, son of Robert Walter and Catharina Leisler, married Elizabeth Oliver, granddaughter of Arent Schuyler by his first wife.[73] Jacob's sister, Sara, wed Arent's son Johannes by his second wife.[74] Their sister, Elizabeth, married Albany quartermaster for the troop Johannes Wendell the Younger, son of the sister-in-law of their aunt Francina.[75] Another cousin, Elizabeth Stevens, daughter of Margarita van der Veen, married official pilot for the port of New York Jacobus Mauritz, son of Jacob Mauritz and Margareta van der Grift.[76] As noted above, Jacob's grandfather was New Amsterdam burgomaster Paulus Leendertsen van der Grift; his uncle was Cornelis Steenwijck, and his aunt, Anna, married first Domine Wilhelmus van Nieuwenhuysen and second Johannes Provoost. And, as a final example, their cousin, Michael Vaughton the Younger, son of Michael Vaughton and Susannah Leisler, married Catharine Donaldson, daughter of John Donaldson, political leader of Pennsylvania's Lower Counties, and Elizabeth Rodenburg, widow of Ephraim Hermans and daughter of Curaçao Vice-Director Lucas Rodenburg. Catharine's mother was Elsie Leisler's first cousin.[77]

When male and female marital alliances are considered, it becomes apparent that a core elite of about two dozen interrelated families dominated eighteenth-century New York. These families included Bayards, Beekmans, Couwenhovens, Cuylers, De Keys, Delanceys, Gouverneurs, Kips, Livingstons, Morrises, Philipses, Provoosts, Schuylers, Staatses, Stuyvesants, Ten Broeks, Van Cortlandts, Van Brughs, Van Rennselaers, Van Schaicks, Walters, and Wendells. All were descendants of Tryn Jonas.[78] Female marriages outside of this kinship network continued, in Dutch fashion, for the enhancement of the family's economic prospects. Robert Walters and Catharina Leisler's daughters, Catharina and Jacoba, for example, married respectively wealthy merchants from Surinam and Jamaica.[79] Elizabeth Rynder's cousin Margriet Stevens, daughter of Jacob Leisler's stepdaughter Margarita, wed a stepson of the governor of Antigua.[80] Margriet's daughter, Elizabeth, married a son of Ulster County sheriff Thomas Noxon.[81] Firth Fabend's study of middling families in rural New York and New Jersey revealed that they, too, followed the marrying patterns of their social betters, consolidating, she writes, "already established marital connections, exchanging siblings in marriage, setting the stage for ever more inter-allied marriages to come, and maintaining for generations their families' grip on political and church offices."[82]

Through advantageous unions, estates were secured and a family's wealth and status preserved for its lineage. New York's political factionalism was, as in the Netherlands, an element of this process. After all, the leaders of court and country or landed and commercial parties emerged out of this core kinship group. Elite allegiances fluctuated. A well-known example is the fluidity of Robert Livingston's loyalties.[83] Another case in point is Jacob Leisler Jr.'s 1712 negotiation of a deal with the formerly anti-Leislerian Lewis Morris, in which Leisler threw his political influence behind Morris in exchange for an Assembly act reimbursing the Leisler family 2,700 pounds sterling, a deal that was later sealed with Morris's son's marriage to Trintje Staats, niece of Jacob Leisler Jr.'s sister Francina.[84] Through the mechanism of contending factions and interelite pacts and deals, New York's elite was able, as the republic's patriciate did, to navigate and retain its privileged position in a constantly changing world of British imperial policies and patronage.

This essay opened with the seemingly incomprehensible marriage between members of two of New York's most famous bitterly feuding families, Leisler and Bayard. It is fitting that the essay ends with the fate of this couple's offspring. Elizabeth Rynders and Nicholas Bayard's daughter Hester married John Van Cortlandt, son of Stephen Van Cortlandt and Catharina Staats and a grandson of Jacobus van Cortlandt. On November 7, 1775, Van Cortlandt was elected New York City and County delegate to the Provincial Congress and served as a delegate to the Second, Third, and Fourth Provincial Congresses in 1775, 1776, and 1777. Elizabeth and Nicholas's son Nicholas served as a member of the New York Assembly in 1787–88. He married in 1762 Catharine Livingston, a daughter of Peter van Brugh Livingston and Mary Alexander, daughter of famed lawyer and surveyor James Alexander. And daughter Judith married Jeremiah Van Rensselaer, son of Johannes Van Rensselaer and Engeltie Livingston. Judith and Jeremiah's son, Johannes, inherited the East Manor estates of Greenbush with the Crailo mansion.[85] The patrimonies of Jacob Leisler's and Nicholas Bayard's lineages were indeed secured.

The oligarchy that began to solidify in mid-seventeenth-century New Netherland dominated New York politics and society for two centuries. Yet, by the mid-eighteenth century the mercantile oligarchy based in the towns was transforming itself into a "landed gentry." Even in this process New York's elite mimicked the patriciate of the republic, where in the late seventeenth century there was a "growing transformation from merchant-administrators to administrator-rentiers."[86] Following the lead of Holland's patriciate, New York's patriciate refocused their capital resources on financing and real-estate development and on industrial development—that is, mining, logging, and farming—of their lands. As Holland's urban elite had, they erected handsome manor houses on their estates, dabbled in the theories of the French and Scottish enlightenments, and maintained a distinctive Calvinist republican lifestyle that set them apart, but not too far apart, from the general population. This lifestyle they successfully retained until the Industrial Revolution, when it was swept away in the "palace revolution" so eloquently described in the novels of Edith Wharton.

Patricia Bonomi noted that "we hear much of 'Patroons' and 'Manor Lords,' of Livingstons, Van Cortlandts, and Van Rensselaers, and have often been encouraged to think of these landed grandees as comprising a sort of neo-feudal aristocracy which imposed both economic and political restraints upon a numerous tenantry." Yet, she provokingly asks, "did this 'aristocracy' differ from that of England, after which it was supposedly modeled?"[87] New York's oligarchy did differ, not because it was modeled after England's aristocracy but rather on Holland's republican patriciate. The Dutch influences in the development of modern America are numerous, but perhaps the most enduring legacy of New Netherland's Dutch is "this habitual factionalism, this politics for its own sake," as Bonomi writes, that "laid the foundation of experience upon which such future architects of party organization as Martin Van Buren would eventually build."[88]

Notes

1. Samuel S. Purple, ed., *Marriages from 1639 to 1801 in the Reformed Dutch Church, New York* (New York: privately printed, 1890), 149 (hereafter cited as *NYGB Marriages*). Bayard brought into the union large tracts of Manhattan land, including Bayard's Farm, containing Smith's Hill, and land originally granted by the Dutch West India Company to "the Company negroes," as well as numerous city properties. I. N. Phelps Stokes, *Iconography of Manhattan, 1498–1909*, 6 vols. (New York: Robert H. Dodd, 1915–1928), 6:70–76. Elizabeth brought an equally large dowry in properties. Her father, Barent Rynders, was at the time of his death in 1726 counted among New York City's wealthiest merchants. Rynders's will, dated February 5, 1725, proved on January, 25, 1726/7, named his wife, daughters Hester and Elizabeth, and son-in-law David Provoost as executors. Wills Liber 10: 241–251, New York State Archives, Albany.

2. Hester, daughter of Jacob Leisler and Elsie Tymens, married Barent Rynders on March 10, 1695/6. Edwin R. Purple, *Genealogical Notes Relating to Lieutenant-Governor Jacob Leisler and His Family Connections in New York* (New York: privately printed, 1877), 14.

3. Edwin R. Purple, "Contributions to the History of the Ancient Families of New York: Varleth," *New York Genealogical and Biographical Record* 12 (January 1879): 35–37 (hereafter cited as *NYGB Record*); Joseph Gaston Baillie Bulloch, *A History and Genealogy of the Families of Bayard, Houstoun of Georgia, and the Descent of the Bolton Family from the Families of Assheton, Byron and Hulton of Hulton Park* (Washington, D.C.: James H. Dony, 1919), 13–14.

4. Adrian Howe, "The Bayard Treason Trial: Dramatizing Anglo-Dutch Politics in Early Eighteenth-Century New York City," *The William and Mary Quarterly*, 3rd ser., vol. 47, no. 1 (January 1990): 57–89.

5. A few such works are Randall Balmer, *A Perfect Babel of Confusion: Dutch Religion and English Culture in the Middle Colonies* (New York: Oxford University Press, 1989); Sung Bok Kim, *Landlord and Tenant in Colonial New York: Manorial Society, 1664–1775* (Chapel Hill: University of North Carolina Press, 1978); Donna Merwick, "Being Dutch: An Interpretation of Why Jacob Leisler Died," *New York History* 70 (1989): 397–399; Robert C. Ritchie, *The Duke's Province: A Study of New York Politics and Society, 1664–1691* (Chapel Hill: University of North Carolina Press, 1977).

6. Patricia U. Bonomi, *A Factious People: Politics and Society in Colonial New York* (New York and London: Columbia University Press, 1971), 59.

7. Dixon Ryan Fox, *The Decline of the Aristocracy in the Politics of New York, 1801–1840*, ed. Robert V. Remini (New York: Harper and Row, 1965), xxiii.

8. Henk van Nierop, "Popular participation in politics in the Dutch Republic," in *Resistance, Representation and Community*, ed. Peter Blickle (Oxford and New York: Oxford University Press, 1997), 272–279.

9. Julia Adams, "The familial state: Elite family practices and state-making in the early modern Netherlands," *Theory and Society* 23, no. 4 (August 1994), 505.

10. M. van der Bijl, "Familie en factie in de Alkmaarse stedelijke politiek," in *Van Spaans beleg tot Bataafse tijd. Alkmaars stedelijk leven in de 17de en 18de eeuw*, ed. E. H. P. Cordfunke (Zutphen: De Walburg Pers, 1980), 13–32; L. Kooijmans, "Vriendschap, een 18e-eeuwse familiegeschiedenis," *Tijdschrift voor Sociale Geschiedenis* 18, no. 1 (1992): 48–65.

11. Henk van Nierop, "Private Interests, Public Policies: Petitions in the Dutch Republic," in *The Public and Private in Dutch Culture of the Golden Age*, ed. Arthur K. Wheelock and Adele F. Seeff (London and Newark, Del.: University of Delaware Press, 2000), 34.

12. Martha Dickinson Shattuck, "A Civil Society: Court and Community in Beverwijck, New Netherland, 1652–1664" (Ph. D. dissertation, Boston University, 1993).

13. For a discussion of the development of oligarchies in New York, see Alice P. Kenney, *The Gansevoorts of Albany: Dutch Patricians in the Upper Hudson Valley* (Syracuse: Syracuse University Press, 1969), particularly the introduction.

14. J. L. Price, *Dutch Society, 1588–1713* (Harlow, England, and New York: Longman, 2000), 129–130.

15. Sara Roelofse was first cousin of Elizabeth's grandmother, Elsie Tymens. Blandina, daughter of Hans Kierstede and Sara Roelofse, married Petrus Bayard, brother of Nicholas's grandfather. For the complex familial connections between Rynders and Bayard, see William Brower Bogardus, *Dear "Cousin": A Chartered Genealogy of the Descendants of Anneke Jans Bogardus (1605–1663) to the 5th Generation—and of her sister, Marritje Jans* (Wilmington, Ohio: Anneke Jans and Everardus Bogardus Descendants Association, 1996), Charts 1, 2, 2-E, 10-H, 10-I.

16. J. Franklin Jameson, ed., *Narratives of New Netherland, 1609–1664* (New York: Charles Scribner's Sons, 1909), 326.

17. It is possible that this myth was first circulated by John Jay after his marriage to Sarah Van Brugh Livingston, Jay being descended from the Loockermans family and Sarah from the Van Brughs. John Reynolds Totten, "Anneke Jans (1607-8?–1663) and her two Husbands, Roelof Jans (or Jansen) and Rev. (Domine) Everardus Bogardus and their Descendants to the third Generation Inclusive," *NYGB Record* 56 (July 1925): 202–203; George Olin Zabriskie, "Anneke Jans in Fact and Fiction," *NYGB Record* 104 (April 1973): 9–10. For a discussion of this myth, see Willem Frijhoff, *Wegen van Evert Willemsz.: Een Hollands weeskind op zoek naar zichzelf, 1607–1647* (Nijmegen: SUN, 1995), 843–846, and Bogardus, 32.

18. Upon marrying an unknown seaman, Tryn moved to Amsterdam, where her children were born. For her early life, see Frijhoff, 611. Kiliaen van Rensselaer employed Roelof Jansz in early 1630 to farm at Rensselaerswijck at ƒ180 per year. Jansz left Texel with Anneke and their two daughters aboard *de Eendracht* on March 21, 1630, and arrived at New Amsterdam on May 24, 1630. A. J. F. van Laer, *Van Rensselaer Bowier Manuscripts: Being the Letters of Kiliaen van Rensselaer, 1630–1643, and Other Documents Relating to the Colony of Rensselaerswyck* (Albany: University of the State of New York, 1908), 57, 63, 202–203, 806. The reasons for the family's removal to Manhattan are unknown. Zabriskie, 1–2.

19. Recent studies of midwifery in the Dutch Republic reveal that midwives enjoyed a "relatively privileged position within the common labouring class." See E. Van der Borg, "Sages-femmes aux Pays-Bas: image et occupation. Les développements dans la pratique de l'obstétrique à Leyde, Arnhem, Bois-le-Duc, et Leeuwarden, 1650–1865," *Histoire des sciences médicales* 28, no. 1 (1994): 57–62.

20. For Dutch patrician marital alliances outside of the Netherlands, see, for example, family entries in Johann E. Elias, *De Vroedschap van Amsterdam, 1578–1795, met een inleiding woord van den archieven der stad Amsterdam, Mr. W. R. Veder*, 2 vols. (Haarlem: V. Loosjes, 1903–1905).

21. Bogardus, Chart No. 1; Frijhoff, 843–846.

22. David M. Riker, "Govert Loockermans, Free Merchant of New Amsterdam," *de Halve Maen* 54 (June 1989): 4–10; Rosalie Fellows Bailey, "Jan Hendricksz van de Water, Skipper of Minuit's ship founding the New Sweden Company, and His Family in the Netherlands," *NYGB Record* 100 (July 1969): 129–140, (October 1969): 225–234. Jacob van Couwenhoven was born in Amersfoort, Utrecht, Netherlands, son of Wolphert Gerretsz van Kouwenhoven, one of five "head farmers" sent by the Dutch West India Company to New Netherland in 1625. Van Cortlandt came from Wijck bij Duurstede, Holland, and had arrived in New Amsterdam aboard the *Haring* in 1637 as a soldier in the West India Company's service.

23. John Romeyn Brodhead, *History of the State of New York*, 2 vols. (New York: Harper and Brothers, 1871), 505.

24. Jaap Jacobs, *New Netherland: A Dutch Colony in Seventeenth-Century America* (Leiden and Boston: Brill, 2005), 345–46.

25. Julia Adams, *The Familial State: Ruling Families and Merchant Capitalism in Early Modern Europe* (Ithaca: Cornell University Press, 2005), 88–89.

26. Bogardus, Charts 2 and 10; Samuel S. Purple, 15–20.

27. Related New York City militia officers were Colonel Nicholas Bayard; Majors Nicholas Demeyer and Abraham de Peyster; Captains Jacob Leisler and Nicholas Stuyvesant; Lieutenants Hendrick Cuyler, Hans Kierstede, and Isaac van Vleck, Cornet Jacobus van Cortlandt; Ensigns Samuel Bayard, Arent Cornelissen, Johannes de Peyster, and Isaac de Riemer. *Collections of the New-York Historical Society*, 76 vols. (New York, 1868–1943), 13: 397–401. Henricus Selijns, Records of the Reformed Dutch Church of New York City, List of Ministers, Elders, and Deacons (ms. photocopy, Holland Society of New York Library, New York City). "Alphabetical List of Members of the Common Council, etc.," *Manual of the Corporation of the City of New York for 1870*, ed. John Hardy (New York: New York Common Council, 1870), 609–662.

28. M. van der Bijl; Kooijmans, 48–65.

29. Bogardus, Charts 2, 2A, 2K.

30. Catharina married Robert Walter on February 4, 1685, *NYGB Marriages*, 56. Susannah's marriage license to Michael Vaughton is dated June 24, 1687, *NYGB Record* 5: 174. *Gray's Inn Admission Register 1521–1887*, page 336, reads: "1685 July 15 JOHN SPRAGGE, late of Uttoxeter, Co. Stafford, now of New York, America, Secretary to the Governor there. Esq.," *NYGB Record* 2: 26; David William Voorhees, "'Fanatiks' and 'Fifth Monarchists': The Milborne Family in the Seventeenth Century Atlantic World" *NYGB Record* 129 (April 1998), 2:67–75 (July 1998), 3:174–82.

31. For the Van Rensselaer estate, see Samuel G. Nissenson, *The Patroon's Domain* (New York: Columbia University Press, 1937), 340–343, and Lawrence H. Leder, "The Unorthodox Domine: Nicholas Van Rensselaer," *New York History* 35 (April 1954): 173–174. For the Delavall estate, see James Riker, *Revised History of Harlem (City of New York), Its Origin and Early Annals* (New York: New Harlem Publishing Co., 1904), 378, 809–810. For the Loockermans estate feud, see Firth Haring Fabend, "'According to Holland Custome': Jacob Leisler and the Loockermans Estate Feud," *de Halve Maen* 67 (Spring 1994): 1–8.

32. For Steenwijck's will, see *Collections of the New-York Historical Society* 26 (New York, 1893), 414–415. To complicate matters, Margareta de Riemer's mother, Elizabeth Gravenraet, widow of New Netherland Domine Samuel Drisius, also died in 1684, naming as her universal heirs daughters Margareta and Machtelt, the widow of her son Nicholas Gouverneur, her son Peter de Riemer, and grandchildren Isaac and Elizabeth de Riemer; ibid., 387–388. Anna Mauritz, widow of Domine Wilhelmus van Nieuwenhuysen, married Johannes Provoost in 1687. See John Reynolds Totten, "Grevenraedt Family," *NYGB Record* 60 (July 1929): 224–226, and 61 (July 1930): 244–245; William S. Pelletreau, *Historic Homes and Institutions and Genealogical and Family History of New York*, 4 vols. (New York and Chicago: The Lewis Publishing Company, 1907), 1: 159–161. Harry C. W. Melick, "The Fordham 'Ryott' of July 16, 1688," *New-York Historical Society Quarterly* 36 (April 1952): 210–20.

33. Adams, *The Familial State*, 76.

34. J. L. Price, *Holland and the Dutch Republic in the Seventeenth Century: The Politics of Particularism* (Oxford, England: Clarendon Press; New York: Oxford University Press, 1994), 83.

35. Jonathan Israel, *The Dutch Republic: Its Rise, Greatness, and Fall 1477–1806* (New York: Oxford University Press, 1995), 392.

36. Price, 83.

37. Herbert H. Rowen, *The Princes of Orange: The Stadholders in the Dutch Republic* (Cambridge, England: Cambridge University Press, 1988), 98–99.

38. Israel, 422–426.

39. Rowen, 131–36, 138. See also D. J. Roorda, *Partij en Factie. De oproeren van 1672 in de steden van Holland en Zeeland, een krachtmeting tussen partijen en facties* (Groningen: Wolters Noordhoff, 1961).

40. "Articles and Conditions for the Government of New Netherland, 1638," in *Documents Relative to the Colonial History of the State of New York*, ed. Edmund B. O'Callaghan, Berthold Fernow, and John Romeyn Brodhead, 15 vols. (Albany: Weed, Parsons and Company, 1853–1885), 1:110–111 (hereafter cited as *NYCD*).

41. Benjamin Roberts, *Through the Keyhole: Dutch Child-rearing Practices in the 17th and 18th century. Three urban elite families* (Hilversum: Uitgeverij Verloren, 1998), 46.

42. David William Voorhees, "For the preservation of their properties and souls: the religious aspect of Leisler's Rebellion" (paper presented at the New Netherland Symposium Kerk en Religie, Woerden, Netherlands, June 4, 1999). See, for example, Henricus Selyns to the Classis of Amsterdam, Sept. 20, 1685, *Ecclesiastical Records of the State of New York*, ed. Hugh Hastings and Edward Tanjore Corwin, 7 vols. (Albany: James B. Lyon, 1901–1916), 2: 907.

43. To prevent continuing violence between Voetians and Coccians, in 1677 the Amsterdam Classis determined to balance ecclesiastical offices between the two. See R. B. E. Evenhuis, *Ook dat was Amsterdam. De kerk der hervorming in de gouden eeuw*, 5 vols. (Amsterdam: W. ten Have, 1965–1978), 3: 125–126, 131–34.

44. Nicholas Bayard, "A Modest and Impartial Narrative, 1690," in *Narratives of the Insurrections*, ed. Charles Mclean Andrews (New York: Charles Scribner's Sons, 1915), 354.

45. Firth Haring Fabend, "'A Mad Rabble' or 'Gentlemen Standing Up for Their Rights?'" (revised version), *The Hudson River Valley Review* 22, no. 2 (Spring 2006): 79–90.

46. Edmund B. O'Callaghan, *Documentary History of the State of New York*, 4 vols. (Albany: Weed, Parsons and Company, 1848–1853), 2: 11–13 (hereafter cited as *DHNY*).

47. Maud Churchill Nicoll, *The Earliest Cuylers in Holland and America and Some of Their Descendants* (New York: Tobias A. Wright, 1912), 7, 13, 17.

48. Ibid., 12, 14; Florence Van Rensselaer, *The Van Rensselaers in Holland and America* (New York: The American Historical Company, 1956), 12–13.

49. *NYCD* 3: 636–648.

50. A Hearty Lover of King William [Abraham Gouverneur?], "Loyalty Vindicated, 1698," in *Narratives of the Insurrections*, 386–387.

51. Unsigned [Nicholas Bayard?], "A Modest and Impartial Narrative, 1690," in *Narratives of the Insurrections*, 351.

52. Willem Frijhoff, "Neglected Networks: Director Willem Kieft (1602–1647) and His Dutch Relatives," in *Revisiting New Netherland: Perspectives on Early Dutch America*, ed. Joyce D. Goodfriend (Leiden and Boston: Brill, 2005), 151–156. Luuc Kooijmans suggests that friendship networks played an increasingly important role among the elite in late seventeenth-century Amsterdam, *Vriendschap en de kunst van het overleven in de zeventiende en achtiende eeuw* (Amsterdam: Bert Bakker, 1997), 17.

53. Descriptions of Leisler's and Milborne's executions are in *New-York Historical Society Collections* 1 (1868): 407–408, and *DHNY* 2: 376–280.

54. David S. Lovejoy, *The Glorious Revolution in America* (New York; Harper and Row, 1972); Robert C. Ritchie, *The Duke's Province: A Study of New York Politics and Society, 1664–1691* (Chapel Hill: University of North Carolina Press, 1977); Charles Howard McCormick, *Leisler's Rebellion* (New York: Garland Publishers, 1989); Randall H. Balmer, *A Perfect Babel of Confusion: Dutch Religion and English Culture in the Middle Colonies* (New York and Oxford: Oxford University Press, 1989); and Donna Merwick, *Possessing Albany, 1630–1710: The Dutch and English Experiences* (New York: Cambridge University Press, 1990).

55. *New-York Historical Society Collections* 1 (1868): 424. The reference is to the labels of "Blacks" and "Whites" applied in the disputes between the Ghibellines and Guelphs in late medieval Florence.

56. Adams, *Familial State*, 35 and chapter 5.

57. Edwin R. Purple, *Genealogical Notes*, 15.

58. Israel, 125.

59. Adams, *Familial State*, 98.

60. Edwin R. Purple, *Genealogical Notes*, 12, 13. A biographical sketch of Robert Walter is in Paul M. Hamlin and Charles E. Baker, *Supreme Court of Judicature of the Province of New York*, 3 vols. (New York: New-York Historical Society, 1959), 3: 196–199. For Abraham Gouverneur, see Pelletreau, 1: 157–160, and Arthur Everett Peterson, *New York as an Eighteenth Century Municipality*, vol. 1 (New York: Columbia University Press, 1917; repr. Port Washington: Ira J. Friedman, 1967), 25.

61. Edwin R. Purple, "David Provoost, of New Amsterdam," *NYGB Record* 6 (1875): 16; Andrew J. Provost, *Biographical and Genealogical Notes of the Provost Family from 1545 to 1895* (New York: privately printed, 1895), 27–29.

62. Ibid.

63. Bulloch, 13–14.

64. Marriage License, Wills Liber 6: 52; *NYGB Record* 3: 92; Marriage Licenses, 28.

65. Howard S. F. Randolph, "The Lewis Family of New York and Poughkeepsie," *NYGB Record* 60 (1929), 131–142, 245–254. Thomas's brother, Leonard, served as a New York City alderman and member of the New York Assembly for the city from 1699 to 1701 and for Dutchess County from 1713 to 1726.

66. Jonathan Pearson, *Contributions for the Genealogies of the First Settlers of the Ancient County of Albany from 1680 to 1800* (Albany, 1872; repr., Baltimore: Genealogical Publishing Company, 1976), 105; John P. Dern, *Genealogical Contribution Reprinted from The Albany Protocol* (Cornwallville, N.Y.: Hope Farm Press, 1981), 560–565. For a discussion of the Morris-Cosby dispute, see Bonomi, 103–139.

67. Deaths, 194; Unrecorded Wills, New York Municipal Archives, was endorsed Aug. 3, 1765, during a dispute over the will of second husband Jochem Staats; *Collections of the New-York Historical Society* 35 (1902): 186–188.

68. Florence Christoph, *Schuyler Genealogy: A Compendium of Sources Pertaining to the Schuyler Families in America Prior to 1800* (Albany: The Friends of Schuyler Mansion, 1987), 16–17; Elizabeth Marting, "Arent Schuyler and His Copper Mine," *Proceedings of the New Jersey Historical Society* 65 (July 1947): 126–140; Wills 11: 48–58.

69. Marting, 130.

70. *New York Gazette,* Dec. 6, 1736.

71. *NYGB Record* 9 (1878): 160; Christoph, 16–17; Peter Schuyler's will dated Mar. 21, 1761, proved May 28, 1762, *New Jersey Wills 1761–1770,* 375; Sir James Balfour, *The Scots Peerage Founded on Wood's Edition of Sir Robert Douglas's Peerage of Scotland,* 9 vols. (Edinburgh: D. Douglas, 1904–1914), 2: 494–495; *New York Journal or General Advertiser,* Jan. 1, 1767; William Nelson, ed., *Documents Relating to the Colonial History of the State of New Jersey,* first series (Paterson, N.J.: Press Printing and Publishing Company, 1908), 25: 263.

72. Edwin R. Purple, *Genealogical Notes,* 11; Bogardus, Chart 10; Supplementary List of Marriage Licenses, *State Library Bulletin History No. 1* (April 1898): 45. Marriage license dated Mar. 7, 1703, Wills Liber 7: 161.

73. Christoph, 58; Bogardus, Chart 10-F.

74. Christoph, 58; Florence Van Rensselaer, 16.

75. *CDNY* 64: 74; 73: 14; Joel Munsell, *Annals of Albany,* 10 vols. (Albany, 1850–1859), 1: 133. Johnathan Pierson, *Contributions for the Genealogies of the First Settlers of the Ancient County of Albany from 1630 to 1800* (Albany: J. Munsell, 1872), 148; Holland Society of New York, *Records of the Reformed Dutch Church, Albany, NY* (Baltimore: Genealogical Publishing Company, 1978), 1: 33; *NYGB Record* 17 (1876): 149; *NYGB Record* 57 (1926): 340; Alexander Du Bin, *Wendell Family* (Philadelphia, n.d.), 3–4; James Rindge Stanwood, *The Direct Ancestry of the Late Jacob Wendell of Portsmouth, New Hampshire* (Boston: D. Clapp and Son, 1882), 21–23. The elder Wendell had been a partner with six others in the Saratoga Patent (1684), consisting of about 150,000 acres north of Albany. The associates in the Saratoga Patent were Cornelis Van Dyke, Peter Philips Schuyler, John Bleecker, Johannes Wendell, Dirck Wessells, David Schuyler, and Robert Livingston, Patent Book 5: 159–165, New York State Archives.

76. Commission, New York Historical Manuscripts 53: 8, Albany; *NYGB Record* 57 (1926): 136b; *New-York Historical Society Collections Abstract of Wills, vol. 3, 1730–1744* (1894), 178–179.

77. Edwin R. Purple, *Genealogical Notes,* 10–11.

78. By the end of the eighteenth century, all of these families counted Tryn Jonas an ancestress; thus they form individual genealogical charts in Bogardus.

79. Bogardus, Chart 10-F; John Walter's Estate [1761], F. Ashton DePeyster Papers, Box 5, New-York Historical Society.

80. Howard A. Thomas, *Noxon Family Showing Connection with Bogardus, Gouverneur, Hogenboom, Leisler, Loockermans, Pasco, Vanderburgh, Stevenson & Other Colonial Families* (New York: privately printed, 1951); Joseph Shannon, *Manual of the Corporation of the City of New York* (New York: E. Jones and Co., 1869), 798–799.

81. Thomas, 5; Bogardus, Chart 10A/5.

82. Firth Haring Fabend, *A Dutch Family in the Middle Colonies, 1660–1800* (New Brunswick and London: Rutgers University Press, 1991), 35–39; Fabend, *Zion on the Hudson: Dutch New York and New Jersey in the Age of Revivals* (New Brunswick: Rutgers University Press, 2000), ch. 6.

83. Lawrence H. Leder, *Robert Livingston, 1654–1728, and the Politics of Colonial New York* (Chapel Hill: University of North Carolina Press, 1961), 117–128.

84. Eugene R. Sheridan, *Lewis Morris, 1671–1746: A Study in Early American Politics* (Syracuse: Syracuse University Press, 1981), 113.

85. Edwin R. Purple, "Contributions to the History of the Ancient Families of New York: Varleth," *NYGB Record* 10 (Jan. 1879): 35–37; Bulloch, 14; Florence Van Rensselaer, 26, 39.

86. Roberts, 13.

87. Bonomi, 5, 7.

88. Ibid., 16.

Why New Netherland Matters

JOYCE D. GOODFRIEND

*A*merica's need for crackerjack founding myths has been pervasive and enduring. The circumstances of New World beginnings dictated that Americans take the opening chapters of their national saga very seriously. Compared to the origins of European domains, which were shrouded in age-old mysteries, the American historical clock had started in relatively recent times. The colonization of North America was the product of specific decisions made by identifiable men from familiar backgrounds. Extracting appropriate lessons from events that were locked into the memories of the founders' descendants was an endeavor of great magnitude, one that had ramifications for generations in perpetuity.

Chroniclers of the American past customarily evaded the fact that their European ancestors were not the first humans on American soil. Until recently most were party to the conceit that history in North America began when Europeans arrived on the continent, a notion that is manifestly untrue. As if the task of construing the meaning of American genesis was not daunting enough, there also turned out to be competing versions of the myths that purported to explain how America's destiny was carved out in the early days of planting colonies. The two most familiar stories of American origins, the ones rehearsed in grade-school pageants and appropriated by filmmakers, revolve around Pocahantas and the Pilgrims and by now have been elevated to the stuff of legend. But the other founding story, which foregrounds the Dutch West India Company colony of New Netherland, has always hovered in the wings.

The Dutch colony's origins go back to Henry Hudson's explorations of 1609 and its date of settlement preceded the landing of the main body of Puritans at Boston by six years. Yet because New Netherland survived for only forty years before it was converted into an English domain and renamed New York, its role in the opening scenes of the American drama has been neglected. Because this transfer of sovereignty took place in 1664 (way beyond the age of firsts), standard English-oriented narratives of American history ordinarily bypass New York when they treat of origins. Compounding the difficulty of making the case for the Dutch founders over the centuries has been the ongoing bias against a non-English variant of the American story.

With the nation already embarked on celebrating the 400th anniversaries of the first North American settlements, the early twenty-first century appears to be a propitious time for rethinking the colonial prologue or, better, prologues, to American history and their connections to the nation's evolution. Russell Shorto's *The Island at the Center of the World: The Epic Story of Dutch Manhattan and the Forgotten Colony that Shaped America*, published in 2004, exposed the layers of Anglocentric bias that enveloped the nation's founding myths and built a persuasive case for considering New Amsterdam the true progenitor of all that is American.[1] The popularity of this book suggests that, in our consciously multicultural America, we may be able to surmount the residue of prejudice against the Dutch founders that still creeps into narratives of both state and national history and finally attach due weight to America's Dutch colony in the historical balance.

The history of New Netherland complicates the narrative of American history in fruitful ways by making clear that non-English peoples played a crucial role in the founding of the settlements that eventually joined together to form the United States. Juxtaposing the saga of New Netherlanders with those of the planters of Jamestown and with the Pilgrims and Puritans of New England reveals the distinctive legacy of this heterogeneous society. New Netherland's version of pluralism, in which various groups of Europeans learned to coexist even as they developed the logic and practices that underlay the enslavement of imported Africans and warred against the local Indians, is patently flawed by modern standards, but it still stands as a noteworthy precedent for the multicultural America in which we now live.

Installing New Netherland as one of the country's points of origin is essential not just to establish regional parity or to satisfy the demands of ethnic chauvinists. We need to recognize the Dutch colony's place in our nation's myths of origin for a far more compelling reason: New Netherland was the site of America's first experiment in diversity. Whatever its shortcomings—and they should not be glossed over—it was a society in which men and women of all ranks and backgrounds vied for the prizes awaiting those who set foot in this new world of abundance. As a consequence its history offers the most candid version of American beginnings, one that highlights the pluralism and materialistic striving at the heart of the American experience.

NEW NETHERLAND had a short history, but it has cast a long shadow on America, especially in the mid-Atlantic region. As the first Europeans in the area, the Dutch colonists inscribed patterns on the cultural landscape that have endured over the centuries. Once they had secured the land from the Indians, they renamed it, choosing names from their own geographical repertoire to describe the new territory's features and to forge links with their Old World homes. The cultural footprint of these Dutch settlers lingered long after the colony had been resectioned into English provinces that eventually became the states of New York, New Jersey, and Delaware. Even in the twenty-first century, traces of New Netherlanders' occupation of the land are still discernible in place names derived from their Dutch originals.[2]

Crucial as New Netherlanders' shaping of the mid-Atlantic in the image of their homeland was for the territory's future map, it was only the initial phase of Dutch influence on the region. Many of the sites, artifacts, and institutions that we associate with the Dutch in New York and New Jersey appeared after New Netherland had ceased to exist as a political entity. The progeny of New Netherlanders elaborated the web of institutions created by the firstcomers, not only in towns that had their beginnings during the West India Company's rule but in new zones of cultural influence carved out in the later seventeenth and eighteenth centuries, primarily in New Jersey. In short, the enduring inheritance of the Dutch in the mid-Atlantic region owes as much to descendants of New Netherland families as to the colony's original settlers.

Making a distinction between the inhabitants of New Netherland and their latter-day heirs is crucial for understanding the dimensions of Dutch influence in the region. On the conceptual level this can be done by imagining New Netherland as more than a geographic space whose history encompassed a brief epoch in the seventeenth century. What I am suggesting is that we move beyond the conventional form of periodization that brackets New Netherland's history with chronological guideposts based on political events and instead define New Netherland in cultural terms. New Netherland may have been dissolved as a political reality by 1674, but it remained a cultural reality well into the nineteenth century, and in this guise indelibly influenced the course of history in the mid-Atlantic region. From a consolidated geopolitical territory ruled from the center at New Amsterdam, it evolved into an amorphous cultural remnant of the former Dutch colony consisting of pockets of Dutch settlement, some created during the West India Company regime and others in new communities staked out in northern and central New Jersey. Here, in freshly formed enclaves, Dutch or culturally-Dutch families transplanted from villages on Long Island and elsewhere perpetuated familiar patterns of communal life centered on the Dutch Reformed church. In effect, they reproduced the variant of Dutch culture into which they had been born.

New Netherland remained a living culture in the mid-Atlantic region through the eighteenth century and well into the nineteenth century. Though the culture was modified with the passage of time and in response to different settings, its defining element was continuity with the ancestral Dutch past. Under British dominion, American variants of Dutch culture flourished in the rural areas of the Hudson Valley, western Long Island, and northern and central New Jersey. In Albany it held its own even as English culture began to make inroads at the time of the French and Indian War. In New York City the grip of Dutch culture receded most rapidly, but even there a loyal segment of the population fought to keep Dutch as the language of worship with a fervor that seems mystifying unless one takes into account the interconnectedness of language and beliefs.[3] Long after the American Revolution and the founding of the new republic, descendants of New Netherlanders still perpetuated time-honored folkways across the region.

The observations of visitors, newcomers, and neighbors leave little doubt that Dutch culture was entrenched in New York and New Jersey. Late eighteenth- and early nineteenth-century travelers marveled at the Dutch face of towns around the region and their observations amount to a catalogue of surviving Dutch ways of speaking, building, furniture making, cooking, and religious practice.[4] Scotsman Hugh Simm, who arrived in Albany on the eve of the American Revolution, described the residents as "mostly dutch which Speak their own language and have a dutch minister."[5] Not much had changed by 1786, when a correspondent of Noah Webster informed the dictionary writer that his crusade to create an American language would meet a stiff wall of opposition in Albany: "The Inhabitants are all, or principally the descendants of the first settlers from Amsterdam who have been taught to read and write their native language, and as in the case with all nations, are strongly prejudiced in favour of it. The English tongue has ever been disagreeable and the majority of them now speak it more from necessity than choice."[6] During the debate over ratifying the new federal Constitution in 1788, the text of the document was translated into Dutch so that the city's voters could read it.[7]

Travelers' accounts from the 1790s register the extent of Dutch cultural influence in the early republic. After explaining that Dutchess County had been "early occupied by the Dutch Settlers, and is still held by their posterity," William Strickland, a Yorkshire farmer, noted that "to commemorate the [early Dutch settlers] most of the grave stones in the [Fishkill] church yard are in the Dutch language, and some in that language have been lately erected."[8] New Englander Jedidiah Morse castigated New York's Dutch for their "unacquaintedness with the English language, and their national pride."[9] The tenacity with which descendants of New Netherlanders clung to their ancestral language and religion, and more generally the ways of their forbears, surprised a visitor from the Netherlands, who repeatedly remarked on the familiarity of local people with the Dutch language as he toured communities in the mid-Atlantic in 1783 and 1784.[10] More than sixty years later, in 1847, an immigrant from Gelderland who moved to Schralenburg in Bergen County, New Jersey, noted that "although the Dutch language is no longer employed in [the] services of the [old Dutch Reformed Church] and is no longer taught in their schools . . . the people in their daily intercourse quite generally speak the old Dutch language."[11]

As they sought to comprehend the microcosms of Dutch culture they encountered on their perambulations around New York and New Jersey in the late eighteenth and early nineteenth centuries, outsiders on occasion seized on the trope of the exotic. In November 1780, during his visit to the country home of Philip Van Horne in New Jersey's Raritan Valley, the Marquis de Chastellux characterized Mrs. Van Horne as "an old lady, who, from her countenance, her dress, and her deportment, perfectly resembles a painting by Van Dyck."[12] Englishman William Strickland, who passed through the Dutch areas of New Jersey in 1794, observed that "the women in their external appearance are the perfect copies of their ancestors, or the modern inhabitants of the retired Provinces of Holland; . . . Exactly such figures may be seen in old Dutch paintings."[13] Strickland, like others, viewed rural Dutch folk as out of place in a forward-looking republic and prophesied that the residue of Dutch culture was on the verge of being swallowed up by Anglo-American culture. Fishkill's "large Dutch church [is] rapidly going to decay probably never to be repaired," he declared while visiting Dutchess County and then predicted that "the use of [the Dutch language] is rapidly declining, and the people are assimilating themselves to the English or American manners and language and with them to their religion also."[14]

Whether admiring or critical, witnesses attested to the buoyancy of the Dutch cultural stream in Albany, the Hudson Valley, Kings County, and northern New Jersey many years after the political demise of New Netherland. But it has been left to historians to assess the significance of the survival of Dutch culture over two centuries in multiple communities across the original domain of the Dutch West India Company. If large numbers of the descendants of New Netherlanders chose not to be absorbed into the dominant Anglo culture surrounding them and instead did their best to replicate the ways of their ancestors generation after generation, first in British America and then in the new republic, does their example constitute more than a curious exception to the general pattern of minority assimilation to the majority? Should we be satisfied merely to point to the Dutch saga as an outstanding example of continuity in the midst of change, one that suggests tempering the near universal emphasis on the forward motion of American society and culture after the Revolution? Scrutiny of the historical record of New Netherland descendants in the eighteenth and nineteenth centuries, much of it hidden away in obscure sources, reveals more than enough evidence to move beyond framing their story in terms of exceptions to rules. Building a case for the historical importance of the Dutch in the mid-Atlantic on this broader documentary foundation should ensure that in future they are allocated a clear quota of influence on the course of the region's history.

Unless one makes the mistake of conceiving of the Dutch communities of New York and New Jersey as hermetically sealed entities entirely closed off from the world surrounding them, validating Dutch claims to a substantive role in the development of these states is not difficult. By shifting our perspective from the static to the dynamic, from tallying tokens of the Dutch occupation of the land—church buildings, houses, barns, artifacts, and town and street names—to documenting just how residents of solidly Dutch rural precincts acted at critical junctures in the historical evolution of their towns, counties, and states, we can begin to reconstruct the concrete ways in which the latter-day Dutch exerted influence on the economy, society, politics, and culture of New York and New

Jersey. Concentrated in numbers, possessed of property in land and slaves, arrayed in cohesive communities, and unified in a single religious denomination, Dutch American farmers, far from being inert vestiges of a former realm, were a force to be reckoned with in the mid-Atlantic region in the eighteenth and well into the nineteenth century.

The descendants of old Dutch farm families in Kings County, New York, though often characterized as oddities devoid of power, stood as economic kingpins dominating rural agriculture, initially reaping profits from wheat production and then seamlessly making the transition to market gardening after the Erie Canal opened other sources of grains to New York City in the years before the Civil War.[15] Their wealth translated into political power in the metropolitan arena. Men who spoke for the descendants of the early Dutch clans, many now peppered with English kin, put their stamp on the economic development of the towns adjacent to Brooklyn. As suburbanization of the area loomed on the horizon, leading Dutch men, many already diversified in their interests, jumped on the modernization bandwagon, in the process amassing ample rewards not only from the division of their land into residential plots but from their involvement in the financial and civic institutions that facilitated the changes underway. Far from remaining passive as newcomers scrambled to capture the benefits of economic transition, the ancient Dutch families of Kings County retained their wealth and status.

A substantial portion of the wealth of the rural Dutch in New York and New Jersey lay in African American slaves.[16] Describing Kings County in 1776, a Hessian officer noted that "Near every dwelling house negroes (their slaves) are settled, who cultivate the most fertile land, pasture the cattle and do all the menial work."[17] Long accustomed to using slave labor to perform agricultural work, Dutch farmers clung to the institution introduced by their forefathers, even as urban elites, Quakers, and transplanted New Englanders organized to promote the emancipation of the slaves in their states. In the political debates on ending slavery held in New York and New Jersey, the elected representatives of these Dutch farmers voiced their pro-slavery views.[18] Describing the 1799 deliberations in the New York legislature, an abolitionist recalled that the Dutch slaveholders "raved and swore by *dunder* and *blixen* that we were robbing them of their property."[19] After an emancipation act was passed in New Jersey in 1804, many Dutch signed petitions for its repeal.[20] Roundly criticized for their recalcitrance on what their detractors deemed an essential moral reform, the Dutch stood firm in their opposition to freeing African American slaves.

Few historians have spelled out the long-term political implications of the patterns of slaveholding that were deeply etched in the mid-Atlantic. One who does so is Kevin Phillips, who prefaces his account of pro-slavery sympathies in the North with a detailed description of New York in 1790:

> [D]istricts where at least one-fifth of the families owned slaves [ran]
> along the Hudson River like a sleeve—a baggy Dutch sleeve, with its

> biggest concentrations in Albany; Hudson Valley towns like Kingston, Saugerties, and Poughkeepsie; and especially Manhattan and its neighboring counties. In farm-rich Kings, Queens and Richmond, 39.5 per cent of white households owned slaves. . . . In the fattest Dutch farming sections of Kings County . . ., the towns of Flatbush and New Utrecht, two out of every three families owned slaves.[21]

Dutch farmers along with their slave laborers were also clustered in New Jersey, especially in Bergen County but also in the Raritan Valley in central New Jersey.[22]

Resistant to losing their human property and by extension their traditional way of life, the Dutch farmers of New York and New Jersey worked to block the movement for emancipation for as long as they could, and when success eluded them, engaged in a variety of ruses to circumvent the legal measures designed to emancipate slaves and protect free blacks. The political clout of Dutch farmers in New York and New Jersey was instrumental in making these the last two states in the North to facilitate African Americans' transition from slavery to freedom.[23]

Within the rural Dutch neighborhoods of New York and New Jersey through the early decades of the nineteenth century, ingrained social patterns reinforced the cultural authority of slaveholding farmers. The first chroniclers of these Dutch communities built around small-scale slaveholding presented the system they had grown up with in terms of a benevolent paternalism. Gertrude Lefferts Vanderbilt, a descendant of slave owners whose saga of Flatbush reflected their perspective, exuded nostalgia for bygone social conventions that, in her eyes, were eminently benign.[24] Never questioning the subordination and exploitation of African Americans that underpinned the paternalistic version of slavery practiced by the rural Dutch, these writers laid the basis for an interpretation of the institution that was still influential in 1950, when Ralph Foster Weld, the preeminent historian of Brooklyn, referred to "the comparatively mild bondage of Dutch farms."[25] In recent decades historians have shattered this roseate image of Dutch slavery and exposed the heart of a system of power relations premised on racial difference. Barely concealed outrage infuses Craig Steven Wilder's account of slavery in Brooklyn, while Firth Haring Fabend is more circumspect in her evaluation of the institution in Dutch New York and New Jersey.[26] Neither, however, flinches at calling attention to the human tragedy at the core of the institution.

In the heavily Dutch towns of New York and New Jersey, enslaved African Americans, as a rule, were woven into the family circle, albeit on unequal terms. A historian of slavery in Dutchess County has concluded that "whites and blacks . . . worked together, ate and drank together, sang and danced together, worshiped together, and slept together."[27] Assessing the negative effects of this enforced closeness on African Americans has taken priority in recent historical work, but the consequences of such familiarity for the descendants of New Netherlanders must not be ignored. Exploring the cultural ramifications of this quotidian intimacy is crucial to understanding the compass of Dutch influence in the mid-Atlantic region.

By virtue of their long-forced cohabitation in Dutch households, African Americans were immersed, willingly or not, in the Dutch language and culture. They may not have wished to become fluent in the tongue of their masters, but they did, as the many advertisements for runaway slaves who spoke the Dutch language demonstrate. If slaves absorbed the language of the men and women on whose farms they labored, it is reasonable to assume that they became versed in at least some of the religious beliefs and practices of a people whose lives revolved around the Dutch Reformed church. Exposure to Reformed Christianity as practiced by descendants of New Netherlanders did not necessarily lead to African Americans' embracing their masters' religion. The exclusionary policies of rural Reformed congregations must have deterred most from formally affiliating with the denomination. But some African Americans did attend Reformed worship, listening to sermons from the gallery, and some apparently acquiesced in being buried in their masters' family graveyards even when custom mandated interment in a separate section of the burial ground.[28]

If the majority of African Americans balked at attending the local Dutch Reformed church, this does not mean that they remained impervious to Dutch religious influence in the family and community. Fragmentary evidence suggests their involvement in the two-day Dutch celebration of *Paas* (Easter).[29] African American participation in the Dutch holiday of *Pinkster* (Whitsunday) is well documented. In 1797 William Dunlap was an eyewitness to community-wide festivities in New Jersey: "The settlements along the [Passaic] River are dutch. It is the holiday they called pinkster. . . . The Blacks as well as their masters were frolicking and the women and children look'd peculiarly neat and well dressed."[30] Perhaps initially regarded by enslaved blacks as just an opportunity for recreation, *Pinkster* soon became embedded in African American life and culture.[31] Over the centuries slaves and free blacks in New York and New Jersey shared in and then reshaped the Dutch holiday. Writing in 1874, a historian of Long Island related that "poor *Pinkster* has lost its rank among the festivals, and is only kept by the negroes; with them, however, especially on the west end of the island, it is still much of a holiday."[32] While the original religious meaning of the holiday for the Dutch was diluted and even subverted, there is no denying that a Dutch cultural form became an integral part of the cultural life of African Americans in various sections of the mid-Atlantic region.

Contemporary scholars of slavery in New York and New Jersey highlight the efforts of bondspeople to resist the domination of their Dutch masters. But given the contours of the enclosed Dutch worlds in which they were forced to live and work, enslaved men and women faced stiff odds in their struggle to keep Dutch culture at arm's length.[33] Ensnared in the orbit of the same Dutch farm families generation after generation, most slave laborers would have found it difficult to withstand the relentless repetition of Dutch religious formulas and rituals. Yet the fact that Dutch Reformed farmers in rural New York and New Jersey wielded considerable cultural influence over their African American slaves well into the nineteenth century has not been considered by the creators of the familiar narrative of the decline of Dutch cultural power in the post-New Netherland era. The Dutch Reformed church may have been limited in its ability to gain converts among British peoples who were linguistically and historically detached from the religious practices of their Dutch neighbors, but in areas where the Dutch formed a numerical majority and exercised dominion over African American slaves, their cultural authority, far from diminishing, actually was augmented.

The prevailing image of the rural Dutch was cast in a static mold that accentuated the timelessness of their way of life. As a discursive strategy, portraying Dutch-descended peoples as a conglomeration of Rip Van Winkles, ill equipped for the fast pace of life in the new republic, was far from innocuous, since it created the impression that the denizens of New York and New Jersey's Dutch districts were disengaged from public life. Though evidence to the contrary abounds, extricating the rural Dutch from the shackles of this deeply ingrained literary convention and situating them on the historical track requires a broad-scale research initiative. Only by investigating precisely how the lives of Dutch men and women intersected with the mainstream of history in New York and New Jersey can we show that they remained agents of change well into the nineteenth century.

Once descendants of New Netherlanders had become proportionally a smaller segment of the mid-Atlantic states' population, the economic and political influence of the formerly robust Dutch communities of the region was diluted. When Dutch culture was no longer practiced except by a miniscule number of people in out-of-the-way places, it lost its standing as a living culture. On Manhattan the process had started early and been accelerated as old timers died off; customs such as New Year's Day visiting faded away, and ancient buildings were obliterated. In 1864, when the cityscape displayed few visible marks of the Dutch presence, a cadre of women with roots in New Netherland assembled a remarkable Knickerbocker Kitchen exhibit for the Metropolitan Fair organized to raise funds to support Union soldiers.[34] Ostensibly a charitable work, this display of Dutch artifacts ranging from *kasten*, furniture, and portraits garnered from the homes of the elite struck a personal chord for women lamenting the dismantling of Dutch cultural authority in New York. Offering the public access to the material remnants of the once-flourishing Dutch culture was a gesture redolent with meaning for people many generations removed from New Netherland but nevertheless keen to install their ancestors on page one of America's historical scrapbook. The Dutch-kitchen exhibit was a milestone in the odyssey of New Netherland's Dutch as they moved from history to historical memory.

By the end of the nineteenth century New Netherland as a cultural reality was all but gone. It had outlasted the New Netherland colony, its birthplace, by more than two hundred years. But the extinction of Dutch culture in the mid-Atlantic region did not mean that descendants of New Netherlanders no longer retained any influence on American life. Individuals whose forefathers and foremothers had walked and talked and laughed and cried in New Amsterdam, Beverwijck, Schenectady, Flatbush, and Esopus would continue to leave their mark all over the United States, some of them attaining national recognition, others content to be celebrated in their families, communities, and workplaces. The demographic impact of these progeny of America's Dutch founders on the national gene pool should not be underestimated. The vast majority of New Netherland's male and female inhabitants elected to remain in the English colony of New York instead of returning to the Netherlands, and their descendants fanned out over the region, most eventually becoming citizens of the United States. Over subsequent generations members of these early families moved across the country, many of them marrying exogamously, and multiplied, so that large numbers of Americans, including many whose surnames are not Dutch, have ancestors who were among the settlers of New Netherland. With their Dutch lineage concealed by English surnames, literary luminaries such as Herman Melville and Walt Whitman are ordinarily not linked to the Dutch culture of their mothers, Maria Gansevoort Melville and Louisa Van Velsor Whitman. Alice Kenney's exploration of the Dutch elements in Melville's work illustrates the possibilities of such an approach.[35] Whitman's journalistic forays into Brooklyn's history, published in the *Brooklyn Standard*, attest to his keen interest in the layers of Dutch history that surrounded him.[36] Research on the Dutch connections of other well-known Americans may complicate their biographies as well.

Ultimately, the historical significance of the proliferation of the descendants of New Netherlanders lies not in the realm of DNA, or even in the fame of notables such as Martin Van Buren and Theodore and Franklin Roosevelt, but in the memory work accomplished by their representatives over the years. Since only a fraction of the thousands and thousands of men and women who could legitimately claim roots in the New Netherland colony consciously capitalized on their cultural heritage, it was left primarily to those affiliated with hereditary associations such as the Holland Society of New York, founded in 1885, to elevate the ancestral Dutch culture into an object of veneration through projects designed to preserve the records and publicize the deeds of their forbears. These self-appointed conservators of Dutch memory in America put a visible face on an impulse that likely throbbed in the veins of many non-affiliated descendants of New Netherland settlers.

Though Holland Society members' efforts to increase the visibility of the New Netherland Dutch on the American historical stage may have been tinctured by ethnic chauvinism, their motives for exalting their Dutch ancestors were more complicated and came from a reading of history that found in the annals of the Netherlands a prototype for the drama of freedom that was being enacted in the United States. This notion was epitomized in the statue of William the Silent that the Holland Society of New York donated to Rutgers University in 1926.[37]

Enshrining New Netherlanders in American historical memory was the primary objective of Dutch hereditary societies. Gifts of family papers, memorabilia, and portraits, as well as Dutch artifacts, to museums and local historical societies were calculated to secure a permanent place for the Dutch pioneers in local and national history. John Watts De Peyster commissioned a bronze statue of his ancestor, merchant Abraham De Peyster, which was placed on Bowling Green in 1896.[38] This act and others like it were designed to alert the public that the Dutch merited a place among the pantheon of heroes associated with American origins.

However important the work of latter-day Dutch activists in commemorating New Netherland's colonists, they were not the only ones involved in fabricating the historical memory of the New Netherland Dutch. Other people, including many not of Dutch ancestry, have contributed to the cause of preserving and publicizing the legacy of the Dutch founders. Since Dutch descendants were not greatly inclined to pick up the pen, others often did. Joel Munsell, a noted printer, assiduously collected and disseminated the annals of the Dutch town of Albany, learning the Dutch language in the process. Munsell wrote to Edmund B. O'Callaghan, an Irish man also engaged in conserving the materials of New Netherland history for posterity, in 1871: "Have put the last letter of index to 4th my Hist. Coll. in hand today. Such a lot of Dutchmen were never put in print before."[39] In the early twentieth century archivist A. J. F. van Laer and historians Mariana Griswold Van Rensselaer, Alice Morse Earle, and Esther Singleton envisioned a more inclusive version of early New York history that accorded the Dutch greater recognition as did Alice P. Kenney and Adrian Leiby in a later generation. Most recently Charles Gehring, the translator of the New Netherland documents, and David William Voorhees, the editor of *de Halve Maen*, have labored to increase the visibility of New Netherland among both scholars and the public.

As the United States has struggled to become a pluralistic nation in practice as well as in rhetoric in recent decades, there has been a dramatic shift in sensibilities. Historians and museum professionals have been in the vanguard of efforts to correct the myopia of previous generations. Committed to the notion that full understanding of how Europeans gained a foothold on this continent can only come from examining the variety of peoples and places involved in the process of colonization, these professionals are dedicated to conveying this idea to a wide range of people.[40] The search for a unitary narrative of American beginnings characteristic of the nineteenth and much of the twentieth century is surely quixotic in an age when transatlantic identities have become the norm and electronic communications have toppled national barriers. But given the perennial opacity of those who construct the narrative of American beginnings, one wonders whether the American public is ready for decentering the opening acts of our national historical drama and casting the Dutch founders as leading players.

My thanks to Annette Stott for her thoughtful comments on my work and for suggesting the term "cultural reality."

NOTES

1. Russell Shorto, *The Island at the Center of the World: The Epic Story of Dutch Manhattan and the Forgotten Colony that Shaped America* (New York: Doubleday, 2004).

2. For examples see Sanna Feirstein, *Naming New York: Manhattan Place Names and How they Got their Names* (New York and London: New York University Press, 2001), and Leonard Benardo and Jennifer Weiss, *Brooklyn by Name: How the Neighborhoods, Streets, Parks, Bridges, and More Got Their Names* (New York and London: New York University Press, 2006).

3. Joyce D. Goodfriend, "Archibald Laidlie and the Transformation of the Dutch Reformed Church in Eighteenth-Century New York City," *Journal of Presbyterian History* 81 (2003): 149–162.

4. On Dutch architecture see Joseph Manca, "Erasing the Dutch: The Critical Reception of Hudson River Valley Dutch Architecture, 1670–1840," in *Going Dutch: The Dutch Presence in America 1609–2009*, ed. Joyce D. Goodfriend, Benjamin Schmidt, and Annette Stott (Leiden and Boston: Brill, 2007), 59–84. On the durability of Dutch religion see Firth Haring Fabend, *Zion on the Hudson: Dutch New York and New Jersey in the Age of Revivals* (New Brunswick, N.J., and London: Rutgers University Press, 2000).

5. Hugh Simm to Andrew Simm, September 27, 1774, in *Discoveries of America: Personal Accounts of British Emigrants to North America during the Revolutionary Era*, ed. Barbara De Wolfe (Cambridge: Cambridge University Press, 1997), 141.

6. Quoted in Jill Lepore, *A is for American: Letters and other Characters in the Newly United States* (New York: Alfred A. Knopf, 2002), 29.

7. *De Constitutie, eenpariglyk geaccordeerd by de Algmene Conventie, gehouden in de Stad von Philadelphia, in 't jaar 1787: en gesubmitteerd aan het volk der Vereenigde Staaten van Noord-Amerika: zynde van ses derselver staaten alreede geadopteerd, namentlyk, Massachusetts, Connecticut, Nieuw-Jersey, Pennsylvania, Delaware en Georgia. Vertaald door Lambertus De Ronde, V.D.M.*: Gedrukt by order van de Federal Committee, in de stad van Albany, door Charles R. Webster in zyne vrye boek-drukkery, no. 36, Staat-Straat, na by de Engelsche Kerk, in dezelvede stad, 1788.

8. William Strickland, *Journal of A Tour in the United States of America 1794–1795*, ed. Reverend J. E. Strickland (New York: New-York Historical Society, 1971), 98.

9. Quoted in Joseph A. Conforti, *Imagining New England: Explorations of Regional Identity from the Pilgrims to the Mid-Twentieth Century* (Chapel Hill and London: University of North Carolina Press, 2001), 105.

10. Carel de Vos van Steenwijk, *Een grand tour naar de nieuwe republiek: journal van een reis door Amerika, 1782–1784,* Uitgave verzorgd door Wayne te Brake (Hilversum: Verloren, 1999).

11. "Hendrik van Eyck's Diary," in Henry S. Lucas, ed., *Dutch Immigrant Memoirs and Related Writings*, 2 vols. (Seattle: University of Washington Press, 1955), I: 471.

12. Howard C. Rice, ed., *Travels in North America in the Years 1780, 1781 and 1782 by the Marquis De Chastellux*, 2 vols. (Chapel Hill: University of North Carolina Press, 1963), I: 119.

13. Strickland, 74.

14. Ibid., 98.

15. Marc Linder and Lawrence S. Zacharias, *Of Cabbages and Kings County: Agriculture and the Formation of Modern Brooklyn* (Iowa City: University of Iowa Press, 1999).

16. Shane White, *Somewhat More Independent: The End of Slavery in New York City, 1770–1810* (Athens, Ga., and London: University of Georgia Press, 1991), 51–53; Graham Russell Hodges, "Slavery and Freedom Without Compensation: African Americans in Bergen County, New Jersey, 1660–1860," *Slavery, Freedom, and Culture among Early American Workers* (Armonk, N.Y. and London: M. E. Sharpe, 1998), 28–58; 156–163; Graham Russell Hodges, *Slavery and Freedom in the Rural North: African Americans in Monmouth County, New Jersey, 1665–1865* (Madison, Wis.: Madison House Publishers, Inc., 1997).

17. Major Carl Baurmeister quoted in Edwin G. Burrows, "Kings County," in *The Other New York: The American Revolution beyond New York City, 1763–1787*, ed. Joseph H. Tiedemann and Eugene R. Fingerhut (Albany: State of New York University Press, 2005), 22.

18. David N. Gellman, *Emancipating New York: The Politics of Slavery and Freedom 1777–1827* (Baton Rouge, La.: Louisiana State University Press, 2006).

19. Erastus Root quoted in Arthur Zilversmit, *The First Emancipation: The Abolition of Slavery in the North* (Chicago and London: University of Chicago Press, 1967), 182.

20. Hodges, "Slavery and Freedom Without Compensation," 28–29.

21. Kevin Phillips, *The Cousins' War: Religion, Politics, and the Triumph of Anglo-America* (New York: Basic Books, 1999), 426–427.

22. Peter O. Wacker and Paul G. E. Clemens, *Land Use in Early New Jersey: A Historical Geography* (Newark: New Jersey Historical Society, 1995), 44.

23. Much can be learned about the political role of the rural Dutch by examining their actions during the American Revolution. On Bergen County, New Jersey, see Adrian C. Leiby, *The Revolutionary War in the Hackensack Valley: The Jersey Dutch and the Neutral Ground, 1775–1783* (1962; repr., New Brunswick: Rutgers University Press, 1980), and Ruth M. Keesey, "Loyalism in Bergen County," *The William and Mary Quarterly*, 3rd series, 18 (1961), 558–576. On Kings County, New York, see Burrows, 21–42.

24. Gertrude Lefferts Vanderbilt, *The Social History of Flatbush, and Manners and Customs of the Dutch Settlers in Kings County* (New York: D. Appleton and Company, 1882).

25. Ralph Foster Weld, *Brooklyn is America* (New York: Columbia University Press, 1950), 157. For the romanticization of Brooklyn's version of slavery, see Craig Steven Wilder, *A Covenant with Color: Race and Social Power in Brooklyn* (New York: Columbia University Press, 2000), 22–23 and 248–249, n. 1.

26. Wilder, 5–41; Fabend, 179–186

27. Michael E. Groth, "Laboring for Freedom in Dutchess County," in *Mighty Change, Tall Within: Black Identity in the Hudson Valley*, ed. Myra B. Young Armstead (Albany: State of New York University Press 2003), 64.

28. On racial segregation in Albany's Dutch Reformed Churches, see Robert S. Alexander, *Albany's First Church and Its Role in the Growth of the City* (Albany: First Church, 1988), 106, 187. On the liberalization of Dutch Reformed church policy toward blacks after 1792, see Graham Russell Hodges, *Root and Branch: African Americans in New York and East Jersey 1613–1863* (Chapel Hill and London: University of North Carolina Press, 1999), 181.

29. David Steven Cohen, *The Dutch-American Farm* (New York and London: New York University Press, 1992), 160.

30. William Dunlap quoted in Cohen, *The Dutch-American Farm*, 161.

31. There is an extensive literature on Pinkster. For useful overviews see White, 95–106, and David Steven Cohen, "Afro-Dutch Folklore and Folklife," in *Folk Legacies Revisited* (New Brunswick: Rutgers University Press, 1995), 39–43.

32. Gabriel Furman quoted in Cohen, *The Dutch-American Farm*, 163.

33. David Cohen has concluded that "many [rural slaves] were culturally Dutch—having Dutch names, speaking the Dutch language, and observing Dutch customs." Cohen, *The Dutch-American Farm*, 145.

34. On the Knickerbocker Kitchen see Rodris Roth, "The New England, or 'Old Tyme,' Kitchen Exhibit at Nineteenth-Century Fairs," in *The Colonial Revival in America*, ed. Alan Axelrod (New York: Norton, 1985), 166–169.

35. Alice P. Kenney, *Stubborn for Liberty: The Dutch in New York* (Syracuse: Syracuse University Press, 1975), 203–204. See also Alice P. Kenney, *The Gansevoorts of Albany: Dutch Patricians in the Upper Hudson Valley* (Syracuse: Syracuse University Press, 1969).

36. Henry M. Christman, ed., *Walt Whitman's New York: From Manhattan to Montauk* (New York: Macmillan, 1963). On Whitman's mother's family, the Van Velsors, see Justin Kaplan, *Walt Whitman: A Life* (New York: Simon and Schuster, 1980), 55, and Jerome Loving, *Walt Whitman: The Song of Himself* (Berkeley, Los Angles, London: University of California Press, 1999), 28–29.

37. Annette Stott, "The Holland Society and the Arts," *de Halve Maen* 59 (Summer 1996), 29–31.

38. See http://www.nycgovparks.org/sub_your_park/historical_signs/hs_historical_sign.php?id=11.

39. David S. Edelstein, *Joel Munsell: Printer and Antiquarian* (New York: Columbia University Press, 1950), 339. On Munsell, see also Kenney, *Stubborn for Liberty*, 338.

40. For an example of this approach see James C. Kelley and Barbara Clark Smith, eds., *Jamestown, Quebec, Santa Fe: Three North American Beginnings* (Washington and New York: Smithsonian, 2007).

PETER R. CHRISTOPH was the director of the New Netherland Project for its first ten years. He now serves as editor of the New York Historical Manuscripts series. He has produced seventeen books and some sixty articles, primarily on New York's colonial history. He was head of the Manuscripts and Special Collections unit of the New York State Library for twenty years and served on the State Education Department's Archives Committee, which led to the creation of the State Archives. He was elected a Fellow of the Holland Society of New York in 1979 and is listed in *Who's Who in America*.

NOAH L. GELFAND recently finished his Ph.D. in Atlantic and United States History at New York University. His dissertation is entitled "A People Within and Without: International Jewish Commerce and Community in the Seventeenth- and Eighteenth-Century Atlantic World." He has worked as a researcher for the Papers of Jacob Leisler Project and has been a Touro National Heritage Trust Fellow at the John Carter Brown Library and a Quinn Foundation Fellow at the McNeil Center for Early American Studies.

JOYCE D. GOODFRIEND is a professor of history at the University of Denver and received her B.A. from Brown University and her M.A. and Ph.D. from UCLA. She is the author of *Before the Melting Pot: Society and Culture in Colonial New York City 1664–1730* (Princeton University Press, 1992), editor of *Revisiting New Netherland: Perspectives on Early Dutch America* (Brill Academic Press, 2005), and co-editor with Benjamin Schmidt and Annette Stott of *Going Dutch: The Dutch Presence in America 1609–2009* (Brill Academic Press, 2007). She has also written numerous essays on the colonial Dutch, including "Writing/Righting Dutch Colonial History," *New York History* 80 (1999): 5–28.

JAAP JACOBS specializes in the colonial history of the Dutch Republic in the seventeenth and eighteenth centuries, in particular the Dutch in the Atlantic World. He obtained his Ph.D. from Leiden University in 1999 and published *New Netherland: A Dutch Colony in Seventeenth-Century America* (Brill Academic Publishers, 2005), of which an abridged version in paperback will appear from Cornell University Press in 2009. He has published various articles on New Netherland and is currently working on a biography of Petrus Stuyvesant. He has been affiliated with the Institute for European Expansion of Leiden University and the Amsterdam Center for the Study of the Golden Age. Through a grant from the Doris G. Quinn Foundation, administered by the New Netherland Institute, Dr. Jacobs was a visiting professor at Cornell University and the University of Pennsylvania during the 2006–2007 academic year. During 2007–2008 he was a visiting professor at Ohio University.

WILLIAM T. "CHIP" REYNOLDS has served for more than ten years as the director of the New Netherland Museum and captain of the replica ship *Half Moon*. A native Floridian, his professional training was in environmental science, with an emphasis on coastal systems. He and his family reside in Selkirk, New York.

PETER G. ROSE, a food historian, is the author of several books, including *The Sensible Cook: Dutch Foodways in The Old and The New World* (Syracuse University Press, 1989; paperback edition, 1998) and, with Donna R. Barnes, *Matters of Taste: Food and Drink in Seventeenth-Century Dutch Art and Life* (Syracuse University Press, 2002). She lectures nationally and internationally on the subject of the influence of the Dutch on the American kitchen.

MARTHA DICKINSON SHATTUCK is the editor of *Explorers, Fortunes and Love Letters: A Window on New Netherland*. She received her Ph.D. from Boston University and has been the editor and researcher with the New Netherland Project since 1988. She has published various articles on New Netherland, was the New Netherland and Colonial editor for *The Encyclopedia of New York State* (Syracuse University Press, 2005), and is currently editing and annotating the New Netherland Papers in the Bontemantel Collection at the New York Public Library.

RUSSELL SHORTO is the author of four books, including most recently *Descartes' Bones: A Skeletal History of the Conflict Between Faith and Reason* (Doubleday, 2008). His earlier book, *The Island at the Center of the World* (Doubleday, 2004), about the colony of New Netherland and its focal point of Manhattan, won numerous awards and was internationally acclaimed. He is a contributing writer at the *New York Times Magazine* and the director of the John Adams Institute in Amsterdam.

WILLIAM A. STARNA is professor emeritus of anthropology at the State University of New York, College at Oneonta. He has published widely on Iroquoians and Algonquians of the eastern United States and Canada, in addition to contemporary state-federal-Indian relations.

JANNY VENEMA was born in the Netherlands and studied at Groningen, after which she taught at a high school in Haarlem. She has worked with the New Netherland Project since 1985. A version of her master's thesis from the State University of New York, University at Albany, was published in 1993 by Hilversum as *Kinderen van Weelde en Armoede: Armoede en Liefdadigheid in Beverwijck/Albany, c. 1650–1700*. She has also published two volumes of high school educational materials, a translation of deacons' account books of Albany's First Dutch Church (1652–1674), and various articles on New Netherland, Beverwijck, and

Rensselaerswijck. In 2003 she received a Ph.D. from the Vrije Universiteit at Amsterdam. Her dissertation, *Beverwijck, A Dutch Village on the American Frontier, 1652–1664* (Hilversum/Albany, State University of New York Press, 2003), describes the founding of Albany and the city's development during the Dutch period. In 2005 she became a Fellow of The Holland Society of New York.

DAVID WILLIAM VOORHEES is the director of the Papers of Jacob Leisler Project at New York University and the managing editor of *de Halve Maen*, a quarterly scholarly journal devoted to New Netherland studies. Formerly the managing reference history editor at Charles Scribner's Sons and an assistant editor of volume four and co-editor of volume eight of *The Papers of William Livingston* (New Jersey Historical Commission, 1979–1988), he received a Ph.D. in history from New York University in 1988. His other published works include *The Concise Dictionary of American History* (Charles Scribner's Sons, 1983), *The Holland Society: A Centennial History 1885–1985* (The Society, 1985), and *Records of the Reformed Protestant Church of Flatbush, Kings County, New York, Vol. I, 1677–1720* (Holland Society of New York, 1999). He was a New York State Council of the Humanities speaker in 1996–1998.

ADRIANA E. VAN ZWIETEN is an editorial and research assistant for the Biographical Dictionary of Pennsylvania Legislators Project. She received her Ph.D. in May 2001 from Temple University in Philadelphia. In October 2001 she was granted the Hendricks Manuscript Award for her dissertation, entitled "'A little land...to sow some seeds': Real Property, Custom, and Law in the Community of New Amsterdam." Her publications include "The Orphan Chamber of New Amsterdam," *William and Mary Quarterly*, 3rd ser., 53 (April 1996): 319–340, and "'[O]n her woman's troth': Tolerance, Custom, and the Women of New Netherland," *de Halve Maen* (Spring 1999): 3–14. She has also presented her research on various aspects of Dutch colonial life at the Omohundro Institute of Early American History and Culture Conference (June 1998) and the Rensselaerswijck Seminars (1998, 2001).

A

Adams, Julia, 130, 134
Adriaensz, Marijn, 52–53
Aertsen, Leendert, 78
African Americans, 153–156
Age of Periwigs, 137
Albany, Duke of (James), 3
Albany, N.Y., 2, 4, 6–7, 44–45, 51, 66–67, 72,
   92, 116, 133, 138–139, 150–152, 154, 158.
   See also Beverwijck
Albertsen, Wouter, 92
Alexander, James, 140
Alexander, Mary, 140
Algonquian, 27, 29–30
Alkmaar, Netherlands, 133
American Revolution, 4, 67, 131, 151–152
Amsterdam Municipal Orphanage, 91–92
Amsterdam, Netherlands, 3, 7, 39, 41–42, 45,
   52, 54–55, 62, 65, 91–93, 96, 98–99,
   105–106, 116–120, 122, 132
Amundsen, Roald, 23
Antwerp, Belgium, 119, 121, 131
Apollinaren, Q., 61
apprenticeships, 59–60, 62, 65, 67–69, 82–84,
   119
Archer, John, 68
Arentsz, Rutger, 83
Aruba, 68

B

Backer, Jochen Becker, 97
Bacon, Francis, 5
Barbados, 41–43, 45
barbers, 59–60, 62, 69
Barentsz, Pieter, 29
Barentz, Geesje, 138
Barentz, Willem, 12, 15–16
Barsimon, Jacob, 40–41
Bassett, Peter, 67
Baxter, Katherine Schuyler, 107
Bayard, Balthazar, 133
Bayard family, 134–135, 139–140
Bayard, Hester, 140
Bayard, Judith, 137, 140
Bayard, Nicholas, 129–130, 132, 135–137, 140
Bayard, Samuel, 129
Beaver Wars, 33–34
Becker, Carl, 129
Beeckman, Jochem, 62–63
Beekman family, 139
Beekman, George, 135
Belfast, Ireland, 138
Bentin, Jacques, 52
Bergen County, N.J., 151, 154
Bermuda, 133
Beverwijck (Beverwyck), 29, 32–33, 63, 65,
   72–76, 92–93, 99, 133, 157. *See also* Albany,
   N.Y.
Blaes, Gerard, 60
Blaeu, Willem Janszoon, 15
Blagge, Benjamin, 135–136

Blanck, Juriaen, 78
Blancq, Abraham, 53
Block, Adriaen, 22
Blommaert, Adriaen, 57
Bloomart, Samuel, 132
Bogardus, Everardus, 53, 130–131
Bonaire, 99
Bonomi, Patricia, 129, 140–141
Bout, Jan Evertsz, 54
Brahe, Tycho, 19
Brazil, 39–41, 45–46
bread baking, 91–99, 107
Breuckelen, 63, 66, 72, 80. *See also* Brooklyn,
   N.Y.
Brim, Johan Dircsz, 65
Brodhead, John Romeyen, 4
Brooklyn, N.Y., 153–154. *See also* Breuckelen
Brunel, Olivier, 12
Bunnik, Netherlands, 50–51, 55–57
Burgomasters' Court, New Netherland, 81
Burnet, William, 138
Buys, Jan Cornelisz, 55–56

C

Calvinists, 41, 120, 122, 134, 140
Campisi, Jack, 28
cartography, 14, 16
Catholics, 41, 105
Cats, Jacob, 121
Ceci, Lynn, 30
celebrations
   folk, 102–111, 155
   religious, 73–74, 77, 96, 102–111, 155
Cherster, Michiel de Marco, 67
child-rearing practices, 76–85
chirugeons. See surgeons
Christiaensen, Hendrick, 22
Christians, New, 43–44
Christmas, 102, 111
Claesen, Tryntie, 78
Clark, James, 67
Clasen, Frans, 77
Classis, 135
Clinton, Hillary, 6
Clock, Cornelis, 66
Cocceians, 134
Cocceius, Johannes, 134
Colden, Cadwallader, 138
Collier, John, 22
Columbus, Christopher, 12, 17, 20
Coorn, Nicolaes, 82
Cortes, Martin, 18
Cosby, William, 138
cosmography. *See* geography, world
Couwenhoven family, 139
Couwenhoven, Jonathon, 135
Croon, Jan, 67
Curaçao, 39, 42–43, 45–46, 66, 68, 95, 99,
   132, 139
Curtius, Alexander Carolus, 66, 81

Hardenbrook, John, 106–107
Haring, 52
Hart, Simon, 121
Hartgers, Joost, 132
Hartgers, Pieter, 132
Haukens, Leonora, 119, 121
Hays, William, 66
Heergrins, Gerrit, 83
Hendrick, Jan, 84
Hendricksz, Gerrit, 77
Hendricksz, Jeuriaen, 55
Henriques, Abraham Cohen, 45
Henry (King of Portugal), 18
Herls, Cornelis, 61
Hermans, Ephraim, 139
Hervey, Jan, 66
Highlands, N.Y., 10–11
Holland, Netherlands, 51–52, 92–94, 97,
    130–131, 134, 140–141, 152
Holland Society, 157
Hontom, Hans Jorisz, 28
Hooft, P. C., 122
Hoorn, Netherlands, 98
Hudson, Henry, 5, 10–23, 28, 72, 117, 148
Hudson, John, 22
Hudson River, 10, 22, 30, 32, 51, 53, 72,
    85, 117
Hudson River Valley, 13, 23, 27–34, 103,
    150, 152, 154
Hughes, Jacob, 66
Huyck, Jan, 63

I

Indians. *See* Algonquian; Iroquois; Mahicans;
    Mohawks; Munsees; Narragansetts; Native
    Americans; Onondagas; Pequots; Tappans;
    Wechquaesgeeks
Industrial Revolution, 140
inheritance
    customs and laws, 78–79
    disputes over, 133–139
Iroquois, 27, 33
Irving, Julia, 111
Irving, Washington, 102–103, 106–111
Irving, William, 108, 111

J

Jacobsen, Geertruyt, 79
Jamaica, 42–43, 45, 67, 133, 139
James II (King of England), 135
Jamestown, Va., 2, 149
Jans, Anneke, 131–133, 135–136
Jans, Marritje, 131–133, 136
Jansen, Hans, 82
Jansen, Hendrick, 135
Jansen, Isaac, 67
Jansen, Marritjen, 82
Jansen, Rouloff. *See* Jansz, Roelof
Jansen, Thymen, 131
Jansz (Jansen), Roelof, 79, 131
Jennings, Francis, 34
Jeuriaensen, Jacob, 62–63

Jews
    Ashkenazi, 40, 44–46
    Portuguese, 44
    Sephardic, 39–46
    Spanish, 44
Jogues, Isaac, 29
John Adams Institute, 8
Jones, Charles W., 106
Juet, Robert, 11–13

K

Kalmar Nyckel, 132
Keizersgracht, 122–123
Kennedy, Archibald, 138
Kennedy, Archibald, Jr., 138
Kenney, Alice, 157–158
Kerkbyle, Johannes, 63
Kieft, Willem, 52–54, 64, 82, 110, 130–131,
    133
Kieft's War, 27
Kierstede family, 135
Kierstede, Hans, 62–65, 67, 130, 132–133
Kierstede, Hans, Jr., 133
Kierstede, Jesse, 137
Kierstede, Jochem, 67
Kierstede, Lucas, 137
Kierstede, Roelof, 65, 67
Kings County, N.Y., 152–154
Kingston, N.Y., 65, 67, 83, 154
Kip family, 139
Kleyn, Leendert Huygens de, 139
Krap, Jacob, 67
Krol, Sebastian Jansen, 63

L

La Garce, 54, 67
La Montagne, Johannes, 61–63
Lager, J. L. de, 105
Lange, Jacob de, 66
Leiby, Adrian, 158
Leiden, Netherlands, 7, 94–95, 97, 119,
    133–134
Leisler, Catharina, 133, 138–139
Leisler, Elsie, 133, 135–136, 138–139
Leisler family, 140
Leisler, Francina, 137–140
Leisler, Hester, 129
Leisler, Jacob, 65, 129, 133, 135–140
Leisler, Jacob, Jr., 136, 139–140
Leisler, Jakoba, 137
Leisler, Mary, 133
Leisler, Susannah, 133, 138–139
Leisler's Council, 138
Leisler's Rebellion, 129
Leverich, William, 67
Levy, Asser, 40–42, 44–46
Levy, Miriam, 42
Lewis, Thomas, 137
Lewis, Thomas, Jr., 137–138
Livingston, Catharine, 140
Livingston, Engeltie, 140
Livingston family, 139–140

van Laer, Adriaen, 83
van Laer, Arnold J. F., 4–5, 117–118, 158
van Leer, Mirjam, 102
van Maesterland, Tryn Jonas, 131–132, 139
van Meekeren, Job Janszoon, 60
van Meteren, Emanuel, 21, 28
van Nieuwenhuysen, Wilhelmus, 138–139
van Putten, Andries Pietersz, 55
van Rensselaer, Anna (van Wely), 73, 75, 118, 121
Van Rensselaer family, 133, 135, 139–140
van Rensselaer, Hendrick, 75–76, 117, 135
van Rensselaer, Jeremiah, 140
van Rensselaer, Jeremias, 68, 74–76, 82, 135
van Rensselaer, Johannes, 76, 117, 140
van Rensselaer, Kiliaen, 51, 65, 69, 73, 75–76, 79, 116–126, 136
van Rensselaer, Maria, 68–69, 76, 107, 116
Van Rensselaer, Mariana Griswold, 158
van Rensselaer, Richard, 118
van Rensselaer-Bowier, H. J. J., 117
van Rensselaer-Bowier, M. W., 117
van Rensselaer-Bowier, M. W. M. M., 117–118
van Rensselaer-Bowier-van Zanten Jut, Mrs. J. M., 118
van Roonhuyse, Hendrik, 60
Van Schaick family, 133, 139
van Schalkwijk, Hendrick Jansz, 55
van Slechtenhorst, Margaretta, 138
van Sweeringen, Schout Gerrit, 67
van Tienhoven, Cornelis, 51–53, 55
van Tricht, Abraham, 65
van Twiller, Wouter, 52, 131–132
van Utrecht, Hendrick Harmensz, 52
van Valckenburgh, Jan, 121
van Vorst, Cornelis, 28, 52
van Vorst, Jacob, 79
van Vorst, Jan, 52, 79
van Wassenaer, Nicolaes, 29
van Wely, Anna. *See* van Rensselaer, Anna
van Wely, Jan, 119, 121
van Wely, Pieters, 117
van Wely, Willem, 119, 121
van Werckhoven, Cornelis, 56
Van Zandt, Cynthia, 6
Vanderbilt, Gertrude Lefferts, 154
Varrevanger, Jacob Hendricksz, 64, 66
Vaughton, Michael, 133, 139
Vaughton, Michael (the younger), 139
Vega, 23
Venema, Janny, 6–8, 92
Verbrugge family, 135
Verbrugge, Gillis, 132
Verbrugge, Johannes Pietersz, 132
Verrazano, Giovanni da, 17
Vesalius, Andreas, 61
Vetch, Alida, 137
Vetch, Samuel, 137
Viele, Cornelis, 68
Vigne, Christina, 51–52
Vigne, Guillaume, 51
Vigne, Maria, 51

Vigne, Rachel, 51
Vigne (Vijne), Jan, 51, 54, 77
Vijne, Jan. *See* Vigne, Jan
Vilna, Lithuania, 44
Voetians, 134
Voetius, Gisbertus, 134
Volckertz, Dirck, de Noorman, 51–52
Voorhees, David William, 158
Vreucht, Peter, 66

W

Waddington, George, 117
Wagenaer, Lucas Janszoon, 15
Walloons, 50–52, 65
Walter family, 139
Walter, Hester, 138
Walter, Jacob, 139
Walter, Jacoba, 139
Walter, John, 138
Walter, Maria, 138
Walter, Robert, 133, 137–139
Walter, Sara, 139
Webster, Noah, 151
Wechquaesgeeks, 53
Weld, Ralph Foster, 154
Wendell family, 133, 139
Wendell, Johannes, 139
Wessels, Hartman, 68
Wessels, Hermann, 67
Wessels, Jochem, 92
West India Company. *See* Dutch West India Company
Weymouth, George, 12, 17
Wharton, Edith, 140
Whitman, Louisa Van Velsor, 157
Whitman, Walt, 157
Whitsunday. *See* Pinkster
Wilder, Craig Steven, 154
Wiltwijck. *See* Kingston, N.Y.
Willekens, Anna, 119
Willemsz, Hendrick, 133
William I (Prince of Orange)(William the Silent), 131, 157
William III (King of England), 136
William III (Prince of Orange), 135
William the Silent. *See* William I (Prince of Orange)
Williams, Thomas, 135
Wilson, Edward, 22
Wilson, Woodrow, 5
Winne, Pieter, 83
Wirtsung, Christopher, 61
Wittewrongel, Minister, 121–122
Wolsum, Magdalena, 139

Z

Zeeland, Netherlands, 94, 130, 134

Membership in the New Netherland Institute

The membership of the New Netherland Institute is open to all and demonstrates a wide diversity of backgrounds, education, and interests. Although some members are, for example, historians, genealogists, or linguists by profession, most have joined because of their interest in areas such as Netherlandic or American colonial history, genealogy, language and literature, and popular or material culture. Some were born in the Netherlands or are descendants of the early settlers of the Eastern Seaboard. Although much of the membership is clustered in the East, many members reside across the United States, in Canada, and elsewhere, in particular the Low Countries.

Membership contributions support the work of the New Netherland Project and the Institute. They ensure that an essential and unique resource, which provides new insights into the early history and culture of one of this country's most important regions, is accessible to scholars and ultimately to the public at large.

Membership Benefits

Individual members receive special invitations to the Rensselaerswijck Seminar and other regularly scheduled and special events, where members have the opportunity to meet others with interests similar to their own; receive a free subscription to the Institute's English-language quarterly newsletter *De Nieu Nederlanse Marcurius*; and are entitled to participate in the New Netherland Institute's members-only e-discussion group. New members receive a framable copy of the 1667 Pieter Goos map of New Netherland.

Benefits of the *family association/dual membership* include all of the above. Dual members receive single copies per dual membership of the newsletter and invitations to events, which extend to all members of a family. In addition, up to three members of a family association can participate in the New Netherland Institute's members-only e-discussion group but must register individually to receive their own username and password. New family association memberships entitle the association to receive one framable copy of the 1667 Pieter Goos map of New Netherland, which will be mailed to the address of record.

Membership Form

NAME _____

ADDRESS_____

CITY _____STATE / PROVINCE_____

POSTAL CODE _____COUNTRY_____

PHONE_____E-MAIL_____

Please circle the type of membership:

Single $35   Family/Dual $60   Organization $60 $_____

I wish to make an additional contribution to support the work of
the New Netherland Project and the New Netherland Institute $_____

TOTAL AMOUNT ENCLOSED $_____

Please make check payable to the New Netherland Institute and mail to
New Netherland Institute, Box 2536, Empire State Plaza, Albany, NY 12220-0563